DETERMINATE SENTENCING

SUNY Series in Critical Issues in Criminal Justice
Donald J. Newman, editor

DETERMINATE SENTENCING

THE PROMISE AND THE REALITY OF
RETRIBUTIVE JUSTICE

Pamala L. Griset

State University of New York Press

Published by
State University of New York Press, Albany

© 1991   State University of New York

For information, address State University of New York
Press, State University Plaza, Albany, N.Y. 12246

Production by Christine Lynch
Marketing by Bernadette LaManna

Library of Congress Cataloging-in-Publication Data

Griset, Pamala L., 1946–
    Determinate sentencing : the promise and the reality of
retributive justice / Pamala L. Griset.
        p.   cm. — (SUNY series in critical issues in criminal
justice)
    Includes bibliographical references.
    ISBN 0–7914-0534–6 (alk. paper) . — ISBN 0–7914-0535–4 (pbk. :
alk. paper)
    1. Prison sentences—Case studies. 2. Prison sentences—New York
(State). I. Title. II. Series.
HV8719.G75   1991
364.6'09747—dc20   90–35293
                                                                          CIP

10 9 8 7 6 5 4 3 2 1

ACKNOWLEDGMENTS

This book would never have been written without the encouragement and wise advise of Vincent O'Leary, University Professor of Criminal Justice and retired President of the State University of New York at Albany. President O'Leary was unstintingly generous in sharing his keen insights with me, and for that I will be forever grateful.

I am thankful also to the people who agreed to be interviewed for this work. That these busy policymakers gave so freely of their time and experience speaks well for those who have made their career in public service.

To Jane Wylen, my gratitude for her dogged pursuit of poor prose, loose logic, and grammatical goofs. To Bob Keeler, thanks for his patience and heroic restraint with the red pen on earlier drafts of this work. And finally, a special thanks to my family, friends, and colleagues for their support and friendship.

DEDICATED TO MY FATHER,
William J. Griset

CONTENTS

1

Introduction

The determinate ideal captured the imagination of a generation of jurists, social activists, policymakers, and academics. Propelled by swirling forces, competing expectations, and hollow promises, it burst forth on the public policy scene with a vigor and popular appeal unmatched in recent history. In this book, I argue that the determinate ideal is a myth founded on false notions of power and purpose.

Until the early 1970s, sentencing policy in the nation was heavily influenced by a set of ideas about the purposes of punishment and the allocation of sentencing authority. With foundations in a century-old paradigm, the rehabilitative ideal encompassed more than a concern with rehabilitating criminals: it legitimatized a set of procedures and structures that shaped sentencing policy throughout the country.[1]

The rehabilitative regime was founded on the assumptions that a criminal sentence should rehabilitate (i.e., change the offender's criminal propensities), deter, and incapacitate; that the allocation of sentencing authority should be determined by the purpose of the criminal sanction; that case-by-case decisionmaking should be encouraged; that future behavior could be predicted; that criminal-justice practitioners possessed the expertise required to make individualized sentencing decisions; that sentences should be indeterminate; that mandatory incarceration and mandatory minimum sentences should be avoided; that judicial discretion should be encouraged; that decisions on the duration of the sentence should be deferred until late in the offender's term; and that the parole board should decide how long the offender remained incarcerated.

The rehabilitative program began to lose its hold on sentencing policy throughout the nation in the early 1960s and thereafter. The retreat from the old order was widespread. Liberals and conservatives, defense interests and law-enforcement interests, claimed that the rehabilitative philosophy was theoretically and empirically flawed, its promises a chimera.

The destabilization of the rehabilitative regime accelerated as each of its tenets became suspect. While the manifestations of discontent varied from

1

state to state, it was evident that a sea change in sentencing philosophy was occurring. The hegemony of the rehabilitative ideal was coming to an end.

As the challenges to the reigning paradigm mounted, reform proposals were inevitably sought. Determinate sentencing, a concept that by then had attained national prominence, appeared a ready-made answer. While determinate sentencing proposals varied by prescription and specificity, they shared basic characteristics. The offender would be informed at the time of sentencing, or shortly thereafter, of the length of the prison term. Penal rehabilitation and other crime-control objectives would be abrogated or minimized in favor of retributive purposes. Discretion would be eliminated or curtailed. Disparity, the by-product of individualized sentencing, would be abolished.

Determinacy was embraced warmly by anti-rehabilitationists espousing the law- enforcement perspective as well as by anti-rehabilitationists favoring the defense position. Law enforcement saw determinacy as the guardian of tough punishment, while defense saw it as the essence of fairness and due process. Faced with this unusual alliance, policymakers, accustomed to the traditional opposition between the left and the right, had cause to wonder what determinacy was really about.

The reasons underlying determinate sentencing's bizarre attraction to both the left and the right were rarely discussed until an attempt was made to operationalize the amorphous concepts underlying the determinate ideal. Once the effort to write down the code began, once the vague was rendered specific, the conflict between the competing expectations of the defense and law-enforcement establishments could no longer be ignored. No calculus could be conjured up to determine whose definition would assert primacy. In the end, proponents became opponents, and no one was satisfied.

Crime Control and Discretion

This book explores the myth of the determinate ideal by asking two questions. First, what happens when a sentencing model ignores the crime-control purposes of the criminal sanction and fails to allocate sentencing authority among criminal-justice decisionmakers? Will crime-control objectives disappear, or will they simply be forced underground? Will decisionmakers stop making discretionary decisions, or will they merely stop accounting for the decisions they make?

The second question builds on the first. What happened to the determinate model, which once seemed destined to sweep the nation as the natural successor to the discredited paradigm? Why did determinacy rise and fall, why did it appeal and then repel? How could the movement for determinate sentencing attract both the left and the right? What is the consequence for public policy when the clash between conflicting ideologies can no longer be ignored?

Controlling Crime Through Sentencing

The determinate sentencing proposals that gained prominence in the late 1960s and early 1970s were rooted in theories of retributive justice, disclaiming reliance on crime-control objectives. Punishment for its own sake, not in the service of an unattainable utilitarian objective, became the banner under which the determinate sentencing forces mustered.

I question whether a sentencing system can ever divorce itself from the pursuit of crime control. Does not the diversity of behavior prohibited by the criminal law necessitate a diversity of responses? If so, will decisionmakers continue to seek to control crime through the imposition of the criminal sanction, even where utilitarian purposes are obfuscated by retributive rhetoric?[2] If the sentencing system does not explicitly accommodate rehabilitation, incapacitation, or deterrence, will these purposes nevertheless operate *sub rosa*, frustrating the objectives of the reform?

The purposes underlying the imposition of punishment on convicted offenders can be categorized in a variety of ways. The discussion here will be limited to the four traditional purposes of the criminal sanction: rehabilitation, incapacitation, deterrence, and retribution.

Crime control is at the heart of all but one of the traditional rationales for punishment. Rehabilitation serves crime control by changing the offender. Incapacitation controls crime by restraining the offender. Deterrence furthers crime control by preventing crime among nonoffenders. Retribution, often referred to as just deserts, alone forsakes utilitarian objectives, pursuing punishment for its own sake—because it is deserved.

Rehabilitation is premised on the belief that the criminal propensities of convicted offenders can be diminished to the point that they will choose not to commit crime. Whether the prescribed treatment is isolation and penitence (the method favored by the Quaker reformers who established Eastern State Penitentiary in Philadelphia in 1829), or congregate-silence (New York's approach at Auburn Penitentiary in 1823), or psychosurgery and other modern therapeutic interventions, the purpose of the sentence has been the same: to control crime by changing offenders into law-abiding citizens.

Incapacitation seeks to control crime by the restraining effects of prison bars. More recently, intensive community supervision and electronic monitoring devices have been added to the incapacitative arsenal. Incapacitation is premised on the assumption that, if free, the offender would continue to offend. Prediction is the cornerstone of incapacitation: who might offend, how likely is the offense, how soon will it occur?

Deterrence assumes that punishment imposed on one offender will induce other potential offenders to refrain from committing crime. The threat of the penalty, coupled with knowledge of its execution on others, will cause citizens to obey the law, deterrence advocates claim.

Rehabilitation, incapacitation, and deterrence are difficult to support empirically. The relative rarity of the criminal event, coupled with the small proportion of crimes that result in an arrest or conviction, make recidivism measures—the typical subjects of studies of crime-control strategies—inherently problematic. Lacking empirical justification, crime-control rationales are vulnerable to attack; nevertheless, recidivism studies remain a staple of the research community.

Retribution is deserved punishment, lex talionis, the tariff due. The crime-control purposes of punishment are future-oriented, that is, they seek to prevent crime by either the convicted offender or the general public. Retribution is backward looking: punishment is inflicted for past conduct. Retribution is not amenable to empirical testing. What is deserved is deserved, and whoever has the power defines the terms.

Removing Discretion or Just Moving It?

The determinate model of the late 1960s and early 1970s ignored the organizational context of sentencing decisions and the day-to-day realities of the criminal-justice system. Rather than allocating authority and responsibility among criminal-justice practitioners, the advocates of determinacy sought to eliminate or severely limit discretion.

Sentencing operates in a complex environment, representing a balancing of competing forces, with decisions about sentences made by various criminal-justice functionaries. The question is not whether sentencing discretion will survive a shift to determinacy, but rather how sentencing authority will be reallocated in the new system. The struggle for justice can easily be transformed into a struggle for power.

Unstructured discretion—the power to make and enforce choices without restraint—was portrayed by the proponents of determinate sentencing as the central evil of the old order. Rather than providing for the just and ordered allocation of sentencing authority, they sought to dismantle discretion. Rather than accepting its inevitability and devising decision rules to guide its exercise, they flayed out against it, devising instead proposals to abolish or tightly circumscribe its use.

What happens when discretion is ignored? Does it disappear? Do decisionmakers stop making discretionary decisions about sentences? Or does the locus of discretion simply shift from one constellation of authority to another, as the gulf between stated and actual policy widens? Rather than being exercised by an unwieldy combination of legislators, parole board members, prosecutors, and judges, did the determinate model merely rearrange discretion, yielding another unwieldy combination of legislators, correctional authorities, prosecutors, and judges, each vying for the power that must be newly distributed?

Linking Purpose and Power

The purposes of the criminal sanction are linked to the allocation of sentencing authority, the linkage turning on whether the purposes are retrospective or prospective. Retribution is a retrospective purpose, focusing on the current offense. (And perhaps also on prior offense-related variables, depending on one's views of blameworthiness.) At least theoretically, serving retributive purposes requires no information that cannot be known at the time of sentencing. Consequently, where the purpose behind the sanction is retributive, sentencing discretion is logically placed with courtroom actors: judges, prosecutors, defense counsel, and probation officers.

Where the objectives of the criminal sanction are prospective, seeking to control crime in the future, the information needed to accomplish the goal may not be available when the sentence is imposed. Thus, serving rehabilitation, incapacitation, or deterrence purposes may require that criminal-justice functionaries operating at the later stages of the criminal process be vested with the authority to exercise sentencing discretion.

What are the implications of failing to allocate sentencing authority in accordance with the purpose of punishment? If purpose and power are not linked, can the sentencing system fulfill its promise?

What Happened to the Determinate Ideal?

The determinate ideal appealed to law enforcement as well as to defense advocates. Yet, interest in the new reform, which at first seemed to be an unstoppable, natural heir to the old order, soon faded as determinate sentencing began to lose its momentum. How did it happen, how could a major public policy proposal that had such universal appeal suddenly attract widespread and vehement opposition?

The answers to these questions lie in the history of the national movement for determinate sentencing, a saga that took two decades to unfold. By exploring how complex phenomena can be made to appeal to people with differing ideological bents, this book attempts to explain how competing interest groups ultimately controlled the fate of the determinate ideal.

The book describes a course of events not uncommon to other areas of public policy. For any proposal to be considered seriously by policymakers, it must receive widespread attention. Consequently, a means of spreading the message underlying the new policy proposal must be found. The resort to rhetoric is common. To attract a larger following, the proposal may be cast in terms of general social values, such as freedom, democracy, or liberty. Such symbols provide cues that elicit a positive response in many people. In sentencing policy, terms like doing justice, law-and-order, and getting tough come immediately to mind. These terms are vague, having no generally accepted meaning. People tend to imbue them with meaning consonant with their own value systems.

Vagueness has a price, however. Expanding the base of support for a policy issue may have untoward consequences, as the original supporters of the policy may lose control over its substance. Generalizing the proposal may attract persons and groups with different ideological agendas, different conceptions of the policy issue, and different opinions about its successful resolution.

Varying and changing definitions of the policy proposal may emerge. As more people are attracted to a particular reform or policy direction, the originators' ability to shape the resolution of the issue may diminish. Other groups may influence policymakers, convincing them that their definitions and solutions are preferable to those of the early policy advocates.

The tensions lurking within a loosely defined policy proposal are not overly apparent, and hence not problematic, while the issue remains vague and undeveloped. But when the policy is fully explicated, when the amorphous becomes concrete, the gulf between the policy's promise and its reality is exposed. Not uncommonly, those who originally endorsed the proposal will be displeased with the attempt to translate it into practice.

The book expands on this perspective to explain how defense and law enforcement advocates could agree that determinacy was a much-needed reform. Cloaked in rhetoric, rife with ambiguities, the determinate ideal was susceptible to selective interpretations. The book documents what happened when the conflicting expectations were exposed, as both sides to the debate realized the true price of the reform.

Book Outline

The questions of purpose and power raised in this first chapter dominate the discussion throughout the book. To better capture the dynamic contradictions inherent in the determinate ideal, an in-depth, case study, using New York as the example, is the focus of much of the book. The New York experience— an odyssey that took two decades to unfold—is placed in the context of the national movement for determinate sentencing.

Chapter 2 begins with a brief history of sentencing reform in the United States and then describes the rehabilitative juggernaut at its zenith. Turning to events in New York, the chapter describes policymakers' attempt to devise the quintessential modern rehabilitative system. Chapter 3 presents the counts in the indictment against the old order put forward by the liberal reformers, both in New York and elsewhere around the nation. Chapter 4 chronicles events in the national movement for determinate sentencing.

The next four chapters focus on New York's twenty-year pursuit of a new sentencing system. Chapter 5 discusses New York's rejection of the rehabilitative ideal, focusing primarily on the law-and-order sentencing movements that flourished under New York Governors Nelson A. Rockefeller and Hugh L. Carey. Chapter 6 chronicles the earlier phases of New York's determinate sentencing movement, from the formation of blue-ribbon commissions, to the support of politically diverse newspapers, to the testimony received at public hearings, to the formation of a sentencing guidelines committee. Chapter 7 documents what happened when the liberal thesis, which had been cross-endorsed by law-and-order and defense advocates alike, was exposed to scrutiny in the process of drafting a determinate sentencing code. Chapter 8 describes the political response to the proposed sentencing code. The concluding chapter summarizes the movement for determinate sentencing in New York and elsewhere around the country in reference to the issues of purpose and power that guide this work.

2

Purpose and Power: A Historical Link

The criminal sanction has historically been used for crime-control and retributive purposes, although the relative importance of the three crime-control objectives of deterrence, incapacitation, and rehabilitation has varied over time. Traditionally, sentencing authority has been allocated according to the purpose intended to be served by the criminal sanction. Crime-control purposes of punishment, with their orientation on controlling future behavior, are best served by placing the power with the officials operating at the later stages of the criminal-justice process, particularly parole boards and prison authorities. Where the purpose of the criminal sanction is retributive, punishing for crimes previously committed, judges are the logical recipients of sentencing authority.

This chapter begins with an overview of the major epochs in the history of sentencing in New York State, where sentencing policy largely mirrored that of other states. The discussion then turns to the reign of the rehabilitative paradigm, when crime-control purposes of punishment and parole board power were at their zenith.

The Colonial Era

Crime control through deterrence was the central objective of penal policy in colonial New York and during the early years of statehood. The severity of the criminal sanction was intended to frighten and thereby deter the would-be offender from committing a criminal act.

Following the European tradition, punishment in eighteenth century New York consisted of a variety of sanctions: stocks, pillories, and other forms of public shaming; fines and restitution orders; banishment from the jurisdiction; flogging, branding, and other types of corporal punishment; and the gallows.[1] New Yorkers were subject to the death penalty for over two hundred crimes, ranging from pickpocketing to horse stealing to murder.[2] The state was not in the business of incarcerating convicted felons; neither were the localities. County jails were reserved primarily for pretrial detainees and debtors.

9

1790–1820: Enlightenment and the State Prison

Deterrence continued to dominate sentencing theory in New York as the ideas of the European Enlightenment philosophers began to influence policymakers during the latter part of the eighteenth century and the early years of the nineteenth century. In his powerful treatise, *On Crime and Punishment,* published in 1767, Cesare Beccaria documented the infrequent and capricious use of the death penalty in England. Claiming that the "severity of punishment of itself emboldens men to commit the very wrongs it is supposed to prevent," Beccaria argued that certainty of punishment, not severity, deterred crime.[3]

Beccaria reasoned that a correspondence between crime and punishment would generate respect for the law. Not only should punishment be proportionate to the severity of the offense, but torture, public spectacles, and excessive use of capital punishment should be abolished, he argued, because they ran counter to the humanitarian principles of Enlightenment teachings and did little to foster obedience to the law.

European humanitarianism was well-suited to New York's populist government. Changing conceptions of the efficacy of extreme punishment culminated in the nineteenth century movement away from capital punishment and towards the creation of the fortress prison.[4]

The New York legislature adopted a new penal code in 1796 abolishing corporal punishment, reserving the gallows for murderers and traitors, and establishing the state's prison system. Fixed terms of incarceration were set by the judge at sentencing. Offenders served the entire sentence, unless released earlier by executive clemency or pardon. Thus was the first version of determinate sentencing born, but unlike its later manifestations this early version embraced crime-control objectives.

During the period from 1797–1801, 15 percent of the offenders committed to New York prisons received life sentences, 11 percent received terms of over five years, and only 10 percent received terms of less than two years.[5] While these sentences may appear severe by today's standards, as substitutes for the gallows they were understandably heralded as a humane and rational approach to crime control.

1823–1877: Prisons and Crime Control

Crime control continued as the primary objective of the criminal sanction during the early days of the prison era, although the emphasis shifted from deterrence to reformation, the precursor of rehabilitation. Paralleling the reform movement led by the Quakers in Pennsylvania, changes in New York's sentencing system were premised on the belief that crime was caused by the criminal's corrupt environment. The penitentiary, home of the penitent, was perceived as the state's optimal response to criminal behavior. By forcing offenders to conform to an orderly routine and by isolating them from temptation, the penitentiary would lead the way out of crime. Changing the offender for crime-control purposes thus became the central objective of the criminal sanction.

The New York State Penitentiary at Auburn was completed in 1823; two years later Auburn prisoners travelled down the Hudson River to build Sing Sing Prison. The New York penal system was run under the silent system: Prisoners slept alone in small cells at night and congregated—silently—during the day to work and eat. Forbidden to even glance at one another, inmates were expected to contemplate their wayward past, do penance, and emerge reformed.

Penitentiaries were enormously popular. Dubbed "the pride of the nation," this newest manifestation of crime control prompted the oft-cited visit in 1831 by Alexis de Tocqueville and Gustave Auguste de Beaumont from France.[6] By 1850 prisons had been constructed throughout the nation.[7]

In practice, the operation of prisons fell far short of the ideals that inspired their creators. Once prisoners became long-term residents, the problems of enforcing the congregate system became painfully apparent. Crowding, widespread corruption, and brutal punishment were routine; guards enforced discipline with racks and cat o'nine tails.[8] Bizarre and brutal punishments, including hanging by the thumbs and the infamous water crib, were part of the prison routine in some institutions.[9] The solution was in need of reform. The climate was ripe for the emergence of a new antithesis.

1877–1970: The Rise of the Rehabilitative Juggernaut

Crime-control objectives continued to dominate sentencing theory in New York from the late 1800s to the early 1970s. Like their predecessors, policy-makers during this era embraced changing the offender through incarceration as the answer to the problem of crime. Their quarrel with their forebears was merely with the means to achieve the agreed-upon ends.

Earlier reformers had been wrong, the new reformers argued, in assuming that all offenders were alike and that all could be changed through a single program—the ubiquitous prison routine. A case-by-case approach to change was needed, they said. Punishment must be tailored to the needs of the individual offender. Regardless of their ideological bent (some located the causes of crime in the environment, others claimed a psychological etiology), these reformers trumpeted an individualized approach to crime control. Different offenders required different treatment programs; one needed only to understand the offender's life history to devise a cure. Some offenders were best changed by treatment in prison; others by treatment in the community. A medical analogue was frequently invoked. Just as the doctor cannot predict the date on which the patient will be restored to health, the judge cannot predict at the time of sentencing when an offender would be rehabilitated. Only the experts, by carefully watching the patient's progress, would be in a position to determine when the cure was effected.

Rather than shrinking from such an empyrean task, rehabilitationists exhibited great confidence in their ability to do good by remaking man. They shared a basic trust in the state and a faith that the experts could be relied upon to exercise their untrammeled discretion benevolently.[10]

The change sought by the new reformers squared poorly with the existing determinate sentencing structure. The new model required maximum flexibility. Offenders would be sentenced to indefinite terms, treatment would be individualized, and when the cure was effected, the offender would be released to the community under close supervision.

Everything about the offender's life was relevant to the pursuit of the ideal treatment program. Rules could not be made in advance. Each case was different, each required a different response. The legacy of the rehabilitationists' innovations in criminal justice is far-reaching: Probation, parole, indeterminate sentencing, diversion, and juvenile courts all rose to prominence under their tutelage.

The first application of indeterminate sentencing is traced to an experiment in 1877 at New York's Elmira Reformatory. Male first-offenders between the ages of sixteen and thirty who, according to the sentencing judge, were likely candidates for rehabilitation were sentenced "until reformation, not exceeding five years."[11] Run with a school-like atmosphere, with instructions in moral as well as academic subjects, inmates were rewarded for good behavior with release. The Board of Managers of Elmira determined the release date, and members of the New York Prison Association, a prestigious philanthropic society, provided services to the releasees.

In time, release decisions shifted from prison authorities to parole authorities. By 1901, indeterminate sentencing and parole release were available in New York for first offenders with sentences of five years or less.[12] The indeterminate sentence was extended in 1907 to all first offenders, except murderers.[13] Indeterminacy and the medical model swept the nation. By 1922 thirty-seven states had adopted some form of indeterminacy and forty-four had parole boards.[14]

Modernizing the Rehabilitative Design

In the 1950s and 1960s the American Law Institute's Model Penal Code inspired a national movement for reform of the criminal law. The drafters of the Model Penal Code sought to prepare the definitive modern statement of the law, and "to stimulate and facilitate the systematic reexamination" of state criminal codes.[15] Sentencing reform was an integral part of the code revision effort. The work on the code began in 1951 and a Proposed Official Draft was approved in 1962.

In 1955 Wisconsin became the first state to pass comprehensive revisions of its criminal law based on the Model Penal Code, followed in 1961 by Illinois and in 1963 by Minnesota.[16] More than thirty states, including New York, ultimately passed derivative criminal codes.[17]

The rehabilitative ideal was the glue that tied the national reform movements together. The code revisionists clung tightly to the prevailing sentencing philosophy. The criminal sanction would control crime by its deterrent, rehabilitative, and incapacitative effects. Retributive purposes were eschewed. The Model Penal Code, its drafters claimed, "necessarily excludes dispositions motivated by merely vindictive or retributive considerations or determined by routine tariffs."[18]

The Model Penal Code matched the allocation of sentencing authority with the purposes of punishment. The drafters sought a "sound distribution of authority between the court and the administrative organs of correction." Authority would be allocated to different criminal-justice functionaries according to the "type of power and responsibility that each is best equipped to exercise, given the time when it must act, the nature of the judgments called for at that stage, the type of information that will be available for judgment and the relative dangers of unfairness and abuse."[19] Believing that insufficient evidence was available at the time of sentencing to make crime-control decisions, the drafters of the model code urged that decisions on the duration of incarceration be "reserved for later times," when there will "be different data and experience to guide the choices to be made."[20]

The Bartlett Commission

A progeny of the American Law Institute's Model Penal Code, New York's new criminal codes—"the most sophisticated legislation yet achieved in the evolution of a twentieth century criminal code"[21]—served as a model for other states.[22] And like revisionists in other states, New Yorkers mounted few serious challenges to the rehabilitative regime when revising their criminal codes. Indeterminate sentencing, discretionary decisionmaking, and expertise were reverently embraced by the members of the New York Temporary Commission on Revision of the Penal Law and Criminal Code (Bartlett Commission).

Created by Chapter 346 of the Laws of 1961, the Bartlett Commission was the direct result of discussions undertaken in the early phases of Nelson A. Rockefeller's first term as governor of New York.[23] The commission devoted its attention first to drafting a penal law, which was submitted as a study bill in 1964 and adopted by the legislature in 1965, with an effective date of 1967.[24] Thereafter, they drafted a code of criminal procedure, which took effect in 1973.

The Pre-1967 Penal Law

The Bartlett committee confronted a penal code that had not been substantially revised in over eighty years. The Field Commission, working during the 1860s and 1870s, had codified many of the state's criminal laws.

In 1881 the Field Commission's work was reflected in a new Penal Code and Code of Criminal Procedure.[25] The new statutory scheme classified crimes into broad categories such as crimes against the person and crimes against property. A minimum and maximum prison term was assigned to each crime.

In 1909 the Penal Code was replaced with the Penal Law, the most significant change being the abandonment of the categorical structure in favor of an alphabetical listing of crimes.[26] Since it was believed desirable to keep degrees of crime mutually exclusive, a multiplicity of separate crimes were created for each offense type. Crimes dealing with similar subject matter were rarely located in the same place, rendering charging decisions arbitrary and cumbersome. Continuous piecemeal amendments yielded a prolixity of narrow and highly specific offense definitions, many of which overlapped. Malicious injury to property, for example, was covered by twenty-five sections and numerous subdivisions; the Bartlett Commission would reduce the number to seven.[27] Thirteen different maximum sentences existed for felonies, resulting in anomalous sentencing patterns, with misdemeanants sometimes being punished more severely than felons.[28]

Labeling the 1909 restructuring "pseudo-alphabetical"[29] and "a hodgepodge conglomeration of amendment upon amendment,"[30] the New York law revision committee observed that "[i]nstead of a modern set of guidelines to help effectuate the *deterrence* of crime and the *segregation* and *reformation* of criminals, the State of New York has a few modern procedures engrafted by amendment upon a structure designed for a retributive system."[31] This was clearly unacceptable to the Bartlett Commission, which believed that the criminal sanction should control crime, not pursue a narrow vindictiveness.

The commission repealed many of the archaic prohibitions of the former law, for example, heating of railroad cars by stove or furnace, dueling challenges, and driving cattle and sheep on sidewalks. The many regulatory prohibitions to which sentences had been attached (for example, selling or giving away "baby chicks, ducklings, or other fowl under two months of age in any quantity less than six") were assigned to specific bodies of law relating to the particular subject matter.[32]

Focus on Sentencing

The Bartlett Commission conceived its task as more than one of reorganizing and clarifying the penal law. It felt obliged to reexamine the "many fundamental principles and concepts of the criminal law."[33] Sentencing reform was high on the list of priorities: "From the standpoint of fundamental importance and need for revision, the single most important area was considered to be that relating to classification of offenses and sentencing."[34] After examining the rehabilitative sentencing structure, the Bartlett Commission found the model's merit enduring. Thus, power would continue to be matched with the crime-control purposes of the criminal sanction.

Paralleling the work of the American Law Institute, the Bartlett Commission classified crimes into broad categories for sentencing purposes. Instead of the three offense categories recommended by the Model Penal Code, the New York drafters recommended five felony categories, A through E.[35]

Purposes of Punishment

Richard Bartlett, former chairman of the Bartlett Commission, told this author during an interview that the members of his commission agreed that crime control was the central objective of the criminal sanction. The new penal law recommended by the commission declared that the purposes of punishment were "[t]o insure the public safety by preventing the commission of offenses through the *deterrent* influence of the sentences authorized, the *rehabilitation* of those convicted, and their *confinement* [that is, *incapacitation*] when required in the interests of public protection."[36] The relative importance of the three crime-control purposes of punishment would be determined by considering the seriousness of the crime of conviction and the characteristics of the individual offender.[37] Retribution was not entirely dismissed, although it was relegated to a boundary-setting role. The commission reasoned that the legislature could consider retributive impulses when setting the outer limits of state intervention—the maximum sentence. But all other sentencing decisions were designed to control crime.

The Bartlett Commission acknowledged the lack of scientific evidence on the link between sentencing and crime control. Nevertheless, the commission maintained that problems with the rehabilitative structure centered on the techniques employed or the manner of implementation, not on the overall design.

> Because...the deterrent effect cannot be measured and...neither the legislature nor the courts can predict with any degree of accuracy whether imprisonment will reform a person or how long this will take, it is difficult, if not impossible, to design a sentencing structure that will assure the accomplishment of the previously stated objectives. The best that can be done with our present knowledge and practical limitations is to construct a system that allows adequate scope for the accomplishment of these objectives.[38]

Thus, according to the Bartlett Commission, limitations of proof were no impediment; they merely justified a more vigorous pursuit of the goal.

Linking Purpose with Discretion

The members of the Bartlett Commission believed that the objectives of the sentencing system and the allocation of sentencing authority were ineluctably interwoven. Like the drafters of the Model Penal Code, the New York revisionists sought to distribute authority according to the power and responsibility that each component of the system was to exercise. Believing that little could be known about the effectiveness of treatment at the time of sentencing, the drafters urged that durational decisions be made at the later stages of the criminal process.

The legislature would serve the retributive function by establishing the maximum sanction for broad classes of criminal conduct, reflecting society's view of the seriousness of that type of offense. Thus, for example, a misdemeanor could not be punished by more than one year in jail, even if such a term was not sufficient to accomplish crime-control objectives. While the boundary-setting function of legislators would thus be influenced by retributive objectives, crime-control objectives would also play a role in determining the maximum sanctions for crime classes. A longer sentence for a misdemeanor would be inappropriately severe, the commission reasoned, because it allowed the state "a degree of control that would be out of proportion to the possible *dangers* to society from the particular criminal conduct."[39]

After setting the outer limits, the legislature would delegate control over sentence length to the courts, corrections, and parole, "each to serve its proper purpose and, within its special sphere of competence, to individualize the sentence."[40] Richard Bartlett recalled in an interview with this author that

> throughout the whole concept was the assumed validity of indeterminate sentencing . . . and that the ultimate responsibility for sentencing should be distributed among the judge, the penal and parole authorities, and the executive. And it was an absolute essential threshold assumption that the sentencing judge could not know everything about this defendant, how he or she would behave or ought to be treated in the future.

The 1967 law made major changes in the calculation of good-time credit to afford "a better distribution of control between the Department of Corrections and the Division of Parole."[41] Under the pre-1967 law, good behavior in prison could result in a reduction from the minimum term, lowering the offender's parole eligibility date; pursuant to a 1962 amendment, an additional one-sixth good-time allowance was deducted from the maximum term.

The Bartlett Commission recommended that good time be deducted from the maximum sentence only. Good time and parole release would function as part of an integrated plan, each to be employed at the proper place to effectuate the achievement of the overall goal. The commission's vision of the allocation of power led it to reason that while the minimum term was being served, the prisoner was working for parole release. Good time should not come off the minimum sentence, the commission argued, because that would interfere with the parole process. Where the offender was denied release by the board, good time off the maximum sentence would provide an incentive for good behavior in prison, they thought. Offenders released because of good time (conditional release) would be supervised by a parole officer until the expiration of their maximum term. The Bartlett Commission thus hoped to protect the community and control crime, regardless of whether the prisoner was released by the board or by good time.

Rejecting Mandatory Sentencing

Mandatory sentences, whether they be mandatory incarceration, mandatory maximum and minimum prison terms, mandatory recidivist laws, or mandatory consecutive sentences, are antithetical to the rehabilitative ideal. Mandatory sentences are passed by legislators far removed from the facts of the specific crime. Rehabilitative theory holds that lawmakers should deal with broad principles, not individual cases. They should therefore not prescribe mandatory sentences, which by their nature are applicable to vastly different types of offenders who commit vastly different types of offenses. Judges need flexibility and should not be shackled with mandatory sentences, the rehabilitationists believed.

The pre-1967 law provided mandatory minimum prison terms for many crimes; where no mandatory minimum was stipulated, the court was required to set a minimum sentence within the statutory limits. The Bartlett Commission reversed this practice and, with the exception of a one-year minimum prison term that was viewed as an institutional necessity, rejected mandatory minimum sentences for all but class A felons.

Offenders convicted of class A felonies would receive a court-set minimum sentence of between fifteen and twenty-five years. The court would decide whether to set a minimum sentence when sentencing class B, C, and D felons; if the court elected to set a minimum sentence, the sentence could not exceed one-third the maximum imposed. The court was forbidden to set a minimum sentence (beyond the standard one year) for class E felons.

In rejecting mandatory minimum sentences, the Bartlett Commission reasoned that "[i]f the court is to be entrusted—as it should be—with authority to decide whether to impose a sanction, it can certainly be entrusted with authority to decide whether a minimum period of imprisonment in excess of one year is necessary."[42]

Unless the court set a minimum prison term, the parole board would determine the minimum period of imprisonment, which would have the same effect as a court-set minimum—it determined when the prisoner would first be considered for release. The parole board could lower its own minimum sentence, but it could not lower the court-set minimum. In setting a minimum, the board would consider the offender's "post-commitment development."[43] It would not base its release decisions on retributive considerations.

The 1967 law established maximum sentences for each felony classification.[44] With the exception of class A felonies, which received a maximum sentence of life imprisonment, the commission gave the court the discretion to set the maximum sentence anywhere within the statutory limits. The Bartlett Commission believed that courts were better equipped than legislators to evaluate the circumstances surrounding the crime and the offender:

In many cases, the court has a substantial amount of information available concerning the offender's history, character, and condition. Thus, the authority to fix the maximum allows the court to tailor the sentence to the many individual considerations involved in each case."[45]

The rehabilitative regime proposed by the Bartlett Commission presented the judge with a variety of sentencing options designed to encourage alternative sentences. Mandatory incarceration was reserved for offenders convicted of class A felonies or convicted of two or more felonies simultaneously.[46] In all other cases, the court could impose a non-prison sentence.

Conditional discharges were authorized for all but class A and class B felonies and certain narcotics offenses. Unconditional discharges were authorized in cases where the court found that imposing conditions on the defendant's release served no legitimate purpose.

The pre-1967 law mandated enhanced penalties for all recidivists. Second and third felony offenders received a minimum sentence of not less than one-half the statutory maximum and a maximum sentence of up to twice the statutory maximum; fourth offenders received a minimum term at least as long as the maximum term that could be imposed on a first offender for that offense.

Warmly embracing judicial discretion, the New York code revisionists rejected sweeping mandatory recidivist laws. The Bartlett Commission claimed that mandating enhanced punishment for repeat offenders forced "the court to blind itself to all relevant sentencing criteria, such as the circumstances surrounding the crime for which sentence is to be imposed, the nature and circumstances of the previous crimes, and the history, character and condition of the offender."[47]

Mandatory recidivist laws were recommended for offenders convicted of a third felony, however. But rehabilitation did not lose its hold in defining the pool of offenders eligible for the mandatory sentences. Previous felony convictions could not be considered unless the second felony was committed after the offender was imprisoned for the first felony and the third felony was committed after imprisonment for the second felony. Thus, "two or more convictions for crimes committed prior to the time when the defendant was imprisoned under sentence for any such conviction shall be deemed one conviction."[48] This sequence formulation proposed by the Bartlett Commission flowed directly from the rehabilitative paradigm: "Only those who persist in committing serious crimes after repeated exposure to penal sanctions" (and their rehabilitative influence) would be eligible for increased punishment.[49]

The pre-1967 code specified when concurrent and consecutive sentences could be imposed. Consecutive sentences were mandated where the offender was simultaneously sentenced for multiple offenses, provided that the offenses were charged in separate indictments not consolidated for trial and provided that the offender was convicted of a felony committed while under sentence for another felony.[50] In other instances of multiple sentences, the court would determine whether the sentences were concurrent or consecutive. If the court failed to specify how the sentences should be served, the pre-1967 law followed the common-law tradition, whereby two or more sentences imposed by the same judge at the same time were presumed to be concurrent sentences. In all other situations multiple sentences were presumed to be consecutive sentences. In practice, this formulation resulted in the imposition of consecutive sentences in most cases of multiple sentences.[51]

The Bartlett Commission abolished all mandatory consecutive sentences and reversed the presumption of the pre-1967 law. Where the court failed to specify how multiple sentences were to be served, the sentences should run concurrently, it said. Reasoning that mandatory consecutive sentences "can only be justified on the ground of arbitrary retribution," the rehabilitation-oriented Bartlett Commission allocated this consequential decision to the discretion of the court.[52]

Passage of the New Penal Law

The Bartlett Commission's proposals were well-received by the New York legislature. The few controversies that arose centered on the decriminalization of certain consensual sex crimes, the abolition of the death penalty, and gun control. The opponents of these aspects of the proposal ultimately prevailed, and the proposal was amended accordingly.[53]

The sentencing provisions were not seriously disputed. The criticism that did exist focused on the too-lenient, too-harsh dichotomy. In a 1968 interview, Chairman Bartlett noted that "[t]he sentence structure was said to be too harsh. Of course ... [a conservative] criticized it as being far too weak. However, the opposition from the liberal members of the two houses did not take the form of negative votes. They simply expressed concern and reservations."[54] (Later, when the same polarized criticisms was voiced by those opposed to another commission's sentencing proposal, the disagreement would not be so easily overcome.)

On approving Chapters 1030 and 1031 of the Laws of 1965, enacting the Bartlett Commission's penal law proposals, Governor Rockefeller announced that "a new scheme of sentencing is provided affording ample scope for both the rehabilitation of offenders and the protection of the public."[55] The statutory modernization of the rehabilitative paradigm was complete.

The McGinnis-Oswald Committee

While the Bartlett Commission was concerned with the statutory modernization of the rehabilitative system, the Governor's Special Committee on Criminal Offenders (the McGinnis-Oswald Committee) attempted to match rehabilitative theory with the day-to-day realities of the criminal-justice bureaucracy. Chaired by Paul McGinnis, commissioner of the Department of Correction, and Russell Oswald, chairman of the Division of Parole, the McGinnis-Oswald Committee was established in 1966 by Governor Rockefeller and charged with recommending improvements in the post-adjudicatory treatment system. In creating the committee, Governor Rockefeller reaffirmed the state's commitment to crime control through rehabilitation: "Any way we can rehabilitate more of these criminal offenders and reduce the number of repeaters will have a significant impact on our crime rate in New York State."[56]

Like other rehabilitationists, the members of the McGinnis-Oswald Committee proposed to link the allocation of authority with the crime-control objectives of the criminal sanction. Retribution, "having no inherent value as a goal of the treatment system," was relegated to a boundary-setting role.[57]

Linking Purpose and Power

The McGinnis-Oswald Committee conceptualized a new sentencing system with three distinct sanction levels: the maximum authorized sanction, the appropriate sanction range, and the actual sanction imposed. Authority was allocated to reflect the purpose served by each sanction level.

The legislature set the maximum authorized sanction based on retribution and the prevention of anomie, thereby demonstrating that the state was prepared to uphold the norms of the society. According to the McGinnis-Oswald Committee, legislators were merely boundary setters; they should not be allowed to impede the flexibility of the other sentencers because "criminal treatment is most effective when administered in accordance with individualized criteria."[58] Legislators, who make their sentencing decisions before the crime is committed, were incapable of case-by-case decisionmaking, the committee reasoned.

The judge determined the appropriate sanction range based on the offense actually committed. The appropriate sanction range served deterrence and prevented anomie, both proper purposes for judges to consider because they have "intimate knowledge of the manner in which the community views particular situations."[59]

The judge and the parole board shared responsibility for determining the actual time to be served in prison. The length of incarceration was designed to reflect the behavior of the offender prior to and during incarceration, in the process serving all of the crime-control purposes of punishment.

The McGinnis-Oswald Committee proposed a complicated and highly theoretical calculus for determining the actual sanction. If the appropriate sanction range included prison, the decision to incarcerate would turn on whether incarceration was required for deterrence and prevention of anomie, or social instability, and whether the offender presented a risk of recidivism. Where deterrence or the prevention of anomie did not require imprisonment, the offender would not be incarcerated if there was no risk of recidivism. If there was a risk of recidivism, the offender would be sentenced to the maximum term of the appropriate sanction range; the maximum term was chosen because "there is no way to forecast the effect that treatment will have and the duration of the risk."[60] The parole board would release the offender when the risk was no longer present.

Where prison was required for general deterrence or prevention of anomie, and the offender posed no risk of recidivism, a definite term of incarceration would be set.[61] (The McGinnis-Oswald Committee did not elaborate further on this proposal, which suggested a form of determinate sentencing.) Where prison was required for general deterrence and prevention of anomie, and the offender posed a risk of recidivism, decisions concerning the actual sentence revolved around the minimum term. Where the crime shocked the conscience, a minimum period of incarceration would be set to demonstrate the state's willingness to uphold the norm. In cases where the crime did not shock core values, a minimum sentence would not be imposed; if a statutory minimum existed, it would not be exceeded by the court.

Where no minimum sentence was specified, the parole board determined how long the offender would remain incarcerated. If a minimum had been set by the court, the board would decide whether an additional period beyond the minimum should be served. The parole board's decision would be based on rehabilitative or incapacitative purposes, "it being inappropriate for them to consider general deterrence or prevention of anomie."[62] All treatment decisions would be reserved for the parole board.

Continuous Custody

Going beyond explicating the modern theory of rehabilitation, the McGinnis-Oswald Committee proposed a detailed blueprint for converting the rehabilitative ideal into bureaucratic practice. A thorough reorganization of the criminal-justice bureaucracy would be required.

Continuous custody, which stood in sharp contrast to the separate systems of probation, prison, and parole, was the guiding principle behind the committee's proposal to fully incorporate the rehabilitative program into the criminal-justice bureaucracy. To avoid fragmentation and overlap of services, the committee recommended that the treatment system be reorganized to conform with the actual function performed, rather than with the juridical label attached to the function. All custody would be administered by one executive agency—the Department of Rehabilitation. Persons in need of supervision (PINS), juvenile delinquents, wayward minors, youthful offenders, misdemeanants, felons, and convicted narcotic addicts would all be treated within the consolidated agency. Although children, youth, and adults would be handled by separate divisions, the divisions would be linked together under a single administrative structure.[63] Distinctions between types of institutions (e.g., prisons, reformatories, jails, training schools) would be abolished; facilities would be used in accordance with the services they provided, not according to artificial labels.[64]

Continuous custody required gradations in the amount of custody needed at any given time—from full-time incarceration, to intermittent incarceration, to community supervision. Incarceration would be only one of several forms of custody, and treatment administrators would be given "latitude (i.e., flexibility) in utilization of custodial instrumentalities so that persons may be released from institutions and returned to institutions in accordance with the needs of the case."[65]

The experts—the administrators of the treatment system—determined the form of custody the offender required. Arguing that the type of custody used and the place of custody were vital treatment decisions, the McGinnis-Oswald Committee reasoned that "such decisions should be made by administrators who specialize in this area, and who are also intimately familiar with the vast array of programs available."[66] The committee noted that a "significant corollary of the principles of flexibility, fluidity and risk taking is that the basic treatment decisions must be left, to the greatest extent possible, in the hands of treatment administrators."[67]

Each offender would be diagnosed by an interdisciplinary panel of experts, who would submit their recommendations to a regional panel charged with preparing a treatment plan. The treatment itself would be performed by interdisciplinary case-management teams, which would periodically review the offender's progress. Offenders could be transferred as needed to other custody statuses, for example, part-time incarceration or field supervision. Rather than starting treatment afresh each time an offender was subject to a new period of custody, a unified file would be created, allowing each period of custody to be viewed as "a building block for treatment rather than as an isolated experience."[68]

A Receptive Legislature: On the Road to Continuous Custody

Continuous custody and the bureaucratic modernization of the rehabilitative system received its biggest boost in the 1970 legislative session. On approving a package of criminal-justice bills recommended by the McGinnis-Oswald Committee, Governor Rockefeller focused on crime control. The bills, he said,

> constitute a major segment of my recommendations to the [New York state] [l]egislature this year, [and] mark a watershed in the treatment of criminal offenders in this state. The changes in State Law embodied in these measures will enable a comprehensive modernization of the state's programs of correctional services, placing it in the forefront of national efforts to reduce criminal recidivism. The bills are a direct result of the nationally significant work of the Governor's Special Committee on Criminal Offenders. Any last-

ing gains in combating crime depend on the prompt and effective rehabilitation of criminal offenders. These five bills together represent a historic step by New York in the treatment of offenders in order to prevent recidivism.[69]

Parole and Corrections Merge

Chapter 475 of the Laws of 1970 borrowed directly from the McGinnis-Oswald Committee's conception of a unified criminal treatment system. The bill consolidated prison and parole services in one state agency, the Department of Correctional Services (DOCS).[70] An institutional parole officer unit was established to administratively integrate the functions of institutional and field parole services. While the merger fell short of the single Department of Rehabilitation urged by the McGinnis-Oswald Committee, it nevertheless represented a large first step towards continuous custody.

The merger was presented as a crime-control measure. On approving the legislation, Governor Rockefeller announced that

> efforts to reduce the rate of crime cannot be truly successful unless the entire criminal-justice system, from arrest through the courts and correctional services, can be made into a more effective instrument for reducing the number of criminal repeaters. The creation of a new Department of Correctional Services, incorporating important concepts expressed in the pioneering report of the Governor's Special Committee on Criminal Offenders, would provide greater coordination and continuity in institutional and field supervisory services for those convicted criminals who require imprisonment. This merging of responsibility would do much to ensure a unified system of rehabilitation and close liaison between the work done in correctional institutions and that of parole officers.[71]

The governor also noted that by "merging responsibility for institutional and field supervision of convicted offenders in one department with unified leadership and direction, a coordinated, consistent and continuous system of rehabilitation can be insured."[72]

A Name By Any Other Name

The McGinnis-Oswald Committee argued for a functional, as opposed to a juridical, organization of the state's treatment services. Following the committee's recommendation, Chapter 476 of the Laws of 1970 was designed to "substantially increase the flexibility of the correctional system by eliminating artificial distinctions among types of state institutions."[73] Correctional facilities would be classified according to the security risk of the inmates—maximum, medium, and minimum. Facilities would be further classified by the function performed, thus permitting "assignment of inmates to facilities according to individual needs."[74]

Chapter 476 was largely a draftsman's exercise. Superintendents replaced wardens; correctional facilities replaced institutions, prisons, reformatories, reception centers, and diagnostic centers; inmates replaced prisoners. One can only wonder what the new arrivals thought about these weighty changes.

Peter Preiser, former Counsel to the Bartlett Commission and executive director of the McGinnis-Oswald Committee, was consultant to the governor's office in 1970. In an interview with this author Mr. Preiser, who helped write Chapter 475, recalled the merger:

> They [the legislature] did buy it—they started. You see they started. I started . . . I got a contract to implement continuous custody, and that's when I rewrote a good deal of the correction law, and that's when I went to merge Parole and Correction. The whole concept of merging Parole and Corrections was to create continuous custody.

The Eve of a New Era

Ironically, just as the synthesis and refinement of the rehabilitative structure was being completed, dissonant voices rose to challenge its dominance. The McGinnis-Oswald Committee's action proposals were hailed by the governor; several were enacted by the legislature. Yet the plan for a unified treatment system was never realized, in part because of a coincidence of timing: The McGinnis-Oswald Committee's proposal was put forward just as a new antithesis was ascending. The faith with which reformers once embraced the rehabilitative ideal stands in stark contrast to the deep-seated skepticism that characterized the acerbic attacks launched on the old orthodoxy. This is not to suggest that allegiance to the rehabilitative ideal would be forsaken in one cataclysmic stroke; major shifts in ideology do not happen without antecedents. Nor is it meant to suggest that the rehabilitative system had never been criticized before; few public policies of major importance escape negative review. Neither was there a single rehabilitative position. Adherents differed on the causes of crime (e.g., environmental, moral, biological); on the relative importance of penal rehabilitation (e.g., the dominant purpose, the sole purpose); and on the measures required to achieve the goal (e.g., educational, vocational, or religious training; psychosurgery). Acknowledging that the prevailing structure was not without its critics and that it meant different things to different people does not, however, diminish the strength of its hold on sentencing policy in New York.

Yet the rehabilitative ideal's hold on contemporary thought would suffer severe, perhaps irreversible damage in the ensuing years. The historian cannot but wonder why support for the old order evaporated so quickly; how ideological positions were reversed so suddenly; and why the traditional components of the rehabilitative design—parole release, indeterminate sentences, and vast allocations of discretion to judges and parole boards—became repugnant symbols of all that was wrong with sentencing policy. That the transformation happened so rapidly only makes the search for understanding more pressing.

3

The Birth of the Determinate Ideal

The rehabilitative paradigm was well entrenched throughout the nation at the end of the 1960s. Serious challenges to the rehabilitative program soon surfaced, however, providing an ideal climate for the ascendancy of a new antithesis. In New York State, just as the McGinnis-Oswald Committee was delivering its blueprint for the bureaucratic modernization of the indeterminate sentencing system, a strong anti-rehabilitationist sentiment emerged to challenge the reign of the rehabilitative ideal.

Discontent with the old order spread quickly. Within the span of a few years, faith in the expertise and in the ability of government to do good would give way to deep-seated suspicion of official actions; the rehabilitationist's threshold assumption that everything that needed to be known about the offender could not be known at the time of judicial sentencing would yield to the opposite assumption; the legislature would cease to function as boundary setter, assuming instead far-ranging sentencing responsibilities; crime-control purposes of punishment would be cast aside in favor of retributive purposes; and confidence in the provident exercise of discretion would erode as mandatory sentencing provisions proliferated.

While the antithesis would not command the same level of support as had its opposite, and while it would never clearly dominate sentencing policy, it served to destabilize the old orthodoxy, eroding the hegemony of the rehabilitative ideal.

A Climate Ripe for a Liberal Thesis

As the historian David Rothman noted in *The Discovery of the Asylum,* significant similarities exist in the development of prisons, mental hospitals, almshouses, and orphanages.[1] Changes in separate areas of social policy are often manifestations of the same, larger phenomena. As with other issues of contemporary concern, sentencing policy rides along on larger waves, following the current of public policy.

Rothman provides a context for understanding the sea change in public

25

attitudes that surfaced in the late 1960s and early 1970s:

> The list of those who have suffered a decline in the legitimacy of their dis-
> cretionary authority was as lengthy as it is revealing: college presidents,
> high school principals and teachers, husbands and parents, psychiatrists,
> doctors, research scientists, and, obviously, prison wardens, social workers,
> hospital superintendents, and mental hospital superintendents.[2]

The attacks on the traditional bastions of authority were contemporane-
ous with the widespread unrest associated with such major social upheavals
as the Vietnam War, the rise of racial and student militancy, urban riots, the
Kent State massacre, and the Watergate fiasco. Seen in this context, the
destabilization of the rehabilitative ideal represents but one manifestation of
a far-reaching alteration in American sensibilities.

Appellate court decisions are instructive barometers of change in society.
The abrogation of the "hands-off" doctrine of post-conviction processes and
the emergence and expansion of the "due process revolution" provided an
ideal environment for challenge and change. Opinions of the Warren Court
and their progeny fed the fires of rights-consciousness that swept the nation.

Influential Supreme Court cases in the criminal realm included *Mempa
v. Rhay*[3] (sentencing is a critical stage in the criminal process requiring the
assistance of counsel), *Morrissey v. Brewer*[4] (parole revocation hearings,
while not passing a critical stage analysis, nevertheless require the rudiments
of due process), *Gagnon v. Scarpelli*[5] (counsel provided on a case-by-case
basis at probation revocation hearings, the decision to turn on a fundamental
fairness analysis), and *Wolff v. McDonald*[6] (modicum of due process extended to inmates at disciplinary hearings where good time is in jeopardy).

Major civil cases concerning the rights of the incarcerated mentally ill
were also influential in creating an atmosphere conducive to reform. They
included *Baxstrom v. Herold*[7] (civilly committing a person—regardless of
any benevolent purpose—to an institution maintained by corrections without
a judicial determination that the person is dangerously mentally ill is a denial
of equal protection) and *O'Connor v. Donaldson*[8] (the state cannot confine a
nondangerous mentally ill person capable of surviving in freedom without
providing treatment). In juvenile justice, the important High Court decisions
included *Kent v. U.S.*[9] (waiver of a juvenile to adult court must be preceded
by a due process hearing), *In Re Gault*[10] (delinquency proceedings that may
result in institutionalization require due process hearings), and *In Re
Winship*[11] (the beyond-a-reasonable-doubt standard for conviction of adults
applies to juveniles).

A common thread runs through these seminal decisions. The police
power of the state bore careful scrutiny and continued monitoring. *Parens
patriae* would no longer justify procedural arbitrariness.

Opinions in these and other Supreme Court cases focused the debate on issues of fundamental fairness, due process, effective assistance of counsel, cruel and unusual punishment, procedural regularity, the right to treatment, the right to refuse treatment, and the least restrictive alternative consistent with public safety (the parsimony principle).

In criminal justice, these ideas translated into a liberal call for less severe sentencing and greater emphasis on non-incarcerative sanctions. Parole boards' decisionmaking authority was criticized as arbitrary and contrary to the rule of law. Discretionary decisionmaking was characterized as evil. Prisoners were romanticized, and popular prison abolitionist literature, such as the social critique presented in Jessica Mitford's *Kind and Usual Punishment,* exhorted against the guard mentality, warned of the dangers of the rehabilitative charade, exposed the lawlessness of prisons, and defended the development of inmate unions.[12] Prisons and prisoners became more visible. From Soledad to Attica to San Quentin to the Tombs, the plight of the incarcerated captivated the liberal imagination.

The Indictment against Rehabilitationism

The rehabilitative paradigm was not without its critics before 1970. In 1964, for example, Francis Allen challenged what he called a "narrowing of interests" prompted by the rehabilitative program. Criticizing its all-encompassing set of practices, Allen observed that the rehabilitative ideal "dictated what questions are to be investigated, with the result that many matters of equal or even greater importance have been ignored or insufficiently examined." Allen warned that

> the language of therapy is frequently employed, wittingly or unwittingly, to disguise the true state of affairs that prevails in our custodial institutions and at other points in the correctional process . . . Too often the vocabulary of therapy has been exploited to serve a public-relations function . . . Perhaps on occasion the requirements of institutional security and treatment coincide. But the inducements to self-deception in such situations are strong and all too apparent. In short, the language of therapy has frequently provided a formidable obstacle to a realistic analysis of the conditions that confront us.[14]

While, as noted by Allen, "most of the counts in the modern indictment of the rehabilitative ideal were expressed by one person or another before the outbreak of the American Civil War," the opposition remained scattered and, in spite of occasional rumblings of discontent, it was not until the end of the 1960s and the early 1970s that disillusionment with the old order became widespread.[15]

The attacks on the rehabilitative ideal were both theoretical and empirical. The current order not only offended the anti-rehabilitationists' sensibilities, it also failed to deliver its promises. The new wave of reformers argued that the pursuit of crime control was a folly and a fraud, and that generous grants of discretion were antithetical to the rule of law. None of the interrelated components of the rehabilitative structure escaped unscathed. Each supporting pillar, as well as the numerous ancillary beams and planks, was scrutinized and found wanting. The rehabilitative ideal was exposed as but a front for sinister motives. The edifice would surely crumble. Or would it?

The major counts in the indictment against the old order centered on issues of purpose and power, as the following discussion illustrates.

Penal Rehabilitation is a Fraud

The anti-rehabilitationists attacked the assumption that the criminal sentence should rehabilitate, that the execution of the sentence should instill in the offender the self-control needed to refrain from future criminal conduct. This preeminent cornerstone of rehabilitation was challenged on both theoretical and practical grounds. Offenders were not sick, they did not require treatment; furthermore, if they were sick, the criminal-justice system was incapable of administering the requisite cure.[16]

The anti-rehabilitationists held that the medical analogue was flawed when applied to sentencing. Coercive treatment could not induce psychological change.[17] Ignorance of the causes of crime undercut the notion of the offender as patient: "There is no reliable device for classifying individuals for treatment purposes and no significant evidence that any one form of treatment is superior to any other."[18] The treatment model was grounded on theories of individual pathology, but the characteristics of the pathology had no known dimensions, the anti-rehabilitationists claimed.[19] Offenders' behavior in the community could not be predicted by their prison behavior;[20] an offender who adopted the appropriate demeanor while incarcerated was as likely as the recalcitrant inmate to commit another crime.[21]

The anti-rehabilitationists recognized the bureaucratic usefulness of treatment. One attack characterized "the latest treatment fad [as merely] a new carrot for the sticks-and-carrot arsenal of managerial control."[22] Treatment was but a subterfuge for organizational goals, they said. "Medicine is allowed to be bitter; inflicted pain is not cruelty, if it is treatment rather than punishment. Under the rehabilitative model, we have been able to abuse our charges, the prisoners, without disabusing our consciences. Beneath this cloak of benevolence, hypocrisy has flourished, and each new exploitation of the prisoner has inevitably been introduced as an act of grace."[23]

The anti-rehabilitationists charged that vagaries of the treatment model helped perpetuate the rehabilitative myth. "What is disagreeable—and vicious —is to cage prisoners for indeterminate stretches while we set about their assured rehabilitation, not knowing what to do for them or, really, whether we can do any useful thing for them."[24] The treatment chimera was characterized as "the foundation, however well surrounded with good intentions, upon which we construct a monstrous apparatus of ignorance and horror."[25]

Penal treatment was said to be empirically invalid, as measured by recidivism rates. The origins of the empirical attack can be traced, in part, to Martinson, Lipton and Wilks's *The Effectiveness of Correctional Treatment,* ironically conducted under the auspices of the McGinnis-Oswald Committee, a group deeply wedded to the rehabilitative ideal. An exhaustive review of the literature on the impact of over two hundred custodial treatment programs on recidivism revealed that one treatment program could not be proven more effective than another in reducing recidivism.[26] These findings led one of the authors to a widely publicized conclusion: "With few and isolated exceptions, the rehabilitative efforts that have been reported so far have had no appreciable effect on recidivism."[27] The Martinson study was strong ammunition for the emerging anti-rehabilitationists, as disillusionment with the impact of rehabilitation on recidivism prompted a "nothing works" refrain. And the final *coup de grâce:* Since most crimes remain unsolved, even if a successful treatment regime could be devised, it would have very little impact on crime, the anti-rehabilitationists claimed.

Incapacitation: The Underside of Rehabilitation

Incapacitation, the second crime-control pillar, was also widely criticized. Like penal rehabilitation, incapacitation's intellectual and moral underpinnings were said to be a myth: Crimes were not prevented by removing some offenders from society, or, if they were, the price was too high for a democracy to pay. Incapacitation rested on prediction, but future criminality could not be predicated with even moderate accuracy, the anti-rehabilitationists held. It was unjust—and unAmerican—to punish an offender now for something that might occur (or might not occur) at some future, unspecified time. Predictions, whether clinical or actuarial, are fixed; offenders are free to change.

Incapacitation depends on a critical assumption: If free, the inmate would have continued to commit crimes. This assumption posed several thorny questions, according to the anti-rehabilitationists: Would the offender actually have persisted in criminal behavior? Will the incapacitated offender merely be replaced by another criminal, especially if the offense involved drug trafficking, vice, organized crime, stolen property, etc? What kind of crimes are harmful enough to justify predictive confinement? How does one balance the harmfulness of the conduct with the likelihood of its occurrence? How many years of incarceration are required for maximum effectiveness? Should all offenders be incapacitated? If not, the question becomes how to selectively incapacitate without risking an intolerable false-positive level— that is, incarcerating many offenders based on a prediction that they would offend if released, when only a few would actually do so.[28] Accurate statistical predictions of an infrequently occurring event, such as serious crime, are not possible; how much error in predictions should society tolerate?

In addition to being attacked as theoretically and empirically unsound, incapacitation was characterized as the perfect facade for the security-minded bureaucracy: "So imprecise is the concept of dangerousness that the punitively minded will have no difficulty in classifying within it all who currently find their miserable ways to prison . . ."[29]

Another anti-rehabilitationist observed that "the sentence purportedly tailored to the cherished needs of the individual turns out to be a crude order for simple warehousing."[30]

The interrelationship between penal rehabilitation and incapacitation was not lost on the anti-rehabilitationists, who noted a

> curious kind of shuffling between rehabilitation and incapacitation . . . within the institutions. Confront an administrator with the fact that his institution is not rehabilitating, and he would tell you he was confining dangerous people; tell him that not everyone inside the walls was dangerous, and he would respond that this was a therapeutic effort designed to rehabilitate the offender.[31]

Discretion is Evil

Individualization of justice is the fundamental organizing principle of the rehabilitative ideal. To conform the sentence to crime-control objectives, judges, parole boards, and correctional officials needed the utmost flexibility, it was believed.

Now, the anti-rehabilitationists declared case-by-case decisionmaking as "*prima facie* at war with such concepts . . . as equality, objectivity, and consistency in the law."[32] The discretionary grants of power legitimatized by rehabilitation were unknown elsewhere in the law, the critics charged.[33]

The consequences of individualization were clear to the new reformers: It was but a short leap from discretion to disparity to discrimination. Individualized justice rendered standards "necessarily nonexistent or so vague as to be meaningless, and review . . . impossible."[34] Without uniform rules or standards, there are "no issues to resolve—there is little occasion to talk or think."[35]

It was obvious to the anti-rehabilitationists that discretion led to disparity:

> What would require proof of a weighty kind and something astonishing in the way of theoretical explanation, would be the suggestion that assorted judges, subject to little more than their own unfettered wills, could be expected to impose consistent sentences.[36]

It was likewise obvious to the anti-rehabilitationists that disparity resulted in discrimination: The powerless suffered the most under the rehabilitative system.[37] A system built on covert practices provided the predicate for systematic discrimination against minorities, it was believed. Secret practices also served organizational ends, such as expediting case processing and controlling inmates, and while there was nothing inherently wrong in this, it should be acknowledged, the anti-rehabilitationists argued.[38]

Expertise, Deferred Decisionmaking, and Parole Release

Indeterminate sentencing's basis in expertise, deferred decisionmaking, and parole release were assailed as "a not so subtle form of torture."[39] Faith in expertise and deferred decisionmaking was said to be based on an unproven science of human behavior, a nascent endeavor that rarely generated reliable data.[40] Offenders were to be held until ready for release, a term lacking in definition. Deferring sentencing decisions until more or better information was available was seen as but a specious tactic for maintaining control over offenders.

Labeling parole "at best an obstacle . . . at worst..a trap," reformers called parole practices covert managerial tools. Suspense about release forced inmates to submit to the prison administrator's whim.[41] Preparing for parole release was a charade, they claimed: "The theory of rehabilitative benefit from the striving for parole is dissolved in an acid certainty among the supposed beneficiaries that the task is to find the muscle or the stratagems for beating a rotten system."[42] The anti-rehabilitationists maintained that offenders' behavior in prison (and hence their suitability for parole) was a poor indicator of future criminality.[43]

Unwarranted State Intervention

Suspicious of state power, the critics of the old order identified state intervention—in its most nefarious manifestations—with the rehabilitative program. They argued that an individual's right to liberty should restrict "the power that we wish to accord the state over the individual. We do not suspect, we know, that such powers tend to be abused."[44]

The benevolence imparted by the rehabilitative model was phony, a thinly veiled disguise for expanding the sphere of the state's authority, they said.[45] Less sanguine than their predecessors about solving the problems of crime, these early anti-rehabilitationists resolved to do better by adopting "a crucial shift in perspective from a commitment to do good to a commitment to do as little mischief as possible."[46]

Liberals First Call for Determinate Sentencing

At the core of the charges against the rehabilitative order was a concern for the plight of the least fortunate and a frustration over the perceived inequity, injustice, and arbitrariness in the application of the law. This was a liberal thesis, replete with liberal notions of parsimony, equal treatment under the law, and concern for society's outcasts.

The creators of the determinate ideal were in the main liberal-minded reformers seeking a better, fairer way to structure sentencing policy. Yet, while left-leaning reformers first sounded the clarion call, they were not alone in their embrace of the new model. By 1975 conservatives had discovered determinacy. In that year conservative academic ideologues Ernest van den Haag and James Q. Wilson published treatises urging the adoption of determinate sentencing.[47] The new reform initially appealed to the right, as it did to the left, because of its promise of certain punishment, yet the two camps would soon take vastly divergent views of the meaning of certainty in sentencing.[48]

Diverse and Undefined: Determinacy Emerges

While there was agreement on the diagnosis of the disease, the liberal anti-rehabilitationists differed widely on the preferred course of treatment. Some reformers urged the abolition of parole, others wanted it restructured; some called for legislatively-set presumptive sentences, others for sentencing guidelines formulated by a sentencing commission.

The reform proposals that gained prominence shared two fundamental characteristics, however. First, each advocated replacing the flawed rehabilitative model with a determinate structure based on retribution and limited discretion. Rather than relying on the criminal sanction to control crime, the creators of the determinate ideal elevated retribution as the primary purpose of sentencing. They supported punishment for its own sake, because it was deserved, not in the service of an unattainable utilitarian objective. Rather than meshing power with purpose by allocating discretion among sentencing functionaries—a hallmark of the rehabilitative paradigm—the new reformers sought to limit or eliminate discretionary decisionmaking.

Second, while the separate renunciations of the rehabilitative order had been explicitly detailed, the suggestions for reform were vague and unformed. The proposals were sketched with the broadest brushes, leaving it for others to fill in the details—and change the substance—of the reforms. By failing to embody the ideal of determinacy with practical effect, the liberal anti-rehabilitationists set the stage for the dissonance that would become the hallmark of the movement for determinate sentencing.

The determinate sentencing proposals discussed below are but a few of the most influential treatises to emerge during the creation stage.

The American Friends Service Committee: Struggle For Justice

Struggle for Justice, the first of the reform treatises of the 1970s, couched its recommendations in symbols of justice, fairness, and basic human rights and dignity, not in concrete proposals for change. Their Quaker tradition provided the Friends with another type of struggle: justifying the quest for reform in a corrupt society. They recognized that "[t]o some extent . . . many of the problems we have dealt with involve complex contradictions, perhaps inherent, insoluble contradictions."[49]

Struggle for Justice begins with the list of grievances presented by inmate rioters in New York City's Tombs jail. The book ends with an endorsement of a prisoners' bill of rights. Their "prison-eye view"[50] led the Friends to conclude that social justice would remain an illusion unless there was a fundamental reallocation of power. They questioned whether, rather than urge reform, they should advocate overthrowing the political system. While this course was not taken, the Friends exhibited conflicting attitudes toward sentencing reform. On the one hand, they said that determinacy would not end inequity in sentencing unless police and prosecutorial discretion were likewise controlled. On the other hand, they proceeded to propose a determinate model without such controls.

Struggle for Justice recommended the abolition of parole release and the end of the indeterminate sentencing structure. The Friends argued that the pursuit of crime control should be replaced with a more just objective: retribution. Sentences should fit the offense, not the offender, they argued. Persons convicted of the same crime should receive the same sentence, although repeat offenders might receive longer sentences than first offenders.

Rather than relegating the legislature to a boundary-setting function, *Struggle for Justice* recommended that the legislature set fixed-length sentences for each offense category. Mitigating factors would be included in the crime definition, rather than being left to judicial discretion. Thus, while never expressly raising the issue, the Friends advocated giving to the legislature the power that was stripped from the parole board and the judge.

Struggle for Justice epitomized the leftist leanings of the early advocates of determinacy. While many liberals might fear giving huge grants of sentencing power to the legislature, the Friends appeared unconcerned because their system was premised on the parsimony principle: Incarceration would be reserved for the very few, and sentence length would be reduced overall. Good-time allowances would be continued, but they would not account for a significant portion of the sentence.

Marvin Frankel: Criminal Sentences: Law Without Order

Like the Friends, then-Federal District Court Judge Marvin Frankel's *Criminal Sentences* was rife with the rhetoric of equality, objectivity, and consistency, not with the particulars of a sentencing system.

Frankel also advocated that sentences should serve retribution, not crime control, and that the punishment should fit the crime, not the criminal. Sentencing decisions should be based on objective criteria and articulated reasons, not on idiosyncratic discretion, Frankel said.

Although calling parole release "the ultimate Kafkaism," Frankel did not call for the abolition of parole release in all cases.[51] Rather, he proposed a dual-track system, with some offenders receiving determinate sentences and others subject to indeterminate terms and parole release. Sentences in excess of six years would be indeterminate; sentences of six years or less would be determinate.

In addition, Frankel outlined what later would be a frequently repeated theme: determinate sentencing based on sentencing guidelines. Frankel envisioned that

> [b]eyond codifying the numerous factors affecting the length or severity of sentences, an acceptable code of penal law should, in my judgment, prescribe guidelines for the application and assessment of these factors . . . I have in mind the creation eventually of a detailed chart or calculus to be used . . . in weighing the many elements that go into the sentence . . . I propose a kind of detailed profile or checklist of factors that would include, wherever possible, some form of numerical or other objective grading . . . I suggest that 'gravity of offense' could be graded along a scale from, perhaps, 1 to 5.[52]

The sentence would be determined by the offender's score on the various factors. To operationalize the sentencing system, a sentencing commission would formulate rules, subject to legislative and judicial approval, "to be considered in individual sentences, the weight assignable to any specific factor, and details of sentencing and parole procedures."[53]

Frankel, like the Friends, leaned hard to the left ideologically. His conceptual model was premised on the parsimony principle and the belief that reliance on incarceration should be reduced significantly.

Norval Morris: The Future Of Imprisonment

Law professor Norval Morris shared the liberal revulsion with the present system; like the others, his agenda for reform was cast in terms of broad societal goals. Respect for the human condition and justice as fairness formed the cornerstone of Morris's polemics.[54]

Morris also endorsed the parsimony principle, arguing that sanctions should be the least restrictive consistent with public welfare. Judges should give reasons for their sentencing decisions, Morris believed, and predictions of dangerousness should be avoided.

Rather than advocating the abolition of parole release, however, Morris's sentencing proposal retained "what is good within the individualized treatment model."[55] The prison term would be reduced, and parole release dates would be determined within the first few weeks of the offender's incarceration.[56] Outright release would be replaced with graduated release.

The Committee for the Study of Incarceration: Doing Justice

The influential report of the Committee for the Study of Incarceration presented the case for the just-deserts model of sentencing.[57] The committee rebuked incapacitation, deterrence, and rehabilitation and elevated retributive purposes above all others.[58] In common with other liberal advocates of determinacy, this group endorsed limits on incarceration (prison terms of no more than three years were recommended) and expansion of alternative sanctions.[59] Disparity would be reduced as like offenders would receive like terms.

Like Judge Frankel, the Committee for the Study of Incarceration proposed the adoption of a system of sentencing guidelines. Also like Judge Frankel, theirs was not a concrete proposal for change, but a set of ideas and concepts.[60] The committee's guideline system was based on five or six offense severity categories and four prior record categories.[61] A presumptive sentence would be assigned to each combination of offense seriousness and prior record. The court would impose the presumptive sentence unless aggravating or mitigating factors were present, in which case the court could raise or lower the sentence by a specified amount (the amount to be specified was unspecified). Between 10 and 15 percent of the sentence could be reduced by good-time credits.[62]

The committee said that they were aware of the difficulties inherent in a guidelines system. They acknowledged that constructing a crime seriousness scale was fraught with peril; establishing sentencing standards without simultaneously establishing prosecutorial standards undercut notions of disparity reduction; unrestrained discretion in the imposition of concurrent and consecutive sentences was a breeding ground for disparity; and the complexity of good-time issues could wreak untold havoc with the objectives of the system.[63] As events would later reveal, the committee correctly pinpointed many of the tensions inherent in the determinate ideal.

Liberal New Yorkers Add Their Voices

Anti-rehabilitationist sentiment was well received in New York State, as it was elsewhere throughout the nation. Inspired by determinate sentencing movements in California, Maine and the federal system, New Yorkers called for wholesale changes in the 1967 Penal Law.

As was true nationwide, the early proponents of determinacy in New York were liberals concerned with reducing the incidence and duration of incarceration. Liberal New Yorkers saw determinate sentencing as a way of ending the ever-increasing reliance on incarceration, introducing the rule of law behind the prison gates, and limiting the scope of discretion.

Attica: The McKay Commission

Forty-three people—thirty-two inmates and eleven correctional personnel—died in the prison riot at Attica Correctional Facility between September 9 and 13, 1971. The Special Commission on Attica (McKay Commission), formed in the immediate aftermath of those grim September days, commented that "[w]ith the exception of Indian massacres in the late 19th century, the State Police assault which ended the four-day prison uprising was the bloodiest one-day encounter between Americans since the Civil War."[64]

The McKay Commission was charged with reconstructing the events surrounding the riot and making "judgments about antecedent causes and subsequent occurrences."[65] The commission saw itself as doing more than investigating a tragic but isolated event: "That the explosion occurred first at Attica was probably chance. But the elements for replication are all around us. Attica is every prison; and every prison is Attica."[66] Although the commission was not charged with making recommendations for reform, it felt obligated to speak out against the litany of sins it had uncovered.

The McKay Commission questioned the quintessential feature of the rehabilitative paradigm. Indeterminate sentencing and parole release were characterized by the commission as "by far the greatest source of inmate anxiety and frustration."[67] Calling parole release decisionmaking "unfair..inequitable and irrational," the McKay Commission urged that release be "measured by clear and comprehensible standards, which were disseminated to inmates in advance. The inmate must be told promptly if he has been granted parole and, if not, exactly why not."[68]

The McKay Commission rejected the rehabilitationists' emphasis on individualized sentencing, portraying disparity as a central evil:

> Disparities in sentences imposed for identical offenses leave those who are convicted with a deep sense of disgust and betrayal.[69]

While stopping short of calling for the overthrow of the current order, the commission nevertheless echoed the prevalent liberal refrain, setting the stage for what would follow.

Citizens' Inquiry on Parole and Criminal Justice

New York's Citizens' Committee on Parole and Criminal Justice (Citizens' Inquiry) was chaired by Ramsey Clark, a liberal reformer who had been Attorney General under President Johnson. The Citizen's Inquiry scathingly debunked New York's parole system, characterizing it as "oppressive and arbitrary," and beyond reform.[70]

The unbridled discretion accorded to the parole board perpetuated the charade of severity, the Citizens' Inquiry claimed:

> Parole allows many actors in the criminal-justice system to hide the real nature of their actions and thereby escape responsibility for them. District attorneys may call for and judges may impose excessively long sentences in the name of law-and-order, knowing that the deferred sentencing process of parole will mitigate their harshness. The parole board's extensive and invisible discretion makes it possible for these officials to mislead the public.[71]

Both the theory and the practice of parole were repudiated by the committee. The goals of rehabilitation . . . are unrealistic and should not shape sentencing and release decisions. At present, society is not able to reduce recidivism measurably by exposing the offender to treatment or rehabilitative programs either in the prison or in the community. Discretionary release and community supervision, which rely on the rehabilitation theory, should therefore be discontinued.[72]

Despite the Citizens' Inquiry's proclamation that parole should be abolished, its recommendations for change were more cautious.[73] Believing that parole reform would be worse than meaningless without simultaneously correcting other aspects of the system, they recommended both long-term and transitional changes. The transitional recommendations included shifting the burden of proof to the parole board, who would have to show why an inmate would not be released, and reducing parole supervision to one year.

The long-term recommendations were representative of the typically liberal leanings of the original proponents of determinate sentencing: Abolish the parole board and parole release, end parole supervision based on rehabilitative theory, enact shorter sentences, increase alternatives to incarceration, open procedures to public scrutiny, and develop a wide range of voluntary programs for offenders—"before, during, and after incarceration."[74]

4

The National Movement for Determinate Sentencing

The rehabilitative edifice appeared to crumble under the weight of the strident challenges against it. The vigorous attack on the old bastion of indeterminacy has been described as "the substantive criminal law surprise of the 1970s."[1]

The determinate ideal caught hold rapidly. Between the mid-1970s and the mid-1980s, all fifty states and the District of Columbia enacted or considered enacting legislation to modify or repeal their sentencing structures.[2] In each instance, the new sentencing schemes were purported to be more determinate than the systems they were designed to replace.

Missing from the national debate over the new sentencing plans were the fundamental questions of purpose and power. In their zealousness for reform, determinate sentencing advocates turned a blind eye on these tough, yet pivotal issues. How would one purpose of punishment be made to supplant another? Precisely how would crime control give way to retribution? If, as the reformers claimed, unbridled discretion was evil, if power should be circumscribed, how would decisions be made in the criminal-justice system? If judges and parole boards would no longer exercise decisionmaking power, would they be replaced and, if so, by whom?

Confronting tough issues requires courage and political skill. Avoiding them is expedient and allows policymakers to move forward unencumbered by the thorny facts. While the determinate ideal was widely hailed as a workable solution to the problems of disparity and discrimination in the criminal justice system, there was little discussion, much less agreement, about how the ideal would be translated into practice. Each state developed its own working definition of determinacy; the resulting mishmash was truly remarkable. The variety of new sentencing models that developed also blunted the message of the original determinate advocates, as each jurisdiction imbued the concept with a different meaning.

The diversity in so-called determinate sentencing structures that have been considered or enacted in recent years is as enormous as the penal codes and political histories that gave them rise. Varying definitions of determinacy make simple comparisons suspect. It is thus not surprising that sources disagree on the number of states that have switched to determinate sentencing.[3]

The original, purist determinate sentencing model had two fundamental precepts: Discretionary parole release was abolished and, with the exception of reductions for good time, prison terms were definite and known at the time of sentencing. Using this definition, at least twelve states have determinate sentencing structures: California, Oregon, Colorado, Connecticut, Florida, Illinois, Indiana, Maine, Minnesota, New Mexico, North Carolina, and Washington. In addition, after nearly two decades of negotiations, the federal government recently adopted a determinate sentencing system based on sentencing guidelines.

The purist model has undergone some rather unorthodox transformations. For example, for years Oregon claimed to have determinate sentencing even though it retained discretionary parole release.[4] Pennsylvania has sentencing guidelines but retains indeterminate sentencing; the guidelines in Pennsylvania apply only to the minimum, but not the maximum, sentence.

Before turning to an in-depth examination of the decline of the determinate ideal in one key state, New York, the discussion to follow highlights the major developments in the national movement for determinate sentencing.

The Legislative Model

Maine

Maine was the first state to adopt a determinate sentencing system. In 1975, the Maine legislature abolished the parole board. Under the new system, judges in Maine sentenced offenders to flat prison terms, representing the time that offenders would actually serve in prison, minus good-time reductions. Unlike other states that would switch to determinacy, Maine also eliminated parole supervision.

Legislative control of the new system was limited. Judges in Maine were given enormous latitude. The legislature stipulated extremely wide statutory ranges from which judges could choose any sentence. The court could impose probation or almost any length of prison sentence for all but a select group of crimes. Mandatory imprisonment was statutorily reserved only for offenders convicted of the top four classes of felonies, and then only if the crime was committed with a firearm.[5]

In the intervening years, Maine policymakers have attempted to reform the reform. In 1983 the legislature empaneled a sentencing commission to recommend sentencing guidelines. The commission was unable to complete its work, and recommended instead that "a new commission be created to continue the responsibilities of this commission."[6] While the commission did not fully explain its reasons for failing to recommend guidelines, it labored under a number of difficulties, not the least being a lack of full-time professional staff, resistance by a very vocal and powerful judiciary, and lack of enthusiasm among several commission members for guidelines sentencing.[7]

In 1986, the legislature reestablished the Maine sentencing commission, but this body also failed to recommend a specific sentencing guideline system. Instead, a new appellate procedure was created with the intent that case law would emerge as a foundation for creating judicially-set guidelines. The Maine legislature thus continues to entrust judges with wide ranging discretion, albeit under a fixed, determinate system.

California

In 1976 California became the second state in the nation to opt for determinacy. Unlike Maine, where judicial discretion was virtually untrammeled, the California legislature overtly set out to limit judges' sentencing authority. The legislature set a presumptive term for each offense type and stipulated specific mitigating and aggravating factors that the court could consider in imposing other than the presumptive term. Sentences could be further increased if certain enhancements were present.

Also unlike Maine, the California legislature claimed to pursue a particular sentencing strategy. Using many of the arguments of the determinate advocates, the legislature embraced proportionality in sentencing as a guiding principle, with penalties purportedly reflecting the seriousness of the offense. Parole release was abolished, although parole supervision was retained. A more detailed description of the genesis, as well as the ramifications of the California system is presented later in this chapter.

Indiana

Indiana's determinate sentencing law was adopted the same year as California's. The Indiana legislature stipulated a set prison term for each of four levels of felonies, although judges were given considerable discretion in choosing aggravating and mitigating terms. Parole release was abolished, but good-time credits were extremely generous, allowing inmates to reduce their sentence by half for good behavior in prison. Correctional administrators in Indiana thus reaped an enormous discretionary windfall, leaving them with previously unheard of (and rarely mentioned) authority to set sentence length.

Legislative sentencing systems were also enacted in Illinois, Colorado, Alaska, New Mexico, Connecticut and North Carolina.[8]

The Sentencing Commission Model

The sentencing commission approach was proposed initially by Judge Marvin Frankel in his 1972 classic treatise, *Criminal Sentences: Law Without Order.* Sentencing commissions have since proposed sentencing guidelines that are now in effect in Minnesota, Pennsylvania, Washington, and Oregon. For federal crimes, a United States Sentencing Commission was created, and their guidelines went into effect in late 1987.

New York, Connecticut, Maine, and South Carolina also established sentencing commissions, but the resulting recommendations were rejected by their respective legislatures. In Connecticut, the sentencing commission developed a sentencing grid based on past sentencing practices, but nevertheless stated that it opposed adoption of its own guidelines. The Connecticut legislature took the commission's advice, rejected the guidelines and established a statutory determinate structure. In South Carolina, the sentencing guidelines commission's proposed guidelines were submitted in 1985, but they failed to win legislative approval. The defeat was in large measure attributable to strong resistance by the judiciary.[9]

Minnesota

In 1978 Minnesota pioneered what soon came to be regarded as the prototypical embodiment of the determinate ideal. Rather than allowing the legislature to set sentences—a process that automatically catapults decisions about sentence length into the dangerous and often draconian world of public opinion and encourages politicians to engage in tough-on-crime posturing—Minnesota became the first state in the nation to establish a commission to promulgate a determinate sentencing system.

The recommendations of the nine-member sentencing commission were adopted by the Minnesota legislature in 1980. The guidelines took effect on May 1, 1981 and have been revised periodically.

The Minnesota commission modelled their efforts after the earlier work of the Federal Parole Board, which in collaboration with the National Council on Crime and Delinquency had developed a system for structuring the parole release decision.[10] Rather than setting presumptive sentences as California did, Minnesota established a sentencing guidelines matrix or grid. The terms "sentencing guidelines" and "determinate sentencing" are today frequently used interchangeably, although in practice the two are not necessarily synonymous. Some determinate systems operate without sentencing guidelines, and sentencing guidelines are used in systems that are not determinate.

The Minnesota guidelines commission made a number of overt policy decisions; later, other jurisdictions would shun being so bold as to plainly state an overall guiding principle. A major explicit decision made by the commission was that the guidelines would be prescriptive or normative rather than descriptive. A prescriptive system is based on value judgments about the correct amount of punishment for a given crime, while a descriptive system is based on statistical examinations of past sentencing practices. While the Minnesota commission studied the historical data, the statistical averages were modified to reflect the commission members' normative beliefs about appropriate sentences.

The commission's study revealed that judges had been basing their sentencing decisions more heavily on offenders' prior criminal record than they had on the seriousness of the instant offense. First offenders convicted of serious crimes, even violent crimes, had been less likely to be incarcerated than repeat offenders convicted of relatively less serious offenses. The commission set out to change this pattern.

Minnesota has a long tradition of and widespread support for alternatives to incarceration. With criminal justice issues being less politically charged in Minnesota than they are in many other jurisdictions, the commission took the stance that imprisonment under the new system would be reserved for violent offenders. Non violent offenders, even recidivists, would receive some form of community-based alternative sentence. An offender's prior criminal record would not be ignored, but its prominent place in the sentencing decision would be reduced substantially. The commission thus opted for a new use of scarce prison space, knowing that the new policy would result in a decisive break with past practice.

The Minnesota legislature charged the sentencing commission with considering prison capacity when setting the guidelines. In other states, similar charges were not followed as literally, but in Minnesota the mandate was embraced warmly as the guidelines' drafters sought to freeze prison populations at their current level. To accomplish this, precise data were needed on the impact of the new system on prison populations. For such projections to be accurate, the ranges in the sentencing grid had to be relatively narrow and departure infrequent so that researchers could estimate sentence length in a given case.

The commission recommended a grid with narrow sentence ranges. Aggravating and mitigating sentences were no more than 15 percent above or below the midpoint of the grid range, which generally translated into ranges of just a few months. For example, the presumptive sentence for a first offender convicted of first degree assault was set at forty-three months; the aggravated and mitigated range was forty-five to forty-one months, respectively.

Departures from the prescribed range were limited to cases involving "substantial and compelling" reasons for imposing a sentence other than that stipulated in the grid. Limiting departures to the infrequent case was not only designed to make impact projections easier, it was also intended to check sentencing disparity by limiting judges' sentencing options.

While the decision to depart from the guidelines grid and impose a different sentence was controlled by relatively stringent rules, there were no rules governing the duration of a departure sentence. An upward departure could result in a prison sentence as high as the statutory maximum and a downward or lenient departure could result in virtually any sentence, including probation. The durational departure rules have since been somewhat structured, as the state supreme court held that upward departure could generally be no more than two times the presumptive term in the guidelines grid.[11]

The Minnesota commission provided guidance on whether prison should be imposed in a given type of case and the duration of imprisonment. But, as with the duration of departure, the commission failed to address questions surrounding the use of local jails, probation, or other alternative sanctions.

Parole release was abolished, parole supervision retained. Offenders would serve two-thirds of their prison sentence in prison and the remaining one-third under parole supervision in the community. The Minnesota commission also endorsed appellate review of sentences. Trial judges were thus forced to follow the guidelines or risk being overturned on appeal.

The commission sought a fail-safe system for reducing prison populations if overcrowding was imminent. In 1983, the system was tested when the population projections indicated that Minnesota prisons would soon exceed their capacity. The legislature expanded the good-time provisions so that enough offenders could be released to make room for incoming inmates.

The guidelines have undergone periodic modifications since their enactment. One change, while not major, is illuminating. The commission originally promulgated a noninclusive list of aggravating and mitigating factors for the court to consider in imposing sentence. Non-enumerated factors could be considered at the court's discretion. In 1983 the Minnesota Supreme Court ruled that it would be appropriate for the court to consider the offender's "amenability" or "unamenability" to probation when considering whether to impose a departure sentence.[12] Rather than focusing on the instant offense and the offender's just-deserts, the Minnesota appeals court opted to endorse a departure factor reminiscent of the rehabilitative paradigm.[13]

Washington

Washington's sentencing guidelines took effect on July 1, 1984. They are modelled closely after the Minnesota system, although Washington's crime scoring system is more complex and requires scoring of the seriousness of the prior offense as well as the instant offense.

Like Minnesota, Washington's guidelines grid contains narrow sentence ranges. The guidelines are undergirded by an explicit, just-deserts statement of the purposes of punishment. As in Minnesota, a noninclusive list of aggravating and mitigating factors is specified, and departure is limited to cases of "substantial and compelling" circumstances. The Washington commission likewise chose violence as a benchmark, opting to reserve precious prison resources for violent criminals. Property offenders, including recidivists, would be less likely to be sentenced to prison. Like Minnesota, the Washington commission expressly geared its guidelines to prison capacity.

While the similarities are strong, the guidelines in Washington are also unique on several points. Not only was parole release abolished, but parole supervision was also eliminated. Offenders serve the sentence imposed by the court less one-third off for good behavior in prison.

Also unlike Minnesota, the Washington guidelines apply to misdemeanors as well as felonies. While Minnesota's guidelines provide no guidance on whether to impose a local jail or a probation sentence, Washington's guidelines control local jail sentences as well as state prison sentences.

Washington went further than other states and confronted prosecutorial discretion directly. Rather than pretending that charging and sentencing discretion did not exist, or that prosecutors did not have a great deal to gain under the new system, the Washington commission attempted to structure prosecutorial discretion by promulgating plea bargaining guidelines.

Finally, also unlike other states, the Washington law operates with an express policy of less severity towards nonviolent first offenders. The court is not required to follow the grid for these offenders, and can instead sentence them to a community based treatment program or a short stay in a local jail.[14]

Pennsylvania

Pennsylvania's sentencing guidelines operate within an indeterminate sentencing system, with the judge imposing a minimum and maximum prison sentence. The court uses the guidelines in setting the minimum prison term. Upon reaching their minimum sentence, offenders are eligible for parole release. The guidelines do not regulate the parole board's release decisionmaking power.

Pennsylvania's guidelines commission was established in 1978. Problems quickly arose. Legislators favoring mandatory sentences withdrew their support for the proposal put forth by the guidelines commission, and the guidelines bill was defeated in 1981. Thereafter, the commission was given a new charge: make the guidelines tougher and give judges more power. The revised guidelines were approved by the Pennsylvania legislature and took effect in 1982.[15]

The enacted guidelines are extremely broad, leaving ample room for discretion and disparity to flourish. For every offense, the guidelines specify three ranges—normal, aggravating, and mitigating. The ranges are enormous, with several years separating the possible sanction for a particular crime. Any sentence within the range may be selected, and no criteria are set forth for determining which of the three ranges to use for sentencing. Mitigating and aggravating factors are not specified; judges are free to concoct their own factors. Departure from the range is permissible. Again, no departure criteria were established.

Federal Sentencing Guidelines

After a twenty-year flirtation with determinate sentencing, on November 1, 1987, the U.S. Congress finally succumbed to the allure of sentencing guidelines.[16] In effect since November 1987, the federal guidelines grid is similar in most respects to that used in Minnesota and Washington. Judges have enormous discretion in departing from the grid, being allowed to do so whenever they believe sufficient mitigating or aggravating factors are present. While departure is relatively unrestricted, judges must record their reasons for not adhering to the guideline sentences.

The federal guidelines have been challenged forcefully since their inception. Opponents argued (and they were upheld in some of the various federal district courts that considered the issue) that the guidelines violated the constitutional separation of powers doctrine. One line of argument held that the sentencing commission represented an unconstitutional delegation of legislative power by the executive to an administrative agency. Another maintained that placing the sentencing commission in the judicial branch of government and vesting the President with the authority to appoint and remove the judicial members of the commission violated the separation doctrine.

To avoid prolonged confusion over the guidelines, the United States Supreme Court moved quickly to decide the issue. On January 18, 1989, in an 8-to-1 ruling, the High Court upheld the constitutionality of the federal sentencing commission's guidelines in *U.S. v. Mistretta*. The Court found that the guidelines did not violate constitutionally required separation of powers among the three branches of government. But the justices did not rule on whether the new system violated due process protections for defendants, thereby leaving open a doorway through which future challenges could pass.

On September 29, 1989, in *U.S. v. Curran*, a federal district judge in Peoria, Illinois struck down a key provision of the guidelines. The overruled procedure involved lenient sentencing of offenders who cooperate with federal officials in criminal investigations. Under the guidelines, only the prosecutor can determine whether to invoke the process that allows for a sentence below the guidelines as a reward for an offender's cooperation in the investigation and prosecution of another offender. The district judge ruled that this aspect of the guidelines violated defendants' due process rights because they could not on their own ask the court to impose a lighter sentence; nor could the judge consider such a sentence unless asked by the prosecutor. At this book goes to press, it is still too early to know whether the district court's ruling will be upheld on appeal.

On November 16, 1989, a federal district judge in Washington, D.C. ruled that the guidelines violate the rights of defendants by giving prosecutors arbitrary power to determine prison terms. The judge took particular objection to the secrecy surrounding the prosecutor's charging decisions. Under a guidelines system, the person who picks the charge in large measure controls the ultimate punishment.

Whether this or other federal court cases will set the stage for a new nationwide test of the sentencing laws remains to be seen. Regardless of the outcome of the current litigation, it is likely that serious challenges to the federal guidelines will persist.

Before turning to an in-depth examination of New York State's odyssey with the determinate ideal, an overview of the movement in California is presented.

The Politics of Reform: California

California's Indeterminate Sentencing Law (ISL), adopted in 1917, carried the rehabilitative model of penology to its logical extreme. Life imprisonment was ordered for robbery, rape, burglary, and most other serious offenses. Judges simply sentenced the offender to the "term prescribed by law," which for most offenses was zero to life or five years to life.

In New York, the parole board was somewhat controlled by the actions of judges and legislators, who set the outer boundaries of sentencing. In contrast, California's parole authority had unfettered discretion in determining sentence length.

The Adult Authority, California's paroling agency, held the real sentencing power in the state, and its control was absolute. The Authority fixed the primary term of incarceration, which was the total time to be served before absolute discharge. The Authority also decided what portion, if any, of the primary term would be served in the community on parole. The Authority could refix the primary term or the parole term as it wished. Throughout most of its existence, the Authority postponed setting the primary term until the prisoner was paroled.[17]

The ISL served many masters. Judges and politicians could escape responsibility for sentence length. They could avoid the political pressure to get tough on crime, instead blaming the Authority whenever a parolee got into trouble.

The ISL was also useful to correctional authorities, giving them a flexible tool for maintaining institutional discipline. Police and prosecutors saw the ISL as a means of keeping dangerous offenders locked up longer. They were right: Time served in California prisons was among the longest in the nation.[18]

California was one of the first states to begin code revisions in the early 1960s patterned on the American Law Institute's Model Penal Code. While it started early, it also gave up the effort early, and California became one of the few states that failed to enact sentencing reform based on the Model Code.[19] California's unwillingness to adopt a new model code may well have been linked to the usefulness of the ISL to politicians and criminal justice practitioners.

Despite its many advantages, paralleling national events, criticism of the ISL mounted during the early 1970s.[20] Not surprisingly, the Adult Authority bore the brunt of the attack. Given its broad discretionary reach and the immunity of other criminal justice actors from responsibility for sentence length, the Adult Authority quite naturally became the focus of public complaints about the criminal sentencing system.

Prisoner's rights and civil liberties groups decried the wide-open discretion of the Authority, which they said produced sentences of barbaric uncertainty. Once the attack began, law-and-order groups joined in, accusing the Authority of failing to protect the public. Conservatives complained that release often occurred too early, liberals that it occurred too late. The Authority's term-fixing practices were categorized by both sides as arbitrary, capricious, and disparate.

Politicians Push for Reform

In 1974, Senator John Nejedly, Chairman of the California Senate Select Committee on Penal Institutions, was casting about "in search of matters possibly ripe for legislative remedy."[21] To further the search, Nejedly hired Michael Salerno, a legislative aide, who, recognizing that the ISL was under attack, concluded that sentencing change was possible. Along with Raymond Parnas, a law professor at Davis, Salerno consulted with key policymakers and criminal justice practitioners.

By November 1974, Parnas and Salerno had prepared a working paper on sentencing that called for specific penalty ranges. Depending on the offense classification, courts would impose a maximum sentence of from five to twenty-five years, three to twenty-five years, three to fifteen years, or three to ten years. The court would state its reasons for the sentence selected. All sentences would be subject to appellate review to determine whether they were disparate from sentences imposed on other offenders for similar crimes. The paper served as a basis for comment at public hearings held in December 1974. Approximately two dozen witnesses testified; with the exception of Los Angeles Superior Court judges, all of the witnesses supported some form of determinate sentencing.[22]

Following the hearings, a revised working paper, the forerunner of Senate Bill(SB) 42 (the first Determinate Sentence Law (DSL)), was released by Senator Nejedly. It called for the abolition of the Adult Authority, and created sentencing categories: each included a mitigated, a presumptive, and an aggravated sentence. The court would select a single definite sentence from the appropriate sentencing triad. Good time could reduce the definite sentence by one-third. Released offenders would be subject to a fixed period of parole supervision. A special provision allowed for the extended confinement of dangerous offenders.[23]

SB 42 was introduced in the Senate on March 4, 1975. It passed the Senate by a vote of thirty-six to one on May 15, 1975.[24] The bill did not fare so well in the California Assembly, however. The Assembly Committee on Criminal Justice held hearings on SB 42 in August 1975. The Committee tabled the bill after receiving negative testimony from the American Civil Liberties Union (ACLU), which claimed that the sentences were too severe, and from the District Attorney's Association, which claimed that they were too lenient.

Liberals Push For Reform

Due process liberals and prisoner support groups were inspired by the popular prison abolitionist literature and other social critiques, such as that put forward by the American Friends Society. They were attracted to SB 42 because of the increased certainty of sentences, the perceived equality of sentences for people who committed similar crimes, and the elimination of the arbitrary power of the Adult Authority. In addition, some liberals believed that SB 42 would result in shorter prison terms. The sentence ranges in the proposed bill approximated the median time served under the ISL; with one-third off for good behavior in prison, under the new system sentences might be expected to be shorter.[25]

A brewing conflict between two liberal groups was evident at the hearings on SB 42 conducted by the Assembly Committee on Criminal Justice. The Prisoners Union, comprised of ex-offenders and others interested in penal reform, attacked the discretion inherent in the rehabilitative model, called for flat-term sentencing, abolition of parole, and elimination of future-oriented sentencing criteria. They supported the bill.

The staff of the ACLU of Northern California, however, expressed serious reservations about SB 42, claiming that the sentences were too long, and that they would get even longer in the future. In addition, the ACLU staff wanted to retain early administrative release for deserving prisoners. Although they too wanted shorter sentences, the Prisoners Union was reportedly outraged at the suggestion of retaining administrative release discretion.[26]

At one point, the Prisoners Union picketed the San Francisco offices of the ACLU, promoting an open confrontation between the ACLU board members and staff. The board members listened to both groups, then sided with the Prisoners Union. The ACLU staff were thereafter forbidden to work against the passage of determinate sentencing.[27]

The Prisoners Union succeeded in eliminating what they perceived as the most objectionable features of SB 42, including extended terms for dangerous offenders. Later, after the passage of the Determinate Sentence Law (DSL), the Prisoners Union and the ACLU sought to prevent the legislature from enacting amendments favorable to law-enforcement interests.

Conservatives Push for Reform

Conservatives thought the DSL would result in more offenders being incarcerated, but they felt that the proposed sentences were too short. Representatives of the state's district attorneys and police opposed SB 42 at the initial hearings of the Assembly Committee on Criminal Justice. The Attorney General's Office, however, spoke in favor of the bill.

Revised versions of SB 42 placated conservative interests. Sentence enhancements were established for prior criminal record, armed felonies, and crimes resulting in great bodily injury. The revised bill also increased sentences for offenders convicted of certain violent felonies—the so-called dirty eight offenses. The Attorney General's Office threatened to withdraw its support if the enhancements were made discretionary rather than mandatory. A compromise was reached: Enhancements would not be mandatory, but judges would have to justify decisions not to increase the sentence whenever enhancing factors were present.

District attorneys, seeking to increase their plea bargaining power, lobbied successfully to prevent the passage of a provision allowing courts, on their own motion, to mitigate, aggravate, or enhance a sentence. The district attorneys clearly did not wish to give judges the power to raise or lower sentences.

California judges had relatively little input in the passage of SB 42. The California Association of Judges spoke out against the bill, but the state's judges were otherwise not united or organized in their approach to influencing sentencing policy, especially in the early stages of the development of the DSL.[28]

A Bid for Containment

In April 1975 Raymond Procunier, Chairman of the Adult Authority, issued directive 75/20, an administrative rule that was widely interpreted as an effort to ward off the onslaught of determinate sentencing.[29] Procunier's directive required that the Authority set an early term-fix for each offender based on the seriousness of the offense and the offender's prior record. A parole date would be established at the offender's first regularly scheduled appearance before the parole authorities.

Procunier's directive set forth rules for standardizing parole's decision-making process. First, parole would consider the primary offense, that is, the most serious offense for which the offender was incarcerated; next, they would decide if the typical or the aggravated term ought to apply in the individual case; third, they would consult a chart attached to the directive to determine the appropriate sentence range; and finally, they would fix a base period of confinement within the appropriate range. Procunier's chart based sentence length primarily on the seriousness of the commitment offense and the offender's prior record, although the parole agent was free to also consider the inmate's age and institutional behavior. The similarity between Procunier's 1975 directive and the determinate sentencing structures that were later enacted in other states is remarkable.

Proportionality and the California Courts

Procunier's bid at containment was quashed by the judiciary. The California Supreme Court and the Court of Appeals played a pivotal role in the adoption of determinate sentencing.

In two key cases, *In Re Lynch* and *In Re Foss*,[30] the California Supreme Court chipped away at the rehabilitative ideal by establishing a proportionality test for sentence length under the indeterminate system.

In Re Lynch

Under the ISL, a first conviction for indecent exposure was classified as a simple misdemeanor, punishable by a short jail term or a fine.[31] A second conviction for indecent exposure raised the crime to a felony punishable by imprisonment from one year to life. In *In Re Lynch,* the California Supreme Court struck down the statute, noting that "legislative authority remains ultimately circumscribed by the constitutional provision forbidding the infliction of cruel or unusual punishment."[32]

The *Lynch* court dismissed the argument that challenges to sentence length under the ISL should focus on the minimum sentence. In regard to a convicted criminal, the court found that "the test is whether the maximum term of imprisonment permitted by the statute punishing his offense exceeds the constitutional limit, regardless of whether a lesser term may be fixed in his particular case by the Adult Authority."[33]

A three-pronged test was applied to determine whether a sentence violated the state's constitutional prohibition against cruel and unusual punishment. Sentences would be compared to the seriousness of the offense and the criminal record of the offender, to other punishments in the same state for more serious offenses, and to the punishment for the same offense in other states.[34]

In Re Foss

The California Supreme Court applied the *Lynch* test two years later in *In Re Foss*. Here the court struck down Health and Safety Code section 11501, which provided increased penalties for second-time narcotics offenders. Defendant Foss was convicted of selling heroin, and he had been convicted fourteen years previously for heroin possession. The prior conviction triggered sentencing under section 11501, thereby mandating a maximum term of life and a minimum term of ten years before first parole eligibility. The *Foss* court found that the ten-year minimum sentence with no possibility of parole release was disproportionate to the offense, qualifying as cruel and unusual punishment.

The *Foss* court noted that it was not deciding whether the life maximum was constitutional. Nor was it taking issue with the ten-year minimum term *per se:* It held merely that ten years without parole eligibility for a second time narcotics offender violated the cruel and unusual punishment clause of the state constitution.[35]

California courts were subsequently inundated with individual challenges to sentences under the *Lynch-Foss* test.[36] These two cases demonstrated to observers that the state's highest court would not hesitate to intervene in the operation of the state's sentencing system. This was troubling to many, and rather than allowing the court to assume authority over sentencing, certain influential Californians looked for a legislative solution.[37]

While they were looking, two other decisions were handed down that had a profound effect on the continued viability of the Adult Authority and the ISL.

In Re Rodriquez

The defendant in *In Re Rodriquez* had served twenty-two years in prison for lewd conduct with a child. Applying the *Lynch-Foss* test, the California Supreme Court held that the sentence was disproportionate to the severity of the offense and constituted cruel and unusual punishment.[38]

Sweeping beyond the case at bar, the court attacked the Adult Authority's primary-term policy. The court acknowledged that the statute did not require the Authority to fix a primary term at less than the maximum sentence imposed. It also noted that the Authority had a long-standing practice of fixing a primary term only in conjunction with granting parole release.[39]

In Rodriquez's case, the Authority had not fixed the primary term at less than the maximum during the twenty-two years of his imprisonment. Rodriquez, who had an I.Q. of about sixty-eight,[40] had been retained because "the Authority cannot predict his future behavior, and because he is believed to lack ability to care for himself and to conform to parole requirements except in a structured living situation with supervision."[41]

The *Rodriquez* Court was clearly dissatisfied with the term-setting practice of the Authority.

> Neither the petitioner in *Lynch*, nor, as shall be shown, the petitioner now before us ever had his term fixed at a number of years proportionate to his offense by the Authority at any time before his punishment became constitutionally excessive, thus irrefragably demonstrating the error of the asserted assumption that the Indeterminate Sentence Law has operated constitutionally with respect to term-fixing since its inception. Such assumption is particularly ironic in light of the express declaration of the Authority that in term-setting its function is "to make the punishment fit the criminal rather than the crime." The Indeterminate Sentence Law is not now being administered in a manner which offers assurance that persons subject thereto will have their terms fixed at a number of years proportionate to their individual culpability... or, that their terms will be fixed with sufficient promptness to permit any requested review of their proportionality to be accomplished before the affected individuals have been imprisoned beyond the constitutionally permitted term.[42]

The court reasoned that the power to grant parole and to change the primary term enables the Authority to give recognition to a prisoner's good conduct in prison, his efforts toward rehabilitation, and his readiness to lead a crime-free life in society. On the other hand, this discretionary power also permits the Authority to retain a prisoner for the full primary term if his release might pose a danger to society.[43]

Because the Authority had "failed to properly interpret and administer the Indeterminate Sentence Law with respect to the responsibility to fix the primary term of a prisoner who is subject to that law,"[44] the court announced that, in the future, absent a prompt fixing of the primary term, the maximum term would be used for the purpose of assessing the constitutionality of the sentence. Therefore, the court reasoned, in determining that *Rodriquez* was not ready for parole, the Authority had either failed to fulfill its responsibility to fix a primary term proportionate to the offense, or had implicitly fixed it at life. In either case, the cruel and unusual clause of the state constitution had been violated.

The dissent in *Rodriquez* warned that the majority's decision had raised "for the first time serious doubts as to the constitutionality of the long-established term-fixing practices under which the penal system of California has functioned for many years."[45] The dissent urged case-by-case decisionmaking, rather than the blanket requirement handed down by the majority, who were "embark[ing] on a new course, armed with enthusiasm but neither compass nor chart."[46]

In Re Stanley

Decided one year after *Rodriquez, In Re Stanley* compounded the Adult Authority's problems.[47] In *Stanley* the California Court of Appeals, citing *Rodriquez*, reasserted that there was a difference between the primary-term decision and the parole release decision.

> The Indeterminate Sentence Law vests in the Adult Authority two distinct discretionary functions: sentence-fixing within the statutory minimum and maximum terms for the inmate's crime and parole-setting. In past years the Adult Authority coupled these two functions by fixing sentence only at the time it granted parole.[48]

At issue was directive 75/20, distributed in April 1975 by Adult Authority Chairman Procunier. The Court of Appeals found the directive, which required that the Authority set an early term-fix for each offender based on the seriousness of the offense and the offender's prior record, to be inconsistent with the objectives of the indeterminate sentencing system and parole release. The Court said that the ISL required the Authority to recognize the "inmate's post-conviction history and his potential for safe release as indispensable considerations in parole setting."[49] Directive 75/20 failed under this analysis. Rather than consider the rehabilitative potential of each offender, the parole directive

> bases the period of confinement primarily upon the nature of the principal
> commitment offense, supplemented by mathematical increments for addi-
> tional precommitment offenses. It recognizes in-prison behavior only as a
> negative determinant, directing extensions of confinement for post-convic-
> tion breaches. It withholds recognition of acceptable in-prison conduct,
> reclamation potential and post-release social safety as affirmative factors
> gravitating toward early release ... Its table of fixed time-increments forms
> a mechanical, across-the-board standard which militates against individual-
> ized consideration. It substitutes a mechanized tit-for-tat in place of dis-
> criminating individual judgment.[50]

The California Court of Appeals continued:

> As presently framed, the Indeterminate Sentence Law is grounded upon the
> assumption that an inmate's in-prison responses supply a basis for measur-
> ing his progress toward rehabilitation, thereby permitting predictions of
> post-release behavior, good or ill, which will supply guidance in fixing his
> release date ... The chairman's directive of April 1975 gives primacy to the
> factor of prior criminality, leaving to silence and implication the factors of
> individual reclamation and post-release expectations ... It disregards the
> law's demand to weigh all, not part, of the relevant factors ... Its reliance
> upon a table of time increments clashes with the statute's discerned demand
> for reasoned individualization. Similar criminal histories may characterize
> utterly dissimilar individuals.[51]

Court as Catalyst

Stanley could easily be interpreted as an attempt to preserve the underlying
spirit of the rehabilitative ideal. Ironically, it was used by opponents of the
ISL to topple the rehabilitative structure.

The court in *Stanley* did not prevent the Adult Authority from administrative rule-making. It merely held that the rules must consider the penal rehabilitation of the offender. Nevertheless, *Stanley,* in spoiling Chairman Procunier's bid at containment, acted as a catalyst, providing the requisite spark to
persuade Governor Edmund Brown, Jr. that legislative action was needed.[52]

After the ACLU and the State Bar Association changed their position
and supported the bill, it became apparent that an unusual coalition had
formed around SB 42. The Prisoners Union and other liberal groups backed
the bill because of the perceived equity and fairness of the new system; law
enforcement interests were attracted to the certainty of punishment, especially for violent and repeat offenders.

After *Stanley,* Governor Brown indicated his willingness to support a
reworked version of SB 42 more favorable to law enforcement. The revised
bill changed the retroactivity provisions to permit the retention of dangerous

offenders and added a discretionary three-year enhancement for each prior violent felony offense where the instant offense was a violent felony. This version was amended four times before it passed both houses in August 1976, seven months after the Stanley decision. The revised bill was passed by the Assembly Committee on Criminal Justice in August 1976; later that month it passed the Assembly by a vote of sixty to seventeen. The California Senate concurred.[53]

The Uniform Determinate Sentencing Law (DSL) was signed by Governor Brown on September 20, 1976, with an effective date of July 1, 1977. Declaring "that the purpose of imprisonment for crime is punishment," the DSL was intended to promote "uniformity in the sentences of offenders committing the same offense under similar circumstances."[54] California thus became the first state to officially sanction retribution as the primary purpose of punishment.

Senate Bill 42

The DSL stipulated a lower, middle, and upper prison term for each felony. The court would impose the middle term unless aggravating or mitigating factors were present, in which case the court could impose the upper or lower term. The court could also impose an additional period of incarceration if an enhancement was charged and proved. Precise rules prescribe the duration of the prison term, but the decision to incarcerate was generally left to the discretion of the court.

Inmates were eligible for good-time reductions of up to one-third. Parole supervision terms were set at one year for most releasees. The new Board of Prison Terms, which replaced the Adult Authority, was responsible for applying the DSL retroactively.

To a large degree, the original version of the DSL represented a middle ground between law enforcement and defense interests. The balance was short lived, however.

Criticism of SB 42 mounted even before it was passed into law. The fragile coalition that had formed around the DSL fell apart quickly as law-enforcement groups sought to increase the severity of the sentencing structure.

Several task forces were formed, ostensibly to consider procedural and technical amendments to SB 42. Governor Brown expressed support for amendments that would "mollify law enforcement."[55] It soon became apparent that far more than technical changes were being proposed.

The Prisoners Union, the ACLU, and other prison-reform groups, hoped to salvage whatever benefits they could from the determinate sentencing law. They urged the legislature to resist pressure to revise SB 42. At first, they met with moderate success. Many of the more drastic proposals were moderated, the base terms were not raised, good time continued to vest, and the push for a separate sentencing system for dangerous offenders was halted.[56]

But defense groups could not prevail for long, and by the late 1970s conservatives began chipping away at the DSL. The creators of the determinate ideal should have shuddered to think what they had wrought.

Modifications in SB 42

Since its origin in 1976, California's new code has undergone sweeping changes. A number of new laws have been enacted to increase the sentences for specific crimes and expand the range between the triad of terms. Changes have been made piecemeal, without any overt effort to maintain the proportionality principle that gave impetus to the original structure. With each change, discretion has grown and the rationale underlying the sentencing system has been further muddled.

SB 476—The Boatwright Bill

The erosion of the new system began even before the DSL went into effect. The Boatwright Bill, SB 476, named for its sponsor, Assemblyman Daniel Boatwright, was introduced in February 1977. Although the legislature was able to resist (temporarily) pressure to raise the triad of base terms, changes made by SB 476 enhanced the discretion of prosecutors and the correctional bureaucracy.[57] Several conservative-sponsored measures were contained in the Boatwright Bill, including raising SB 42's caps on enhancements, extending the length of parole supervision from one year to eighteen months, and changing the retroactive sentencing provisions of SB 42 to make it easier to hold "dangerous" offenders longer.

California entered the determinate era with little opportunity to plan for the successful implementation and monitoring of the new policy. The Boatwright Bill was signed by the governor as emergency legislation on June 29, 1977, two days before the effective date of the DSL. The last-minute changes left sentencing decisionmakers scurrying for copies of the new law.

SB 709 and SB 1057

Conservative pressure to increase sentences for violent and repeat offenders resulted in the passage of SB 709, signed on September 5, 1978, with an effective date of January 1979. The original four penalty groupings of SB 42 were expanded to ten groupings. With a wider range of choices, prosecutorial discretion increased accordingly.[58]

A companion bill, SB 1057, increased the discretion of parole decisionmakers. It extended parole supervision periods to three years for offenders sentenced under the DSL and to five years for lifers. The ever present spectre of parole revocation and return to prison served as a constant reminder that, in spite of the rhetoric, sentences remained uncertain under the new determinate structure.

SB 13

SB 13 was passed in 1979 and became effective on January 1, 1980. Aimed at violent sex offenders, SB 13 required severe enhancements for sex offenses involving weapons or great bodily injury to the victim. A ten-year enhancement for each previous incarceration for a violent sex crime was mandated where the defendant had two or more prior incarcerations for a sex crime and where the current offense was for a violent sex crime.

Caps on consecutive sentences for violent sex offenses were eliminated. Each sentence imposed in multiple-count sex cases was to be fully consecutive to any other sentence. While these provisions severely curtailed the discretion of the parties once the factors justifying an enhancement were proved, there was no requirement that enhancements be charged at all. Like the decision on whether to imprison the offender, the new law gave no guidance on when it would be appropriate to enhance sentences. It merely said that once a decision to enhance (or incarcerate) was made, controls would be placed on the duration of punishment.

The Victim's Bill of Rights

In addition to legislative actions, popular referenda were used to further alter SB 42. Proposition Eight of 1982, known as the Victim's Bill of Rights, covered a wide range of criminal and non-criminal-justice issues.

In addition to prohibitions on plea bargaining, the legislation required an extra five-year term for each prior serious felony conviction where the defendant presently stood convicted of a serious felony. The prior conviction need not have resulted in a period of incarceration (the criteria generally used in applying enhancements for previous convictions). Serious crimes included armed or unarmed burglary of a residence, robbery, felonies in which the defendant inflicted great bodily injury on a person other than an accomplice, felonies in which the defendant used a firearm or a dangerous weapon, sale of drugs to minors, and attempts to commit a serious felony.

Prosecutorial discretion grew in direct proportion to the growth of enhancements. In retrospect, it is difficult to understand how the defense advocates of the DSL so seriously underestimated the control that prosecutors' would gain over the new system.

The Work Incentive Law

The original version of the DSL allowed inmates to earn good-time reductions of up to one-third off the definite sentence. Three months could be earned each year for good institutional behavior and one month for participation in prison programs. Several protections were built into the good-time provisions to increase the determinacy of the sentence. Good time was to be lost only for serious misconduct, the maximum loss for each incident was thirty days, two levels of review were designated, and previously earned good time vested (that is, once earned, it could not be taken away).

The Work Incentive Law, effective January 1983, increased good-time credits to one day for each day served for participation in work assignments or educational programs, thus giving correctional authorities control over 50 percent of the offender's sentence.[59]

The Work Incentive Law also gave correctional authorities increased power over procedures for awarding and crediting good time. While the maximum loss per incident was previously thirty days, offenders were now subject to substantially greater penalties. For example, one year could be lost for battery on a non-prisoner that resulted in great bodily injury; 180 days could be lost for a single act that could be prosecuted as a felony, even if it was not so prosecuted; and 90 days could be lost for serious disciplinary offenses.

Vesting of good time, a quintessential feature of determinacy, was abolished by the Work Incentive Law; restoration by prison officials of previously lost good time, the enemy of certainty, was adopted. Like prosecutors, prison officials were turning into the real winners under the new system.

Recent Changes in the DSL

Continuing to approach change in a piecemeal fashion, the California Legislature spends a great deal of time tinkering with the DSL. Recent amendments have increased the severity of the penalty triads and the number of offenses requiring imprisonment.[60] With each change, discretion grows, proportionality declines, and purposes become more confused.

Given the complexity of the DSL, it is easy for practitioners to become enmeshed in the mathematics and mechanical rules of the system, rather than being involved in the substance of sentencing individual offenders. Dissatisfaction with the DSL has remained widespread. The California legislature passed a Sentencing Guidelines Commission Bill in 1984, patterned on the Minnesota model later used by the New York Committee. The commission bill was vetoed by Governor Deukmejian, who has long been an ardent supporter of tough-on-crime measures and the DSL.

Have Discretion and Crime Control Disappeared?

The DSL was designed to limit case-by-case decisionmaking. Yet, the breadth of discretion inherent in the new system is manifest. Discretion is most evident in the decision to incarcerate: While the duration of incarceration decision was precisely structured by the legislature, courtroom players retain control over the in-out decision.

California's Judicial Council is charged with promulgating aggravating and mitigating factors. The council has been criticized for failing to firmly structure the departure decision. The rules are said to justify virtually any sentencing outcome, hardly an effective way to contain discretionary decisionmaking.[61]

In addition to determining whether to depart from the base terms, the courtroom actors decide whether to impose enhancements. Enhancements significantly increase sentences. For example, two years can be added to the base term for using a firearm; five years can be added for a prior conviction for a violent sex crime where the instant conviction is for a violent sex crime. Generally the court has the discretion to impose consecutive sentence enhancements or to allow the offender to serve several sentences concurrently.[62]

While precise durational requirements exist once the decision to enhance has been made, the decision to move for an enhancement in the first instance is left to the discretion of the parties. California prosecutors thus have unfettered charging discretion. If the prosecutor elects to charge an enhancement, the court retains the discretion, with few exceptions, to impose or to strike the enhancement once proved. As with the aggravating and mitigating factors, enhancements provide courtroom actors with powerful bargaining chips.

Research indicates that California prosecutors have used the enhancement provisions to increase their sentencing discretion by electing not to charge enhancements in many cases where the evidence would support such a charge or sentence. One study reported that violent prior prison term enhancements were charged in only 36 percent of the cases where the offender had actually served such a sentence; nonviolent prior prison enhancements were charged in 44 percent of the cases where the offender had served such a term; enhancements for injury were charged in 36 percent of the cases where the victim had been injured; and firearm enhancements were charged in 87 percent of the cases where firearms had been used in the crime.[63]

Thus, in practice, discretion has not been eliminated. It has shifted simply from one constellation of authority to another. Sentence length has not become certain, as the changes in the good-time laws give prison officials control over half of the sentence.

Nor has crime control been toppled, but it has been disguised, as can be seen from the Judicial Council's guidelines for the prison decision. In determining whether to incarcerate a defendant, judges are advised to consider whether the offender is remorseful and whether he represents a danger to others, considerations far removed from the traditional retributive concern with the seriousness of the offense.[64]

Some of the aggravating and mitigating factors address retributive concerns, while others are clearly aimed at crime control. For example, one aggravating factor considers whether the "defendant has engaged in a pattern of violent conduct which indicates a serious danger to society."[65] California policymakers thus continue to try to control crime through the imposition of the criminal sanction, despite rhetoric to the contrary.

Summing Up Events in California

The passage of determinate sentencing law in California was made possible by an unusual coalition of conservatives and liberals, who joined together to destroy the indeterminate structure and abolish parole release. Decisions of an activist Supreme Court provided additional incentive for change. The fragile coalition that had formed around the idea of determinate sentencing fell apart quickly, however, as law-and-order interests prevailed in securing severe sentencing measures in subsequent revisions of the law.

The remainder of this book centers on New York State's pursuit of the determinate ideal.

5

The Attack on the Rehabilitative Regime in New York

As it was elsewhere across the country, the rehabilitative paradigm was well entrenched in New York's statutory scheme at the end of the 1960s. Serious challenges to the rehabilitative program soon surfaced, however, as New York legislators, led by Governors Nelson A. Rockefeller and Hugh L. Carey, emasculated the rehabilitative sentencing structure. Commitment to flexibility, treatment, and expertise would quickly give way to a complex array of mandatory sentencing provisions, restrictions on parole release, and mandatory plea-bargaining rules. As will be seen throughout the following discussion, the erosion of rehabilitative sentencing provided the perfect predicate for the capture of the determinate ideal by conservative law-and-order advocates.

The Rockefeller years: From Rehabilitation to Retribution

Nelson A. Rockefeller was first elected governor of New York in 1958. The Rockefeller administration in New York coincided with a time of national interest in the problem of crime, especially drug-related crime. Rockefeller's public pronouncements during his fifteen-year tenure as governor reflected the national preoccupation with drug crimes: Thirteen of the Governor's fifteen annual State of the State Messages were a call-to-arms over drugs.

Changes wrought in the treatment of drug offenders during Rockefeller's administration graphically illustrate the diminution of the rehabilitative model in New York, as New York moved from treating to punishing narcotic offenders.

Rehabilitating the Addict Offender: New York Leads the Way

Nelson A. Rockefeller did not begin by locking up narcotics offenders. Quite the contrary. Rockefeller launched the most extensive (and expensive) drug treatment program in the nation. Claiming that drugs directly or indirectly accounted for over half of all the crimes committed in the state, Rockefeller was originally committed to treating narcotics offenders.

The governor's drug program began slowly. By 1960 Rockefeller would boast a fifty-five bed experimental program at Manhattan State Hospital for the treatment of addict offenders.[1] By 1961 treatment centers had been established in three state hospitals, with a total in-patient capacity of 155; each treatment center operated an after-care program.[2]

In 1962, calling for a "fresh attack," Rockefeller pushed for expanded treatment of narcotics offenders. The legislature responded by passing the Metcalf-Volker Bill, authorizing non-penal treatment for certain narcotics offenders, who could elect, with the court's approval, to receive in-patient treatment at a state hospital, followed by after-care.[3] Upon signing the Metcalf-Volker Bill, Rockefeller called narcotics addiction "one of the most pressing medical and social problems we face." The governor predicted that his bill would

> save hundreds and ultimately thousands of young narcotics addicts from a life of enslavement to drugs by offering them medical treatment instead of prison in situations where their crimes are not serious.... Many narcotics addicts under arrest whose most serious failing is their own tragic addiction will be given an opportunity ... to become self-respecting and self-reliant members of society through State hospital treatment and rehabilitation.[4]

The Narcotic Addiction Control Commission

The Metcalf-Volker Act allowed the addict offender to elect in-patient treatment and after-care instead of a prison or jail sentence. Many addict offenders apparently chose the latter course, rather than have the state "help them become constructive citizens in our society."[5]

Pledging to "fight crime with an all-out attack on a prime cause of crime, narcotics addiction," Rockefeller pushed in 1966 for compulsory hospitalization of addict offenders. "It is high time," the governor said, "that we in New York pull back the curtain, take a good, hard look at the tragic reality of narcotics addiction, and assume the leadership in taking decisive steps to eliminate this spreading disease."[6]

Chapter 192 of the Laws of 1966 established The Narcotic Addiction Control Commission (NACC) in the Department of Mental Hygiene. Founded on the assumption that addiction was a disease and rooted in the conviction that the disease had reached epidemic proportions, NACC became New York's response to narcotics addiction. Addicts could be certified to NACC in three ways: civilly, after conviction of certain crimes, or after arrest but before conviction. NACC received $75 million for capital construction and $6 million for operational expenses. In signing the enabling legislation for NACC, Rockefeller announced that "the new rehabilitation program will help addicts return to normal, useful and healthy lives. It is indeed a major step toward solving a major health and law enforcement problem."[7]

The special sentencing rules would apply to most narcotics addicts, regardless of whether the underlying offense involved drugs. If the addict offender was convicted of a misdemeanor or a prostitution offense, the court was required to certify the offender to NACC; if the conviction was for a felony, the court could exercise its discretion and impose an indeterminate prison sentence or certify the offender to NACC. Felony offenders could be held by NACC for up to five years; misdemeanants and youthful offenders could be committed for up to three years.[8]

In 1967 NACC expanded its operation by purchasing fourteen privately owned facilities, making agreements with New York City and private agencies for 2,800 beds, establishing four narcotics units in correctional facilities, and placing drug rehabilitation units in facilities operated by the Department of Mental Hygiene. Rockefeller's conviction that forced treatment was the best approach was evident when he announced that "[f]or the first time in our history we can look forward with hope that real progress will be made in controlling addiction, in helping our addicts build useful lives for themselves and in restoring security to our homes, our streets, and our neighborhoods."[9]

In the first ten months of operation, NACC served more than 2,000 addicts. That apparently was not good enough for the governor, who promised to have by 1969 "8,000 addicts off the street—where they threaten people—and under treatment, where they can help themselves."[10]

Rockefeller initially claimed great victory for the mandatory treatment of addicts. In 1969 the governor reported that over half of the released addicts had not returned to drugs.[11] In 1970 he announced that over 10,000 addicts were receiving treatment—5,000 in NACC facilities and aftercare programs and 5,000 in accredited public and private facilities. "We must continue to reach out, to experiment with new methods of treatment and rehabilitation," the governor said.[12] Rockefeller urged the expansion of the state's methadone program to treat an additional 20,000 addicts, at a cost of $15 million.

Yet, despite his commitment and conviction, drug abuse continued to haunt the governor. Rockefeller's frustration with the ever-rising tide of narcotics offenders was becoming more and more evident. In 1971 he wrote:

> How can we defeat drug abuse before it destroys America?... Drug addiction represents a threat akin to war in its capacity to kill, enslave and imperil the nation's future; akin to cancer in spreading deadly disease among us, and equal to any other challenge we face and deserving all the brainpower, manpower, and resources necessary to overcome it ... Are the sons and daughters of a generation that survived the great depression and rebuilt a prosperous nation, that defeated Nazism and Fascism and preserved the free world, to be vanquished by a powder, needles, and pills?[13]

Rockefeller's commitment to fighting drug abuse nevertheless continued, as did the obduracy of the drug problem. By 1971 there were over 10,000 addicts in rehabilitation facilities and after-care status and another

9,000 in public or private programs funded or accredited by the state. Sixty-five million dollars in matching state funds had been allocated to local programs, and $200 million in loans had been arranged to help acquire new facilities.

The governor's growing disillusionment with treatment and rehabilitation was clear:

> Despite all our efforts and the investment of millions of dollars, narcotic addiction and drug abuse continue to plague our society, and to spread a net of fear and despair . . . New York has embarked upon the world's most comprehensive programs for the prevention of drug abuse, and for the treatment and rehabilitation of narcotic addicts and drug abusers. New York has invested more and done more than all of the forty-nine other states and the Federal government combined. In prevention, New York has mounted the Nation's largest drug education effort and also supports 226 local Narcotics Guidance Councils to assist communities in developing their own locally-based anti-narcotic efforts. In law enforcement, New York has also set the pace. It has provided narcotic control training for local law enforcement officials. We have set strict penalties for professional drug pushers and we have been a leader in coordinating the law enforcement efforts of the various states and the Federal government. In treatment and rehabilitation, New York's preeminence is unquestioned. In 1966, with the establishment of the Narcotics Addiction Control Commission, New York launched the Nation's most comprehensive program for removing narcotics addicts from the streets, and for helping them overcome their malady through treatment and rehabilitation. New York State—in this effort—is employing every viable treatment method known and is funding research into all other methods which show any substantial degree of promise.[14]

Although his mounting desperation was evident, it would be another two years before the governor was ready to cast aside the rehabilitative sentencing structure.

The Nation's Toughest Drug Laws

By 1973, having "tried every possible approach to stop addiction and save the addict through education and treatment," (at a cost of over $1 billion) Rockefeller said that he felt constrained to "tell it like it is: We have achieved very little permanent rehabilitation—and have found no cure."

Rather than trying to improve his treatment apparatus, the governor did a complete reversal, saying that the state needed "an effective deterrent to the pushing of the broad spectrum of hard drugs."[15]

NACC would no longer treat offender addicts. Instead, in a flip-flop so complete as to make his previous embrace of treatment even more remarkable, Rockefeller proposed mandatory life prison sentences, without the possibility of parole, for anyone convicted of selling or conspiring to sell any quantity of hard drugs (originally defined as heroin, amphetamines, LSD, methadone, and hashish).[16] Possessing or conspiring to possess more than one ounce of heroin, cocaine, opium, or morphine would likewise result in a mandatory life sentence.[17] Plea bargaining, youthful offender treatment, probation, and parole release would be abolished for these offenders.

Not content to leave the task to the official law enforcement apparatus, the governor proposed a $1,000 bounty to anyone providing information resulting in the conviction of a drug pusher. Rockefeller said that the bounty offer "could wreak havoc within the ranks of pushers—for they will live in constant fear from never knowing who is buying drugs for evidence to turn them in."[18] The "masterminds" of the drug world would be taken care of by a 100 percent state tax on all proceeds from the sale of drugs and by confiscating drug traffickers' cars and other property. Prosecutors would receive additional resources through special narcotics courts in New York City.

Rockefeller's proposal received a chilly reception from all sides. The New York Chapter of the American Civil Liberties Union called it "a frightening leap toward the imposition of a total police state."[19] Robert McKay, former chairman of the Attica Commission, said that the proposal was "completely counter to everything the civilized world has been working for."[20] The New York State District Attorney's Association, the New York City Police Commissioner, and other law enforcement officials likewise opposed the measure.

Undaunted, Rockefeller drummed up support for his plan, getting a warm endorsement from leaders of New York City's black community. One of the black leaders, Reverend Moore, called the governor a hero because "he has seen the preponderance of failure, of doom and devastation, and as he stands there he has done something that is very hard to do, and that is to admit failure from all the other programs that we have tried."[21] Another remarked that the governor's program was not sufficiently tough. For this zealot, nothing short of the death penalty would do.

Rockefeller ultimately prevailed; although he had to make concessions, including dropping the life without parole provisions and agreeing to support mandatory recidivist laws. The drug laws passed the legislature handily.[22] With the signing on May 9, 1973 of the "nation's toughest drug law," New York's retreat from the rehabilitative paradigm had begun.

Under the provisions of Chapter 276 of the Laws of 1973, judges would no longer exercise discretion over whether to incarcerate or impose an alternative sanction for drug cases. Mandatory incarceration was required for all class A, B, and C drug offenses. Not only was the in or out of prison decision removed from the judiciary, but sentence length decisions were also taken from them. An array of minimum minimum, maximum minimum, minimum maximum, and maximum maximum prison terms fully undercut the old sentencing structure.

Chapter 276 raised the ante for drug offenses by creating three subdivisions of class A felonies based on the quantity of the drugs sold or possessed: A-I, A-II, and A-III. The maximum sentence for all class A felonies was life imprisonment. Class A-I drug offenses were assigned a minimum minimum of fifteen years and a maximum minimum of twenty-five years; class A-II drug offenses were assigned a minimum minimum of six years and a maximum minimum of eight and one third years; class A-III drug offenses received a minimum minimum of one year and a maximum minimum of eight and one third years. All class A drug offenders released from prison would be subject to lifetime parole supervision.[23]

Chapter 276 also restricted plea bargaining opportunities for class A drug offenders. Where the indictment charged a class A drug felony, the court could not accept a guilty plea to other than a class A felony.

The Rockefeller drug law's plea bargaining restrictions produced an anomalous result. Whereas the most serious class A-I and class A-II offenders could plead to a class A-III felony (which only carried a minimum sentence of one year in prison), an offender indicted for a class A-III felony had to plead to a class A-III felony or risk trial. Thus, at least theoretically, the small time dealers were being punished at the same level as the kingpins; put differently, the biggest benefits were reserved for the worst offenders.[24]

Rockefeller did not confine his drug net to drug offenses because he associated most crimes with drugs. In the governor's view, burglary and robbery were committed to pay for the offender's addiction; assaultive behavior was the crazen result of mind-altering drugs.[25] The drug laws included stiffer penalties for a variety of non-drug offenses, including robbery and burglary, and mandated incarceration for all class A and B and certain class C and D felonies. In addition, all violent crimes committed by people under the influence of hard drugs would be punished with life sentences.

Second Felony Offender Laws

The rehabilitative model of sentencing was further challenged in New York by the passage of companion legislation to the drug bill. Discretionary sentencing of second felony offenders was abolished by a bill passed at the same time as the drug laws. The second felony offender laws were agreed upon as a compromise to overcome legislative resistance to Rockefeller's drug program.

Similar legislation had been proposed, to no avail, by powerful Assembly Republicans for years. Now the recidivist statute became a negotiation chip to pave the way for passage of the drug laws. Ironically, while much of the effect of the 1973 drug laws has been diluted over the years by subsequent legislative amendments, the second felony offender laws, which passed virtually unnoticed in the furor surrounding the drug debate, continue today to shape the state's sentencing policy and fill the state's prisons.

Under the new law, Chapter 277 of the Laws of 1973, all second felony offenders were subject to mandatory incarceration and mandatory minimum sentences.[26] In addition, plea bargaining restrictions required that an offender charged with a second felony plead to a felony.

Why the Turnabout?

Why did Governor Rockefeller abandon treatment of drug offenders? The rising crime rate cannot explain the governor's retreat from rehabilitation—it had been rising for several years. Perhaps the answer is more idiosyncratic.

According to a biography of Rockefeller written by Joseph Persico, a former speech writer for the governor, Rockefeller was at a party with William Fine, president of Bonwit Teller Department Store and chairman of a drug rehabilitation program called Phoenix House. After a discussion about the drug problem, Rockefeller asked Fine to go on a special fact-finding mission to Japan, where addiction rates were the lowest of any major country. As Persico tells the story:

> Fine agreed to go and financed the trip himself. He flew there and spent a weekend conferring with Japanese health officials. He came away with the apparent secret to the Japanese success against drugs—life sentences for pushers. He returned and submitted a report to Governor Rockefeller. For two months, he heard nothing. Then he met Nelson at another party at which Ronald Reagan, then Governor of California, was also present. Fine intrigued Reagan with his account of the trip and his report on the experience. Reagan wanted to know if he might have a copy. Fine crossed the room to check with Rockefeller, who delivered a firm no. This thunderbolt was to be hurled by him.[27]

Another, equally plausible, interpretation of Rockefeller's turnabout was given by Howard Shapiro, a former counsel to the governor. Speaking at a 1982 conference commemorating the Rockefeller era, Shapiro stressed Rockefeller's strong personal commitment to doing something about the ravages of drugs:

> There is a constant theme from the beginning to the end of the Rockefeller administration about his concern for drug abuse. It starts off with deep concern about the addicted: extensive effort, many programs and lots and lots of money (over $1 billion—and those were big, big dollars in those days) spent for treatment, rehabilitation, and education of drug users. There were the Special Narcotics Courts. There was the beefing up of the State Police. There was an effort to try to establish an effective coordination between federal and state and New York City drug enforcement officials, not always successful or harmonious, but it was a major effort. Then, finally, to cap this theme, in late 1972, out of the blue, the Governor announced to his staff that he would seek very harsh penalties for drug crimes ... I think that

he may have developed a deep personal frustration. Here was a problem that he felt very strongly about, to which he had devoted a great deal of this own time and attention and a lot of the State's money. Yet the efforts had been unsuccessful. It was very frustrating.[28]

A second speaker at the conference also attributed Rockefeller's turn-about on drugs to the governor's persistence:

He got hold of something, and he did not let go until he finally got what he wanted out of it in the way of a solution. I think that, more than anything, explains the ultimate drug proposals that he made. It is part of a larger pattern of persistence.[29]

Regardless of the reasons behind Rockefeller's radical shift, the 1973 drug laws and second felony offender laws were watersheds in the destabilization of the rehabilitative regime.

The drug and recidivist laws also reflected the rising conservatism of the state legislature. Indeed, the toughening-up of the legislature was evident even before the passage of the 1973 mandatory sentencing laws. In a 1968 interview, Richard Denzer, Executive Director of the Bartlett Commission, commented on the significant change from the early 1960s to the late 1960s:

In fact, when we drafted the [felony murder] provision in 1965, the mood of the people and the legislature was quite different from the mood today. We have moved from what might have been called an era of civil liberties to an era of street crimes and riots. The latter era has caused the legislature to stiffen its back.[30]

Nelson Rockefeller resigned from office at the end of 1973 and was temporarily followed as governor by Malcolm Wilson. In January 1975, a new governor, Hugh L. Carey, took office, and again the rehabilitative sentencing system was challenged from the Executive Chamber.

Governor Carey's Retreat from Rehabilitation

The erosion of New York State's rehabilitative sentencing structure escalated during the administration of Democrat Governor Hugh L. Carey. The 1978 passage of the Juvenile Offender Laws and the Violent Felony Offender Laws reflected the state legislature's growing conservatism on issues of crime and punishment.

Special treatment for juvenile criminals was a hallmark of the rehabilitative ideal.[31] Spiraling media coverage fed the public's fear of crime in general and juvenile crime in particular. As public preoccupation with juvenile crime mounted, so too mounted the pressure on the new governor to "do something" about juvenile crime.

Governor Carey's response to youth crime paralleled Rockefeller's odyssey with drug offenders. Each began by urging allegiance to the rehabilitative paradigm, each invested considerable time and energy in finding a solution, only to be frustrated by the apparent hopelessness of the quest, and each ended by forsaking rehabilitation and embracing retribution.

Treating Violent Juvenile Criminals

Interest in juvenile justice reform was sparked in 1974 by the activity of two legislative study committees—the Assembly Subcommittee on the Family Court and the New York State Select Committee on Crime, chaired by Republican Senator Ralph Marino.[32] The committees concluded that juvenile crime was on the rise and that the existing sentencing structure did not adequately protect the public.

Reform was obviously needed, but whose reform?The Assembly Democrats wanted to strengthen the Family Court's authority to deal harshly with violent juveniles; the Senate Republicans wanted a waiver-up system, whereby juveniles arrested for the most serious crimes could be waived, or transferred, to adult criminal court for prosecution. Along with the Assembly, Governor Carey opposed the waiver-up concept and continued to push for strengthening rather than abandoning the juvenile treatment system.

The Cahill Commission

In response to pressure from Democrats and Republicans, Governor Carey appointed a commission in June 1975, chaired by Dr. Kevin Cahill, to study the problems of juvenile violence. Peter Edleman, the new director of the State Division for Youth (DFY), who, like Carey, opposed waiver-up, assumed an active role in the commission's deliberations.[33]

The Cahill Commission gave its blessing to the governor's program and urged that waiver-up be avoided. The commission said that "nothing would be gained and much would be lost by legislation that transferred or waived such young children to the overburdened criminal justice system in which all the worst defects of the juvenile-justice system are exaggerated."[34]

Rather than forsaking the rehabilitative model and the Family Court, the Cahill Commission recommended specific sentencing structures for violent juvenile criminals.[35] The Cahill report became the basis for the Juvenile Justice Reform Act of 1976, which as enacted in Chapter 878 of the Laws of 1976 continued exclusive jurisdiction over juveniles with the Family Court and provided special procedures for sentencing fourteen and fifteen year olds convicted of enumerated serious crimes.[36] The rehabilitationists had prevailed, at least for the moment.

The Juvenile Justice Reform Act of 1976 passed the legislature by a wide margin, although Republican Senators continued to urge waiver-up to adult court.[37] Having successfully resisted pressure for waiver-up, Governor

Carey announced that "the counterproductive approach of transferring the responsibility for rehabilitating these children to the adult criminal justice system" had been rejected: "This bill is a thoughtful approach to the serious problem of increasing juvenile violence and provides for both community protection and an opportunity to devote some earnest efforts towards saving members of our next generation."[38]

Not surprisingly, pressure to get tough on juvenile crime did not abate with the passage of the 1976 legislation. The Senate Research Service issued reports during 1977 stressing the continued ineffectiveness of the juvenile justice system.[39] The Senate Committee on Crime and Correction considered a tougher waiver-down proposal. Waiver-down would give the adult criminal court original jurisdiction over designated youths, allowing discretionary transfer to Family Court. (The waiver-up proposals had continued original jurisdiction with the Family Court, allowing for discretionary transfer to criminal court.)

Nineteen seventy-eight was a gubernatorial election year, and Carey's Republican opponent, Perry Duryea, campaigned mightily against the governor's refusal to sign a death penalty bill. Duryea chided his opponent as "soft on crime," never a good label for a politician but especially troublesome in the frenzied atmosphere of "unrelenting media coverage"[40] of the crime issue. Governor Carey was nevertheless able to resist a waiver system—up or down—during the 1978 regular legislative session. Instead, Chapter 478 of the Laws of 1978 broadened the Family Court's authority over juveniles.[41]

And Then the Bomb Exploded: Willie Bosket

To many people, Willie Bosket symbolized all that was wrong with the rehabilitatively-inspired juvenile justice system: It was insufficiently punitive. It was widely reported that Carey, taking a beating at the opinion polls from Duryea and hammered by the press, seized on the case of Willie Bosket as a means of shedding the politically damaging epithet "soft on crime."

Recently released from DFY, fifteen-year-old Bosket was convicted of brutally and wantonly gunning down two elderly subway passengers. Under the provisions of the 1976 law, he could only be incarcerated for the maximum five year term, until he reached twenty-one years of age. Long Island *Newsday* reported that the

> 1976 law suddenly wasn't good enough. Carey, who had been against adult-court jurisdiction, had a change of heart: Right after the sentencing, on a June 29 airplane trip, Carey told reporters he would accept a bill that could keep juvenile offenders in prison for life. 'I'm going to make sure that a kid like this doesn't get out,' Carey said.[42]

The stage was set for the Juvenile Offender (JO) Law of 1978.

Carey's staff was apparently stunned by the governor's complete turnabout. They were also unable to persuade him to back down from his hard-line campaign statements following the Bosket affair. The legislature was called back to Albany for a special crime session, and a hastily drafted bill was handed to the legislators as they entered the chambers.[43]

The juvenile offender and violent felony offender laws passed the legislature by an overwhelming margin. New York's flip-flop was complete: From rehabilitation to retribution, Carey found his electable image.

Juvenile Offender Law

The JO law applied to juveniles aged thirteen to fifteen charged with murder and those aged fourteen or fifteen charged with other specified serious crimes. Adopting the hard-hitting waiver-down approach advocated by the Senate Republicans, Chapter 481 of the Laws of 1978 vested original jurisdiction with the adult criminal court. Youths could thereafter be waived down to Family Court if requested by the district attorney, the grand jury, or the judge.

Special sentencing provisions were applied to juvenile offenders convicted in criminal court. They would be committed to the custody of the Division for Youth and confined in secure facilities until released or transferred to adult corrections upon reaching their twenty-first birthday. DFY could, however, transfer the youth to adult corrections any time after the youth reached sixteen years of age. The parole board, not DFY, would thereafter make the release decision.

The JO law slashed fiercely and unequivocally at the rehabilitative structure. Its provisions were mandatory. Alternative dispositions, such as probation or less restrictive placement, were prohibited.[44]

Violent Felony Offender Laws

Just as the second felony offender laws passed virtually unnoticed in the tumult surrounding the 1973 drug laws, so too the violent felony offender laws passed easily in the midst of the frenzied political attacks on juvenile crime. Both laws had been unsuccessfully championed for years by key legislators. In the electorally volatile atmosphere surrounding the assault on juvenile offenders (or in the equally hot days of the drug law negotiations) these previously unpopular remedies became irresistible. There is a second, more profound analogue between the violent felony offender laws and the second felony offender laws: Both laws continue to shape sentencing policy in New York State.

The violent felony offender laws singled out certain ostensibly violent offenses for mandatory sentencing and created the habitual offender categories of second violent felony offender and persistent violent felony offender. Mandatory sentencing provisions were attached to each violent felony classification.[45] Plea-bargaining restrictions were intended to further curtail discretion. Offenders indicted for violent felonies were required to plead to violent felonies—that is, unless they were willing to risk trial.

The two new recidivist categories likewise required stringent mandatory sentences. To qualify as a second or persistent violent felony offender, the predicate offense(s) and the instant offense had to be violent felonies. Minimum sentences varied by crime class.[46] The maximum sentence for a persistent violent felony offender was the same regardless of the crime class: life imprisonment.

Assembly Debates

On July 18, 1978 at one a.m., the Senate passed the juvenile offender and the violent felony offender laws by a vote of fifty to two. The following night, it was the Assembly's turn to overwhelmingly pass the bills. Although several members of the Assembly voiced opposition or reservations, it is apparent from the transcripts of the debate that most viewed the passage of the tough crime package as a *fait accompli*. A few revealing (and none too subtle) excerpts from the Assembly debate on Chapter 481 of the Laws of 1978 follow.

One assemblyman equated the juvenile offender legislation with the Rockefeller drug laws, which were

> like a small cloud that drifted over this State and passed off into the Atlantic Ocean. That's the effect it had on drug addiction in this State, and this bill, I submit, is going to have about the same effect on juvenile crime ... [T]he vote is predictable. This bill is going to pass, there is no question about it.[47]

Another noted the full swing of the sentencing pendulum with respect to lenient treatment of youths:

> I think that if someone were to write a song here tonight the song should be "Where Have All the Liberals Gone?" I stand here and I hear people who I considered to be liberals capitulating. Capitulating to the hysteria that is in the street, and it is a justified hysteria.[48]

The late night session was summed up well by one legislator who remarked:

> You've got a Governor that is a chameleon—he changes. He changes because the polls showed that he hasn't been doing his job for 3 1/2 years. Where was he all that time? ... It's a tough bill, yes, because the Governor even said it: "I can be tough on crime, I can be tougher than anybody else." I'm surprised that he hasn't advocated maybe we should take the hands of these thirteen year olds and chop them off, and then politically he can put a sign around them and say, "Vote for Carey because he's tough, he making tough decisions." That's what he has done, so let's say it as it is.[49]

Parole Reform

Judicial sentencing discretion was not the only tenet of rehabilitationism under attack. Anti-rehabilitationists flailed out against discretionary parole release and its association with expertise and the prediction of dangerousness.

One of the earlier indications that discretionary parole release was in trouble in New York was evident in the report of the McKay Commission, which was established in the immediate aftermath of the 1971 massacre at Attica prison. The McKay Commission criticized the parole board and urged that parole release decisions be "measured by clear and comprehensible standards, which were disseminated to inmates in advance. The inmate must be told promptly if he has been granted parole and, if not, exactly why not."[50]

New York's parole system was challenged more vigorously in 1975 by the Citizen's Committee on Parole and Criminal Justice. These reformers called for the abolition of the parole board, the end of parole release and supervision based on rehabilitative theory, shorter sentences and narrower ranges of indeterminacy, extended use of alternatives to incarceration, open procedures, and a wide range of voluntary programs for offenders.

The following year parole release was further attacked in an influential report by the staff of the Democratic Assembly Codes Committee, which at the time was considered a bastion of liberalism. The report was an odd mixture of rehabilitative rhetoric and anti-rehabilitative policy recommendations. On the one hand, the Assembly staff disparaged retribution and warned that abandoning "attempts to rehabilitate offenders accomplishes nothing except giving up an effort which at its least can be termed humane and compassionate, and at its most, is an investment in an ordered society which is well worth the price."

On the other hand, the codes report captured the prevalent tone of contemporary criticisms of rehabilitationism: "Are we to believe that the [Parole] Board makes accurate, fair, and uniform decisions when it follows no specific written criteria, spends only a few moments with each inmate and his file, utilizes no predictive devices, sets unrealistic minimum periods of imprisonment and then refuses to release the inmate at his first release hearing because of his past record and the severity of his offense, and allows the courts to set the tone for minimal due process standards at their hearings? We cannot believe it, and we cannot urge strongly enough that the time is long overdue for reform of the Board's decision making process."[51]

The Parole Reform Act of 1977

The two primary recommendations of the Assembly staff report were enacted by the legislature the following year with the creation of an independent Division of Parole in the Executive Department and the adoption of written criteria to structure the parole release decision. The Parole Reform Act of 1977 allowed the state to hew closely to the rhetoric of rehabilitationism while simultaneously retreating from the principles undergirding the rehabilitative paradigm.

Under rehabilitationism, New York judges were encouraged to hand over to the parole board the responsibility for setting minimum sentences. Allocating such vast discretion to the parole board was intended to provide the flexibility needed to make deferred sentencing decisions based on their expert opinion of the offender's readiness for release.

The Parole Reform Act, Chapter 904 of the Laws of 1977, required the board to adopt written guidelines for the exercise of its discretion in fixing minimum periods of imprisonment and in making parole release decisions. The guidelines were to plainly articulate release criteria, thereby giving inmates and the public a clearer understanding of the parole process.[52] It was left to the parole authorities to devise the guidelines. With the help of outside advisors, including developers of the federal parole guidelines, the board created a two dimensional grid, with offenses arrayed, according to severity, along the vertical axis and criminal history scores arrayed along the horizontal axis.

In signing the Parole Reform Act, Governor Carey said that the legislation was aimed at eliminating disparity: "[T]he bill is intended primarily to reform the paroling process in this State to remove the inequities that numerous studies have cited... [and to ensure] that similarly-situated offenders are treated similarly."[53]

Parole Reform and the Political Climate

In an interview with this author, Clarence Sundrum, who was Assistant Counsel to Governor Carey in 1977, said that parole reform was the result of the Carey Administration's felt need to "do something about sentencing reform." According to Sundrum, the idea

> had been kicking around within the Chamber from as early as the Governor came in. It was always something we talked about. In fact, I think we had initially made some overtures to the Office of Court Administration to try to get them to launch an initiative on doing some training for judges so that ... there would be a more defensible exercise of discretion by judges in different parts of the state. That never went anywhere because, like most officials who have discretion, nobody wants to see it limited or circumscribed in any way ... [Having given up on changing judicial sentencing decisions] we tried to get the parole board to compensate for the idiosyncrasies of the judges across the state by having the board take into consideration some kind of uniformly applied statewide factors, such as the severity of the crime, the offender's background, mitigating circumstances, and so on, and come up with some presumptive sentence ... We tried but it was an imperfect attempt because, particularly with the predicate felon laws, there were an increasing number of people coming to state prison with a minimum

sentence set by the judge. Parole couldn't do much with that, and they were stuck with it.

Governor Carey's former counsel continued:

So this [parole guidelines] was sort of an outgrowth of having tried to get the judges to act more consistently. We were trying to do what we thought we could control best. Since we couldn't control the judges, it was easier to control an executive agency ... I think there were a lot of concerns about how feasible it was for the parole board to do all these things because that board has primarily been used to going in and interviewing prisoners and determining when to release them. And what we were trying to get them to do was to start thinking in a more global sense about sentencing policy and the goals of incarceration, etc. I think they were not up to the task. But they worked with us on it, and I think [Parole Chairman] Hammock particularly began to see more and more the possibility of this kind of function really enhancing the status of the parole board, which didn't have much status at that time.

Edward Hammock, former Chairman of the New York State Division of Parole, agreed with Mr. Sundrum's assessment of the motivation behind requiring the parole board to use guidelines.

There was always, at least in my opinion, a reluctance to directly deal with some of the major actors in criminal justice because of the difficulty that that presents. Judges became a favorite target, but as it became less fashionable to jump on judges, there was a need to make somebody else a whipping boy. The nature of paroling authorities was that their activities would take place in prisons long after the public glow of the case had dissipated, so this after-the-fact kind of process was always left to its own and became the subject of an occasional movie, but other than that, it was kept away from the public eye. Parole board members were stereotyped—nobody knew any. Nobody knew any of their names, and nobody cared to know any. But if we want to beat up on somebody in criminal justice, which is the way this process operates, then let's beat up on somebody that's not there to defend himself—somebody that we can't see. Let's go for the mystery man. So it was a matter of convenience ... The real target of the legislature was the judiciary. They were going for judicial discretion, which except for A felonies under the 1967 Penal Law, was extremely broad. So every time I read a comment about the broad and unfettered discretion of the parole board, I knew that they really meant the broad and unfettered discretion of the judiciary. In my opinion, the parole board was never the target, it was always the judges. The parole board was the fall guy. That was the way you could go after the judges without making it so terribly apparent.

The next chapter begins the discussion of New York's decade-long flirtation with the determinate ideal.

6

New York Embraces the Determinate Ideal

The mandatory sentencing provisions of the Rockefeller drug, the second felony offender, the juvenile offender, and the violent felony offender laws were pushed through the New York State legislature to placate law-and-order concerns, while parole guidelines owed their origin to a liberal thesis. Yet each signaled the demise of the rehabilitative ideal in New York State.

Mandatory sentencing and parole reform occupied policymakers' attention during the 1970s. Once these laws were enacted, New York policymakers searched elsewhere for something to reform. What they found was determinate sentencing. Born in a crucible of liberalism, the determinate ideal was quickly captured by law-and-order enthusiasts.

The Morgenthau Committee

Created by an Executive Order of Governor Carey in December 1977, the Executive Advisory Committee on Sentencing was named after its influential chairman, New York County (Manhattan) District Attorney Robert M. Morgenthau. Ironically—given the natural law-and-order leanings of prosecutors—the Morgenthau Committee's report was a paragon of liberalism.[1]

The Morgenthau Committee endorsed the anti-rehabilitationist rhetoric prevalent throughout the nation. It cited favorably the works of the seminal, standard-bearing liberals, including Marvin Frankel (*Criminal Sentences*), the Committee for the Study of Incarceration and its executive director, Andrew von Hirsch (*Doing Justice*), Jessica Mittford (*Kind and Usual Punishment*), and the American Friends Service Committee (*Struggle for Justice*).[2]

The Morgenthau Committee also endorsed the mainstay of the liberal determinate ideal: the parsimony principle. They argued that sentences should be "the *least severe sanction* necessary to achieve legitimate sentencing objectives."[3]

Like other anti-rehabilitationists, the members of the Morgenthau Committee elevated retributive purposes over crime-control objectives. Rehabilitation was rejected as a legitimate sentencing objective: "[W]e conclude that rehabilitation should *not* be a justification for imposing a term of confine-

77

ment, nor should it influence the length of a prison sentence."[4]

Incapacitation fared little better than rehabilitation as a purpose of punishment, although its theoretical legitimacy was accepted. The problem with incapacitation, the Morgenthau Committee said, was "a basic one: We cannot predict with accuracy whether or not an offender will commit future crimes."[5] The inadequacy of prediction techniques and the large number of resulting false positives "severely limits" incapacitation as a sentencing purpose, the committee said.[6]

While they claimed to be abandoning prediction, the Morgenthau Committee was not about to abandon prior criminal record. The apparent contradiction was explained away: Prior record was being used retributively rather than in an attempt to control crime. "Repeat offenders merit additional punishment because of their sustained unwillingness to abide by the law."[7]

Declaring deterrence "a manifestly proper objective of sentencing,"[8] the Morgenthau Committee bemoaned the lack of empirical evidence regarding the deterrent effect of different types and lengths of sanctions. "Only an incorrigible ideologue would regard such evidence as conclusive one way or another," the committee said.[9] In spite of the absence of proof, they subscribed to the view that certainty, rather than severity, of punishment was more likely to reduce crime.[10]

The Morgenthau Committee repeatedly argued that *doing justice* was the primary purpose of punishment.[11] An implicit synonym for retribution, *doing justice* required that crime-control purposes not determine sentencing decisions; rather "[j]ustice must dictate the boundaries of sentencing."[12] Thus, in common with other anti-rehabilitationists, the members of the Morgenthau Committee elevated retributive purposes over crime control.

Indeterminate sentencing was proclaimed a failure and parole release a charade. While parole guidelines were seen as an improvement over previous practices, their very existence underscored the problem. Why should parole perform a judicial function? If the judge and the parole board were applying the same criteria to the release decision, why should the former's sentencing decisions be superseded by the latter's?[13]

In addition to rejecting parole guidelines, the Morgenthau Committee rejected voluntary guidelines promulgated by the judiciary, which they said had "done little to promote consistency in its own decision-making."[14] As with other major public policy issues, sentencing questions should not be decided by the judiciary alone, the committee maintained.

The First Call for Sentencing Guidelines

The Morgenthau Committee recommended that New York adopt a determinate sentencing structure in the form of sentencing guidelines. The committee's sentencing system was in major respects similar to the guidelines system endorsed by the Committee for the Study of Incarceration, and, later in a series of publications by the committee's executive director, Andrew von Hirsch.[15]

The Morgenthau Committee's proposal was constructed around the appealingly simple concept that like offenders should receive like punishments. The determination of who was alike would turn on the seriousness of the conviction offense and the offender's prior criminal record.

Doing justice required fairness, consistency, and uniformity of sanctions, all of which could be achieved, the Morgenthau Committee reasoned, by the adoption of sentencing guidelines. An independent sentencing commission would formulate the guidelines. The deliberations of the sentencing commission would be open to the public under the state's sunshine provisions, thereby making the commission publicly accountable. Yet, the commission "would be removed from partisan politics,"[16] thereby insulating it from political pressures.

The sentencing commission would have nine members: four criminal justice experts, three active trial court judges, one district attorney, and one public defender. The governor, the legislature, and the Administrative Board of the Judicial Conference would each appoint three members to the committee.

The Sentencing Grid

The sentencing commission would devise a sentencing guidelines grid. Offenses would be distributed along the vertical axis of the grid according to their seriousness. Consistent with the broad range of discretion available under the rehabilitative system, the existing statutory definitions of crimes included conduct of widely dissimilar severity. Thus, to ensure that offenses of equivalent severity received similar punishments under a determinate model, the sentencing commission would redefine and redistribute the statutory elements of crimes based on the extent of harm caused by the offense.

The vertical axis of the sentencing guidelines grid would contain the prior record categories. The Morgenthau Committee suggested that these categories be based on variables such as the number of prior felony and misdemeanor convictions, prior incarcerations, whether the offender was on probation or parole at the time of the instant offense, or whether the offender had previously had probation or parole revoked because of a conviction for another offense.[17] The committee continued to justify its reliance on prior record on retributive, not crime-control, grounds.

The guidelines would specify a range of sentences for each combination of offense and prior criminal record category. In keeping with the requirements of determinacy, the range would be narrow. The higher term would not exceed the lower term by 15 percent.[18] The court would impose a sentence from within the range, which would represent the actual amount of time that the offender would serve, minus good time. There would be no discretionary parole release.

The guidelines sentences were not mandatory. The court could depart from the guidelines and impose a different sentence if aggravating or mitigating factors were found to be present. The sentencing commission would specify the most common departure factors, and the court would decide in a particular case if other factors warranted a sentence outside of the guidelines.

While providing for a measure of flexibility, the committee recommended that unlimited departure from the sentencing grid not be allowed. The sentencing commission would establish a narrow range for departure sentences. The court would state its reasons for sentencing outside of the guidelines, and all departure sentences would be eligible for appellate review. The prosecution would have the same right of appeal as the defense.

Good time would be limited to 20 percent of the sentence. Higher allowances would undermine the uniformity and certainty of sentencing, it was thought. Inmates could lose up to ninety days of previously earned good time for each serious disciplinary violation.[19]

All releasees would be subject to a fixed period of parole supervision. Offenders serving prison terms of up to two years would be supervised for one year; offenders serving terms in excess of two years would be supervised for two years. A serious violation of a condition of parole supervision could result in reincarceration for up to six months.[20]

The sentencing commission would have two years to prepare its guidelines, which would be issued as regulations, becoming effective 180 days after submission.[21] Although the committee was silent about the implementation recommendation, it is clear that this proposal could generate tremendous opposition, as the legislature would not be prone to blithely relinquish its traditional power to veto or alter a proposal from such a committee.

Following the adoption of the guidelines, the sentencing commission would continue to conduct research and make recommendations for any necessary modifications in the guidelines.

At first blush, it seems contradictory that a committee chaired by a district attorney would join with defense interests in calling for determinate sentencing in the form of sentencing guidelines. Yet, the contradiction is easily explained. The sentencing system proposed by the Morgenthau Committee was painted in broad brush strokes; many of the recommendations were vague and inherently ambiguous. As long as the determinate ideal remained loosely defined, it was easy for both law enforcement and defense interests to endorse its principles, as each side read into the reform its preferred meanings. Not until the vague was rendered specific would the differences in ideology be apparent.

Public Hearings: The Determinate Ideal Endorsed

The public had ample opportunity to tell the policymakers what they thought about determinate sentencing and the guidelines structure. The Morgenthau Committee held four days of public hearings in the fall of 1978—two days in New York City and one day each in Albany and Buffalo. Forty-eight witnesses testified. The next year, the Senate and Assembly Joint Codes Committee held three days of public hearings—one day each in New York City,

Albany, and Buffalo. Twenty-seven witnesses' testimony was preserved from the legislative hearings. The following discussion is based on the testimony of the seventy-five witnesses appearing at these two hearings.[22]

For this book, the witnesses' testimony has been read and coded on two fundamental variables: position on determinate sentencing and ideological affiliation. Coding witnesses' sentencing stance was relatively simple as most of them directly endorsed or rejected the concept of determinate sentencing, or favored or opposed the formation of a sentencing guidelines commission. Coding the witnesses' ideological stance was less straightforward then coding their position on determinate sentencing, as few witnesses overtly identified themselves as conservative or liberal. While the simplistic classifications of liberal and conservative ignore the many subtleties surrounding an individual's beliefs, there can be no denying that pervasive differences of mind-set identify the opposing forces and underlie their arguments. In criminal justice, the traditional ideological categories of liberal and conservative are roughly analogous to the positions of defense and law enforcement interests, respectively. To determine whether a witness was orientated more to the left or the right, a set of decision rules were followed, and they are discussed in depth in Appendix I.

Morgenthau Committee Hearings

Of the forty-eight witnesses testifying before the Morgenthau Committee, forty-five (93 percent) were classified according to ideological position. Of these forty-five, thirty-six (80 percent) represented defense interests and nine (20 percent) represented law enforcement.[23]

Forty-six (96 percent of the testifying) witnesses were identified by their position on determinate sentencing. Of these, twenty-nine (63 percent) favored determinate sentencing and seventeen (37 percent) were opposed.

Forty-three witnesses (90 percent) were matched on both ideology and position on determinate sentencing. The results are as follows:

Morgenthau Committee Hearings (1978)

Witnesses' Position on Determinate Sentencing

Ideology	Favored	Opposed	Total
Defense	22 (65%)	12 (35%)	34 (100%)
Law-Enforcement	5 (56%)	4 (44%)	9 (100%)
Total	27 (63%)	16 (37%)	43 (100%)

Assembly and Senate Joint Codes Committee Hearings

Twenty-seven witnesses' testimony was preserved from the Assembly and Senate Codes Committee hearings.[24] The ideological positions of twenty-six

(96 percent) of the witnesses could be classified. Of these, eighteen (69 percent) were categorized as defense-oriented and eight (31 percent) were identified as law-enforcement oriented. All of the twenty-seven witnesses were identified on their position on determinate sentencing. Seventeen (63 percent) were in favor and ten (37 percent) opposed.

The following distribution was obtained for the twenty-six witnesses who were matched on both dimensions.

Assembly and Senate Hearings

Witnesses' Position on Determinate Sentencing

Ideology	Favored	Opposed	Total
Defense	10 (56%)	8 (44%)	18 (100%)
Law-Enforcement	7 (88%)	1 (12%)	8 (100%)
Total	17 (65%)	9 (35%)	26 (100%)

Of the seventy-five witnesses appearing at both sets of hearings, seventy-one (95%) were categorized by affiliation. Fifty-four (72%) were classified with defense interests and seventeen (23%) were classified as law enforcement.

Positions on determinate sentencing were determined for seventy-three (97%) respondents. Of these, forty-six (63%) favored determinate sentencing and twenty-seven (37%) were opposed.

Sixty-nine (92%) witnesses were matched on both dimensions. The distribution is as follows:

Combined Scores from Morgenthau and Legislative Hearings

Witnesses' Position on Determinate Sentencing

Ideology	Favored	Opposed	Total
Defense	32 (62%)	20 (38%)	52 (100%)
Law-Enforcement	12 (71%)	5 (29%)	17 (100%)
Total	44 (64%)	25 (36%)	69 (100%)

Interpreting the Findings

The number of cases available for examination are small, and it is thus not possible to generalize these data to other situations. The findings are nevertheless instructive.

Born of a liberal promise, determinate sentencing was soon equally embraced by conservatives as well as liberals. How could this be, when these groups have such different ideologies? The answer lies in symbols, not facts;

in rhetoric, not reality. While the determinate ideal remained abstract, people with diverse world views could read into it their own preferred meanings. Later, once the abstract was rendered concrete, once the grand notions were reduced to statutory proscriptions, the differences between the interests of law enforcement and defense would become all too apparent.

The findings reveal another pattern. By the late 1970s, liberals were beginning to demonstrate a fair degree of skepticism that this would be a real reform, with about 39 percent of the defense witnesses opposing the adoption of determinate sentencing. Reacting to what they no doubt saw as the takeover of the ideal by law enforcement, these witnesses were unwilling to risk a further hardening of the state's sentencing policy.

Uncovering Crime-Control Objectives

Many prominent individuals testified before the Morgenthau Committee and the Assembly and Senate Joint Codes Committee Hearings. Those speaking in favor of determinate sentencing included Judge Marvin Frankel, New York City Mayor Edward Koch, and Senator Edward Kennedy.

Robert Morgenthau testified on behalf of his committee's report before the Joint Codes Committee Hearings. The Manhattan District Attorney told the committee that rehabilitation was not a legitimate goal of sentencing. In a revealing colloquy, Mr. Morgenthau expounded on the crime-control purposes of punishment. While sentencing guidelines could not cure crime, he claimed that "by increasing the certainty, consistency and uniformity of criminal sanctions, our sentencing laws will come closer to realizing their full potential for crime control."[25] He went on to explain how crime-control objectives would be achieved:

> I think what we are trying to say in the report is that incapacitation is one of the things that should be considered in sentencing, and you get at that by looking at the prior criminal record of the defendant because you are trying to predict from that the likelihood of a crime being committed. That is certainly one of the goals.

One member of the panel, Senator Halperin, questioned the District Attorney on the apparent contradiction between his testimony and his committee's recommendation: "It seems as though the Committee did not think highly of that goal [incapacitation] for sentencing, but from what you are saying, you do feel that it is a rational approach to trying to reduce crime?" Mr. Morgenthau answered: "It is certainly one part of it. We try to get into that by looking at the prior criminal record, because if somebody committed a lot of crimes in a short period of time, it is predicted that they will do it again. That certainly would be cranked into the sentencing guidelines."[26]

So much for the renunciation of crime control.

A Law Enforcement or a Defense Reform?

New York legislators were not unaware of the curious attraction that determinate sentencing held for both defense and law enforcement. Melvin Miller, then the Chairman of the Assembly Codes Committee (the Assembly committee responsible for criminal-justice issues), and currently Speaker of the Assembly, commented during the hearings about the strange bedfellow characteristic of determinate sentencing:

> There is, listening to witnesses throughout the State of New York, a school of witnesses that come before us, and tells us that this sentencing model means that people will spend longer terms in jail, that is why they support it. We have, from the so-called more liberal community, witnesses who appear before us and tell us you are going to spend less time in jail because the whole thrust of the Morgenthau Commission report was that jail was the last expedient, something we prefer not to use except in those very limited cases where we cannot think of any alternative.[27]

As Assembly Speaker Miller observed, witnesses had their own view of determinate sentencing. Some thought that determinate sentencing would promote equality and fairness because prison sentences would be less frequent and shorter. Others believed it would ensure certainty of punishment and longer prison sentences.

In an interview with this author, Assemblyman Richard Gottfried summed it all up:

> The impetus [for determinate sentencing] was, ironically, originally from the left. The earliest reference in New York was the McKay report, which proposed it as a remedy for inmate grievances regarding disparity in sentencing. There was further liberal impetus from those who thought it would be a mechanism for shortening sentences, putting limits on the parole board and not keeping inmates in suspense too long . . . Between 1971 and 1978 there was not that much discussion of determinate sentencing, except for prison reform advocates. The current impetus was fueled by the Morgenthau report and by the popularity of the concept outside of New York, especially in the federal system and in California. Public appeal of determinate sentencing grew as it was identified as a get-tough measure—which was partly because "determinate" sentencing sounds tough. Also, the public perceives parole as letting inmates out early rather than late. The public thinks that abolishing parole would result in longer sentences. They are right . . . Morgenthau was not a liberal initiative . . . If you appoint Bob Morgenthau to head a committee on criminal justice, you are saying something about how it should turn out.

Assemblyman Gottfreid continued:

People packaged the message of determinate sentencing for themselves. On the left, they deluded themselves in thinking it was a gimmick they would get through and would come out OK. On the right, it was a combination of rhetoric and accurate perception of what would happen. Look at the phenomena of "get government off our backs"; it started with the left but then its biggest spokesman is Reagan.

Judge Peter McQuillan, former member of the Bartlett Commission, agreed that, as expanded by the Morgenthau Committee, determinate sentencing was "conservative-oriented. It was generally the prosecutors talking in favor of it, not the judges or the defense side. It was conservative oriented."

James Yates, then counsel to the Assembly Codes Committee and currently chief counsel to the Speaker of the Assembly, commented that

> I think it was a liberal notion that was co-opted and went awry. I think the Attica experience dramatized disparity and so most people wanted to try to rectify disparity. That's what the parole guidelines were intended to do . . . Some conservatives started to realize that we can eliminate disparity and it would be basically blaming the judges for the disparity, and we'll take away discretion from the judge, and if you take away discretion from the judge, that means naturally more for the prosecutor, and so I think that it was the search for the liberal ideal gone awry.

Mr. Yates attributed the growth of the movement for determinate sentencing to a power bid by prosecutors:

> Basically, some prosecutors said "The judges can't do it, so we'll do it." That is not what was ever really intended in the beginning of determinate sentencing . . . Here was the problem of disparity, and all of a sudden prosecutors came up with the bright idea that said "Hey, if you give me the power, I'll be able to do it," and so that is when it went awry.

Mr. Yates commented on the reception of the Morgenthau Committee's report by the legislature:

> I don't think the Republican conservatives to the liberal Democrats, or anything in between conservative Democrats and liberal Republicans—I don't think anyone thought that much about it. I don't think they [the legislators] are as quick to assume that judges can't handle the discretion. I think there's a lot of wariness within the legislature about district attorneys in control of the sentencing functions. Plus the easiest tag—the one that you heard most publicly as a criticism—was that the report was calling for legislative abdication of its control over sentencing. But I don't think that deep down inside that that was the main issue why it didn't go forward. I think that people just weren't so sure that they wanted a system where prosecutors would basically set the sentences by the charges. And I don't think that

the case for disparity was made. A lot of people think that disparity is based on things like geography. I think that there are a fair number of legislators who think regional disparity is a plus.

Mr. Yates continued:

We had hearings.... I think that led to part of the confusion and ambiguity about whether this was a liberal or conservative measure. People were all confused there. Some of the district attorneys liked it, some did not. Some of the defense bar liked it, some did not. It really cut across all those normal ideological lines. And plus it had that banner and label of reform ... It left enough room for people to draw their own mental image, and then go ahead and like it ... There was a lot of legislative suspicion. We weren't doing it.

Then there started to be some public push for it.... We were getting a weird amalgam of liberal and conservative press supporting it, each because they saw something different in it. So you had the *New York Times* calling for definite sentencing, you had Kennedy calling for definite sentencing, you had the *New York Post* calling for definite sentencing, and Carey kept calling for it. But we [the Assembly Codes Committee] were basically holding off, and plus we kept being mischaracterized in our opposition, being against it because the legislature didn't want to give up to some commission powers to set sentences. It was a straw man that was basically set up. It was one of the arguments and one of the considerations, but in all honest reality and candor, I would say it probably was the third or fourth ranked in consideration in opposition to the bill. But it's just a handle that's convenient for newspapers, and if you're going to write a quick, cheap editorial, you'd sit there and say the legislature doesn't want to give up its sentencing power. So we were under our pressure. The Governor kept pushing on it.

The Determinate Forces March On

Following the issuance of the Morgenthau Committee's report, Governor Carey continued to avow a commitment to control discretion and eradicate disparity, the twin pillars of the rehabilitative regime. In his 1980 Annual Message, Carey said that the Morgenthau Committee report had "gained national recognition as a comprehensive and professional study."

Perhaps anticipating the tortuous path that determinate sentencing would follow, the governor cautioned that "[i]t is important that the momentum for sentencing reform not be lost. I ask that we enact legislation to ensure greater certainty of punishment for the guilty and to reduce unjustified sentence disparity among persons who commit similar offenses."[28]

Despite repeated pronouncements by Governor Carey concerning the need for sentencing reform, a sentencing guidelines commission was not established following the issuance of the Morgenthau Committee's report.

Indeed, there was no official indication that a viable replacement to the indeterminate structure had been found.

In an interview with this author, Scott Fein, former Assistant Counsel to Governor Carey, explained that

> many of those in government thought that it [determinacy] was a good idea, but there were still unanswered questions, for example, would it control disparity, what about prosecutorial guidelines? The decisionmakers were hesitant about implementation and concerned about the implications. The issue never crystallized [during the Carey administration]. California's experience with determinate sentencing was in its early stages and difficult to evaluate. People realized that adjusting sentences could have broader implications than anticipated. They thought it best to look at disparity—Morgenthau had said there was a lot of disparity—and at the other subsidiary issues.

Arthur Liman, a prominent New York City attorney and member of the McKay and Morgenthau Committees, said in an interview that he believed that the Morgenthau proposals

> were too radical for Governor Carey in that they contemplated delegating to the commission the power to fix sentences. Stanley Fink [who later became Speaker of the New York State Assembly] was a member of the Morgenthau Committee, but it was very, very clear that he did not believe it was politically feasible. I believe that Governor Carey reached the conclusion that he would get nowhere in trying to translate the committee's recommendations into law.

Edward Hammock, who at the time was the Chairman of the Board of Parole, had a different explanation for why a sentencing guidelines commission was not formed following the report of the Morgenthau Committee.

> In my opinion, Governor Carey was never committed to determinate sentencing. It seems that the people in power were looking to avoid a tremendous upheaval in the way we did things, for fear that it would throw all the balances off. Everybody's early information on determinate sentencing was that it led to higher commitment rates, an increased number of inmates. . . . Even though the 1973 and 1978 legislation might result in increased commitments, people felt that the continued existence of the parole board would serve as a potential hedge against any significant problems that that created. So, whereas emotionally, and to some extent philosophically, there was some move toward determinate sentencing, politically and in terms of existing resources, there had to be a reluctance to get out of what appeared to be a bit of a frying pan into the fire.

Two More Sentencing Commissions

Still ostensibly joining in the attack on the rehabilitative ideal, in 1981 Governor Carey announced that the Morgenthau Committee had "identified disparity and uncertainty in the sentencing of criminal defendants as one of the major problems in our justice system. Lack of uniformity and certainty in sentencing undermines the deterrent effect of our criminal laws and breeds justifiable resentment among defendants treated more harshly than others who committed similar offenses."[29]

Governor Carey's solution to the disparity problem was somewhat different than that recommended by the Morgenthau Committee, however. Rather than appoint a sentencing guidelines commission, the Governor sought to eliminate unjustified disparity by establishing

> a sentencing panel to develop advisory standards to assist judges in making sentencing decisions ... With these advisory standards to guide judicial discretion, and with detailed information concerning sentencing practices of judges throughout the State, which will also be provided by the Panel, judges will be better able to impose sentences which are both appropriate for the individual case and consistent with sentences imposed by other judges in similar cases. The sentencing panel will, for the first time, open the entire sentencing process to public scrutiny and will establish an exchange of information among the various elements of our criminal justice system that play a role in sentencing—prosecutors, judges and the parole board. The panel will produce more consistent and coordinated sentencing practices by all judges of the State.[30]

In addition, the panel would assist district attorneys in developing plea bargaining standards and review standards used for the parole release decision.

The governor stressed that this was an action, standard-setting committee, not another study group. But Carey never got his sentencing standards. Despite protestations that this commission would do more than study the problem, another study commission was being created. Actually, two study commissions were formed. The first, the Executive Advisory Commission on the Administration of Justice (Liman Commission) heartily endorsed determinate sentencing. The second, the Advisory Commission on Criminal Sanctions (McQuillan Commission) sought to contain and divert support for determinacy. Both commissions rendered their reports and recommendations in 1982; their contradictory focuses served to confuse the issue and diffuse support for the new sentencing model.

The Liman Commission

The Liman Commission was created on March 19, 1981 by Executive Order of Governor Carey. It was not intended to be a sentencing commission;

rather, the Liman Commission was charged with developing proposals for "better coordination among the various state criminal justice agencies and between state and local criminal justice programs."[31] But Arthur Liman, the commission's chairman, who was also President of the Legal Aid Society of New York City, was keenly interested in the problems of prison crowding and their relationship to the sentencing structure. Consequently, among other subjects, the commission investigated the state's sentencing system.

In its first of four reports, the Liman Commission attacked the state's prison system. Crowding had reached dangerous levels, it said, and if steps were not taken to reduce the prison population, New York's prisons, like those in other states, would be subject to federal receivership and supervision. Under present policy, the state was "drifting toward disaster."[32]

Rises in prison populations were a direct result of sentencing policy, the Liman Commission reasoned. Sentencing policies had "vacillated between periods of tough, but unenforceable, mandatory sentencing laws and periods of nebulous indeterminate sentences. The present sentencing laws combine the worst aspects of each approach," the commission claimed.[33]

In juxtaposing mandatory minimum sentences on the indeterminate sentencing structure, the legislature had created "a confusing hybrid," the Liman Commission said. They criticized the lack of standards, without which, they said, sentencing decisions would remain idiosyncratic, oscillating with the predilections of individual judges. They castigated the natural by-product of the rehabilitative system, disparity. It was simply wrong for similar offenders to receive dissimilar sentences and dissimilar offenders to receive similar sentences. Sentencing guidelines would "bring clarity, rationality and stability" to sentencing and "bring an end to sentencing disparity."[34]

The Liman Commission's guideline system paralleled that of the Morgenthau Committee in most respects. Both urged that guidelines be established by an independent commission; that the sentence imposed be the sentence served, minus good time; that parole release be abolished; that the guideline sentences reflect the seriousness of the offense and the offender's prior record; that departures from the guidelines be based on the existence of aggravating or mitigating circumstances; and that both the people and the defendant be allowed to appeal departure sentences.

Arthur Liman, responding to a question about the level of dissent among commission members over the sentencing proposals, said:

> No, there was not much dissent. I think what I was dealing with was the fact that there was a report [the Morgenthau Committee report], which most of us agreed with, to try to revise the sentencing laws, to come up with guidelines, and to do it through a commission that would be insulated somewhat from political pressure.

The members of the Liman Commission diverged from their predecessors on the Morgenthau Committee on only two major areas. First, they proposed that, rather than being self-executing, the guidelines promulgated by the sentencing commission be subject to executive and legislative veto. If not rejected within sixty days of submission, the guidelines would become law. This proposal was designed to "preserve the legislature's voice in determining punishment."[35] Arthur Liman noted in an interview that he had "reached the conclusion that no legislator or governor would delegate that kind of total power to a commission, and so I added the variant of a layover provision before the legislature."[36]

Second, the Liman Commission's concern with overcrowded prisons led them to recommend that guidelines explicitly conform to correctional resources. The commission praised Minnesota's sentencing guidelines efforts, and urged that the Minnesota model be copied in New York so that the guidelines could be fashioned to avoid unrestrained prison growth. If policymakers were unwilling to account for prison populations, they should increase correctional resources to accommodate increased populations, the committee said.[37]

The McQuillan Commission

In addition to appointing the Liman Commission, Governor Carey established the Advisory Commission on Criminal Sanctions (McQuillan Commission) "to promote the equitable administration of the criminal laws and eliminate unjustified sentencing disparity."[38] In creating the McQuillan Commission, the Governor stressed the necessity of treating like offenders alike.

Carey said that the

> concept of fairness in sentencing depends, in large measure, upon the imposition of similar penalties upon similar offenders who commit similar crimes. The Advisory Commission on Criminal Sanctions will be responsible for formulating advisory sentencing criteria to aid judges in reaching sentencing decisions. The criteria will be based on existing sentencing norms and practices. In order to determine these criteria, the Commission will evaluate current sentencing practices and identify those factors which have proven to affect the nature of a sentence, including the charge at arrest, the conviction and the criminal history of the defendant.[39]

The McQuillan Commission was put in an unenviable position: Governor Carey wanted it to develop sentencing standards for judges, while the legislature wanted it to study sentencing patterns and provide baseline data. While the enabling legislation called for the commission to do both, in the end the legislature won, and the commission refused to issue sentencing standards.

A bid at containment   The commission's chairman, Judge Peter McQuillan, had been counsel to the Bartlett Commission in the 1960s when the rehabilitative paradigm was at its zenith in New York and elsewhere around the country. Judge McQuillan's prior association proved significant: His commission's report was permeated with all of the trappings of the rehabilitative model.

Despite its mandate, the McQuillan Commission declined to provide advisory guidelines. To provide such guidelines, it reasoned, would be a purely normative exercise, based on "our [the members'] collective but personal evaluations."[40] Rather than recommending guidelines, the McQuillan Commission recommended that judges base their sentencing decisions on their individual perceptions of the appropriate sanction.

As had the rehabilitationists on the Bartlett Commission, the members of the McQuillan Commission linked the purpose of punishment with the allocation of sentencing discretion. They advocated a dual track sentencing system whereby indeterminacy would be retained for prison sentences in excess of five years, and determinacy would be instituted for prison sentences of five years or less. The Commission reasoned that sentences of five years or less represented concerns for proportionality and deterrence, and could therefore be made by the court at the time of sentencing. Predictions of behavior were consequently irrelevant with shorter sentences, they said, and therefore the determinate model was most appropriate. In addition, in cases involving shorter sentences, the parole board currently based its release decisions almost exclusively on factors known at the time the judge imposed sentence. The release function should be turned over to the court in these cases, the commission asserted, rather than to allow the parole board to reconsider judicial decisions about the seriousness of the underlying offense.

Sentences in excess of five years reflected rehabilitation and incapacitation concerns, the McQuillan Commission believed. Decisions about longer sentencing should not be made at the time of judicial imposition of sentence and should await further information about the offender as it developed during the course of his incarceration. Because judges have "no unusual ability to prophesy," the commission recommended that the crime-control objectives of rehabilitation and incapacitation be pursued by those familiar with the long-term offender's prison conduct: the parole board. The commission claimed that the indeterminate system had the "virtue" of delaying the release decision until a "time when that decision can intelligently and fairly be made."[41]

Good time for determinate sentence offenders would be set at 20 percent.[42] A parole supervision period would be attached to each definite sentence in excess of one year. Offenders sentenced to two years or less would receive eighteen months of supervision; offenders sentenced to more than two years would be supervised for thirty-six months.[43]

The dual track was not, the McQuillan Commission protested, a reluctant compromise between conflicting ideologies. Rather, the proposed system would "harmonize the two systems by taking from each that which is conceptually sound and meets the practical needs of the People of the State."[44]

There would be no need to form a sentencing commission to set sentences for offenses covered by determinate sentencing, the McQuillan Commission explained. Instead, they demonstrated in their report how the legislature could convert the existing indeterminate sentence ranges into narrower ranges from which the court could select a definite sentence.

Rejecting the prevailing wisdom   In sharp contrast with the widespread disillusionment with discretion so evident in other quarters, the McQuillan Commission demonstrated little suspicion of the misuse of power. They acknowledged that incapacitation required a prediction of future conduct, but argued that the indeterminate structure "reduces the risk of error by postponing the release decision to a time when more informed judgments can be made."[45]

The McQuillan Commission acknowledged that "[i]mplicit in our decision . . . is our rejection of many of the arguments advanced by proponents of a total definite sentence scheme."[46] They questioned the evidence behind the common "nothing works" refrain, noting that the debate sparked by works such as *The Effectiveness of Correctional Treatment*[47] had not been resolved.

The commission was not prepared to abandon the crime-control purposes of sentencing. While predictions were difficult, they said, "if the [Parole] Board is allowed to concentrate its energies upon those inmates receiving longer prison sentences, it will be better able to perform this critical function."[48] Given the insufficiency of definitive evidence, abandoning rehabilitation and incapacitation would be "an adventurous experiment which should not be undertaken."[49]

According to the McQuillan Commission, disparity was not as serious a problem as was generally perceived. The attack on disparity spearheaded by the Attica riot no longer made sense, they claimed. With the advent of parole guidelines, the disparity engendered by release decisions had been minimized.[50]

The McQuillan Commission criticized the Morgenthau Committee for recommending that the sentencing commission promulgate its guidelines as regulations, which would become effective 180 days thereafter. Self-executing guidelines, the McQuillan Commission reasoned, would require a delegation of power by a legislature known for jealously guarding its prerogative in setting criminal-justice policy. Neither a wholesale delegation of authority nor a legislative veto approach would be approved by the legislature, the McQuillan Commission warned.

The response   The dual track system was neither fish nor fowl, a confusing hybrid. As a result, the McQuillan Commission served as a buffer against the expansion of determinate sentencing—a bid at containment that would diffuse support and confuse supporters. With such an oblique endorsement, it is perhaps surprising that the momentum for determinate sentencing was not lost altogether.

James Yates described the legislature's motivation in establishing the McQuillan Commission:

> The Governor was pushing for determinate sentencing, but we [the Assembly Codes Committee] basically kept saying "Well, we're buying a pig in a poke. We don't know exactly what the sentencing patterns are out there, and we don't know if there is disparity, and we don't know what its basis is and how you would eliminate it. We don't even really know what sentences people are getting on the average. Let's create a commission." So that would be the idealistic way of saying that's why we went ahead and created the commission. That and the practical political answer ... There were so many people who were opposed to it. It was just a convenient way of putting it off for a year. I wouldn't call either more compelling as the reason it happened. I would just say there was a contingent of people who wanted one, and the other contingent wanted the other, and they all agreed let's have a commission.

Mr. Yates continued:

> I was getting extremely frustrated while we were holding off on the Morgenthau report in 1980, 81, and 82. I was getting extremely frustrated by having a liberal group walk in to me and say "we've got to have definite sentencing, it'll be a reform." I'd sit there and say "thank you." They'd walk out the door, and the next group in would be a prosecutors group saying "We've got to have definite sentencing, it'll be a reform." And I was just getting dizzy and saying "this is crazy, and let's paint the picture here so that you can see what people are talking about. Let's have a common language. It's like we have to take a logic or philosophy course. Let's settle our terms here first and our definitions and then we'll get on from there."

Mr. Yates summed up the legislative response to both the Liman and McQuillan Commissions:

> The Liman Commission wasn't meant to be a sentencing commission, it was meant to be an administration of justice commission. There were a lot of things within the administration of justice that needed repair. The Assembly got back a report that basically took some of the Governor's agenda that had languished in the Assembly over the last two or three years, and rubber stamped it. And so we, to be honest, dismissed it in an offhand fashion, saying "well, there goes the Governor's commission endorsing previously stated Governor's positions, trying to force the Assembly to do things that we've already got reservations about." So I don't think the Liman and Morgenthau reports were seen as two reports in conflict, I think it was another Governor's press release versus a report.

Mr. Yates said that the McQuillan Commission's report

> lacked an appealing principle. It lacked some kind of easily stated and convincing rationale behind it. Because of that people would get confused ... It

wasn't a coherent principled position, and therefore it wasn't readily adoptable... I think the McQuillan Commission did not perform the function that we had intended for it. The Governor wanted to set up something like the guidelines commission to promulgate sentences—some kind of sentencing scheme. The legislature clearly didn't want that, they wanted a study first. What the legislature had approved, both Senate and Assembly, was a good snapshot of what's out there—good data base research... If you look at the wording of the implementing statute... it talks about their job is to access, and study, and report and nowhere in there does it say to recommend guidelines, because that was clearly not what we wanted them to do. Now I think from the Governor's end after the appointments were made, there was continued pushing... to make it more like a guidelines commission, that is, come up with a solution, don't just study. And in that regard they came up with a solution that nobody liked, and that was the end of it. But I don't think they were supposed to come up with a solution. That was not what we had created them for. So we were disgusted from this point of view.[51]

Justice Peter McQuillan recalled that there was confusion surrounding his commission from the start:

The problem was that after the commission got underway, Carey announced that he would not seek reelection. So we worried from the start that there would be no audience. We were unanimous in not favoring determinate sentencing. The dual track was a concession[52]... The arguments in favor of determinate sentencing are not impressive. The parole board acts responsibly by and large... The reception [to the report] was not really pondered over. There was no follow through.

Asked if he would characterize the report as instrumental in containing the spread of determinacy, Judge McQuillan said that, while he had never thought of it that way, he "would be happy to think so."

Edward Hammock, former Chairman of the Parole Board, believed that the McQuillan Commission

took the practical approach. He didn't sell determinacy. He said, "Look, for those who want it, let's give it to them. But let's give it to them where it doesn't really hurt the system. . . . The McQuillan Commission's system makes most sense because you retain the ability to screen those people that you're most worried about. So his view was totally practical. But his buy-in to determinacy wasn't based on any great love for it. He just recommended that you could do it without damaging everything too badly.

The Media Supports Determinate Sentencing

Determinate sentencing continued to capture New Yorkers' attention in spite of the less than wholehearted endorsement by the McQuillan Commission. Like the general public, newspapers appealing to law-and-order advocates as well as those geared to the tastes of more moderate and liberal audiences supported the new sentencing structure. It was thus not surprising that adherents of law-enforcement and defense perspectives continued to read their preferred meanings into the determinate ideal. Despite the strong support from all quarters, the New York State legislature remained resistant to enacting a program that both law enforcement and defense labeled a reform.

The following discussion is based on the coverage of determinate sentencing by two New York City newspapers that frequently take divergent positions on public policy issues. The *New York Post* has long been a law-and-order stronghold, a voice for tough punishments. The *New York Times* is a more liberal to moderate newspaper, often supporting alternative sentencing and reduced reliance on incarceration.[53]

The New York Post

In 1977 a *New York Post* editorial claimed that Americans were "agonizing over the issue of whether 'rehabilitation' of criminals is possible or whether we should simply admit that we lock people up to punish them. Period."[54] Calling the rehabilitative system disparate and inconsistent, the *Post* lauded the federal governments efforts to institute sentencing guidelines.

People read their own preferred meanings into vaguely defined policies. The writers at the *New York Post* clearly did just that when the paper reported in 1979 that the Morgenthau Committee had called for the "creation of a commission to formulate more *strict* and uniform sentencing procedures."[55] It is difficult to imagine a case of a greater selective perception: The Morgenthau Committee had recommended that sentences be the *least severe* consistent with the public welfare—hardly a call for strict sentencing. Perhaps the *Post* (and rightfully so) was responding to the identity of the committee's chairman, not the content of their report.

The following year the *Post,* calling the current system "inconsistent, ineffective, unjust and lacking in credibility," urged the legislature to adopt determinate sentencing. In another example of the *Post's* selective misreading of the Morgenthau Committee's report, it equated the passage of determinate sentencing with crime control. It chastised the legislature for failing to act on the Morgenthau plan: "[I]f the Legislature fails to take up the issue, the crime wave itself will insure that the people of this city make it a major issue in the coming election."[56]

Following the retirement of Hugh Carey and the subsequent election of Mario Cuomo as governor, the *Post* increased the frequency of its coverage of determinate sentencing. Noting that the creation of a sentencing commission was supported by powerful state legislators from both political parties, the *Post* said determinate sentencing would "bring equal, and possibly *tougher* sentences for the same crime in all courts of the state." [57]

A 1982 editorial, entitled "End Fraud In Sentencing To Boost The War

On Crime," called the sentencing system a "failure and a fraud." The *Post* urged governor-elect Cuomo to adopt determinate sentencing. Adopting the Morgenthau Committee's recommendations, the *Post* said, would "lead to a major break-through for New York City in the battle against crime ... The present system of sentencing distorts the whole criminal justice process. It should be scrapped. The bipartisan support of the Legislature for doing so should encourage Cuomo to make it one of his top priorities."[58]

The New York Times

Unlike the *New York Post,* the *Times* covered the release of the Morgenthau Committee's report without reading in to it its own sentencing preferences. The paper cautioned, however, that the Morgenthau structure "may lead to longer sentences and give prosecutors, who control the plea-bargaining process, too much power."[59]

Following the issuance of the Morgenthau Committee's report, the *Times* noted that "[w]ith startling speed, a new rationale for criminal sentencing has emerged. Rehabilitation is out, punishment is in." [60]

In a March 1980 editorial, entitled "Dawdling on Determinate Sentencing," the *Times* declared itself strongly in favor of determinate sentencing.

> Curiously, the New York Legislature, which gets so riled up about crime every election year, has dawdled on the proposal ... Opponents of the plan say the Parole Board uses the same criteria for setting prison terms, so why replace them? Besides, they observe, stricter sentencing standards could swell the population of already crowded prisons. These arguments underestimate the corrosive effect of the cynicism that is bred by the appearance of capriciousness in determining who goes to prison and for how long. Public confidence is undercut when sentencing is decided not at trial but behind the Parole Board's doors. The Morgenthau plan would inject predictability, without rigidity, into the sentencing process.[61]

The support of the Mayor of New York City, Edward I. Koch, for determinate sentencing was applauded in a 1981 *Times* editorial. "The Mayor is right to want to narrow the discretion of judges in sentencing; the punishment for crime should be more consistent and predictable."[62]

Following the gubernatorial election of Mario Cuomo, the *Times* ran an editorial urging the new governor to push forward on the Morgenthau Committee's plan. It stated:

> The reason for all the uncertainty [in criminal justice] is a process called indeterminate sentencing, once considered a humanizing reform. Governor Cuomo and New York legislative leaders show laudable interest in reforming the reform. Though the task is perilous, it is worth pursuing.
>
> Indeterminate sentencing grew from the tradition of trying to rehabilitate prisoners ... Lately this ideal of rehabilitation has fallen on hard times ... In

effect, the board resentences the convict, appraising the trial record and other information in proceedings that the public rarely sees. The resulting uncertainty and potential for abuse mislead the public and disturb any student of the process.[63]

Determinate Sentencing Gets Back on Track

Between 1979 and 1982 determinate sentencing was very much alive as a policy issue in New York. The popularity of the concept nationwide, the support of the New York media, the recommendations of the Morgenthau and Liman Commissions, the advocacy of two governors, and the support of law-enforcement and defense-oriented criminal justice practitioners keep the movement for determinate sentencing on policymakers' agenda.

While determinate sentencing remained a viable option, it failed to gather and sustain the momentum necessary for success. Some legislators were suspicious of a policy issue that attracted both defense and law enforcement. It is possible that the contradictions surrounding the determinate ideal would never have been exposed had Mario M. Cuomo not been elected governor of New York in 1982.

Mario Cuomo Pushes for Determinate Sentencing

In his first Annual Message, New York's new governor announced that it was "past the time to take a fresh look at the entire criminal justice mechanism." The punishment should fit the crime, not the criminal, Governor Cuomo said.

> Sentencing must be fair, consistent and uniformly imposed. To achieve those goals we need a comprehensive reform of all sentencing procedures. Judges now exercise vast discretion when imposing sentence. The result is widespread disparities, which undermine the ability of our sentencing laws to do justice or to control crime. To remedy that, I will propose a complete restructuring of our sentencing laws that judges throughout the State will be required to follow.[64]

Unlike Governor Carey, who merely talked about the validity of the determinate ideal, Governor Cuomo backed up his rhetoric with action. Early in 1983 he directed his staff to draft a bill establishing a sentencing guidelines committee.[65] Negotiations on what became Chapter 711 of the Laws of 1983, the enabling legislation for the Committee on Sentencing Guidelines (Bellacosa-Feinberg Committee), were conducted over several months by staff of the Assembly and Senate Codes Committees and the Governor's office.

John Poklemba, currently the governor's Director of Criminal Justice and Commissioner of the Division of Criminal Justice Services, who was then counsel to the former Director of Criminal Justice, explained why Governor Cuomo was attracted to the determinate ideal.

> The main reason that the Governor supported it is that it makes the process more open and honest. It takes the decisionmaking out of the faceless parole board and gives responsibility for sentencing to the judge, who has been elected. It removes uncertainty and eliminates disparity. The Governor feels that defendants who commit similar crimes should receive similar sentences.

Scott Fein, former assistant counsel to both Governors Carey and Cuomo, recalled in an interview that

> Governor Cuomo adopted Liman's recommendations in his campaign. We started work on 711 as soon as Governor Cuomo came in. The Governor was the moving force, but everyone else soon contributed. Morgenthau was still behind it. The expectation was that the legislation would be the product of the studies that had preceded it. The fact that it [Sentencing Guidelines Committee] was a legislative, judicial, and executive commission demonstrates the commitment—all three entities necessary to make and enforce the law coming together.

James Yates (then Counsel to the Assembly Codes Committee) said,

> When Governor Cuomo became governor he had an era of cooperation, whereas we had said no on a routine basis to Carey in the criminal-justice area. In the first year when there was a love match going on, the Assembly wasn't quick to say no...Once the Assembly withdraws its opposition, then as long as it carries the law and order banner...the Senate is going to go along with it. Once the Assembly gives in, even though the Senate might not approve it, they are not going to be willing to step down. So anyway, Cuomo called for it, and so we went ahead...It wasn't all Cuomo's pressure, though ...We'd started to see more and more of the impact of the 1978 laws and started realizing that sentencing was running wild...We were pumping more resources into the system, and we started getting more and more commitments, plus the length of time was going up because of the mandatory minimums. The biggest surge in prison population was probably in 1980–81. By 1983 we were starting to say maybe this discretionary system is not so discretionary. Maybe in fact we have a definite system, but it's a one-sided definite system. It's definite so that a judge can't show leniency, but it's not definite if he wants to go higher...I think there was more receptiveness to the idea coinciding with Cuomo coming in and pushing for it.

Matthew Crosson, former Assistant Counsel for Governor Cuomo and currently chief administrator of the Office of Court Administration, said that

> there was a fairly strong feeling for doing it [Chapter 711] in the executive. There was also opposition to the concept at fairly critical places in the leg-

islature. The legislature was willing to do a committee and study it. The fact that the bill was passed does not mean that it was supported by important people. They had voiced skepticism when it was passed.

James Cantwell, then the Counsel to the Senate Codes Committee, agreed with Mr. Yates's assessment of what happened in the legislature. Passage of the bill did not signal approval of determinate sentencing. According to him,

[The] Senate had not made up its mind on determinate sentencing, but used 711 to get hard information. The Morgenthau Committee had supplied a theoretical basis, but no one had satisfied the Senate on what you would get with determinate sentencing. Liman didn't, McQuillan tried to give actual numbers, but the sample was often too small when broken down by crimes.

Assemblyman Gottfreid agreed:

There was growing discomfort on both the left and the right with the idea. Determinate sentencing gained some of its strength from the people who said it's a fine idea, but it has a few problems, let's study it—all the while hoping never to have to deal with it.

Negotiations on Chapter 711

The negotiations and legislative debates over Chapter 711 foreshadowed the controversy that would later engulf the guidelines commission. The major negotiation points centered on the following components of the legislation.

Committee make-up The Morgenthau Committee had recommended an independent sentencing commission with nine members, but Chapter 711 created a fourteen member panel. At the insistence of the Senate leadership, no legislators could serve on the committee. This was seen by the negotiators as a clear indication of the Senate leadership's desire to distance itself from the committee's work and the ultimate product of that work.

Enactment The Morgenthau Committee had recommended that the guidelines become law 180 days after being issued by the sentencing commission. Recognizing that the legislature would be unwilling to yield its sentencing power so totally, the Liman Commission had recommended that the legislature be allowed to veto the guidelines. Governor Cuomo's original proposal, consistent with the Liman Commission's report, put the committee's proposal before the legislature on an all-or-nothing basis; the guidelines would take effect unless vetoed by one House. Even in this diluted form, however, such an enactment provision was unacceptable to the legislature. Reserving the right of the legislature to make line-by-line changes in the guidelines, the negotiators of Chapter 711 provided that the guidelines would have no force unless enacted into law.

Mr. Cantwell recalled that the enactment clause was

> the major issue in the negotiations over Chapter 711. The Senate felt that the purpose of 711 was to educate the Senate, so a veto would not be sufficient. Setting sentences is a legislative function, passing on the legislature is a governor's responsibility—they are elected to do this. It [the sentencing committee] was an information gathering experience."

Rehabilitation   The Morgenthau Committee had denounced rehabilitation as a purpose of punishment. While it was accepted from the start of the negotiations that rehabilitation would not be included in Chapter 711 as a purpose of punishment, it was also accepted that it would not be expressly abrogated. Consequently, Chapter 711 endorsed all of the traditional purposes of punishment except rehabilitation. The negotiators were leery over engaging the legislature in a debate over the purposes of punishment; as the excerpts presented below from the Assembly debates over Chapter 711 demonstrate, the negotiators had valid reasons for trying to avoid a showdown in the legislature on the objectives of the criminal sanction.

Parole release   The clear intention of Chapter 711 was to abolish parole release. The governor had stated publicly that the parole board was insufficiently sensitive to prison crowding; Parole Chairman Hammock had sharply retorted that parole release was governed by statute, and that prison crowding was not an enumerated factor to be considered in making the release decision.

Prison capacity   While the negotiators wished the committee to consider prison resources in formulating the guidelines, an express link to resources was considered politically unacceptable.[66]

Inspect and reduce   This provision, included at the insistence of the Assembly leadership, was aimed at controlling prosecutorial discretion. As developed by the negotiators, the inspect and reduce provision gave the court the authority to reduce an indictment to charge a lesser included offense.[67]

Time to report   The legislature gave the guidelines committee eighteen months to complete its recommendations. The negotiators realized that any delay in submitting the recommendations would seriously undermine the chance for careful consideration of the committee's product.

Most/least severe sanction   Consistent with the Morgenthau Committee's report, the negotiated bill presented to the legislature provided that sanctions be the least severe consistent with the enumerated principles of punishment. The call for least severe sanctions did not survive legislative scrutiny, however, as the following excerpts from the Assembly debates on Chapter 711 reveal.

The Assembly Debates the Parsimony Principle

Chapter 711 was sponsored in the Assembly by Melvin Miller, then Chairman of the Codes Committee.[68] In describing the bill to his colleagues, Assemblyman Miller said that it was intended "to bring some rationality to the scheme."[69] The new structure would alleviate disparity and end the "helter-skelter" sentencing provisions of the current law, he said.[70] While Chairman Miller was looking for rationality, it is obvious that his Assembly colleagues were looking to control crime through the imposition of the criminal sanction.

The debates centered around section 2(2) of the bill, which originally read: "The sanction imposed shall be the least severe measure consistent with the principles of sentencing set forth herein." An amendment was offered by Assemblyman Saland for a "relatively simple" change[71]: The word least would be replaced with the word "most". Reasoning that each of his Assembly colleagues had campaigned on a get-tough-on-crime platform, Mr. Saland argued that it would be incongruous for the Assembly to adopt as a guiding principle that sentences should be the least severe.

Others agreed. Assemblyman Hoblock said:

> I don't think there is anyone in this House, with perhaps a few exceptions, that has not campaigned in 1982, and previous years, on some form of determinate sentencing ... something we should do about the criminal activities and those who appear to be getting away with criminal activity in the State, but yet we are supporting, without this amendment, a concept that is somewhat contrary to what most of us have been saying.[72]

Calling this the most significant criminal justice bill of the year, Mr. Hoblock called for bipartisan support of the amendment to change "least" to "most".

Chairman Miller tried to deflate the criticism by claiming that "least" was being read out of context, distorting the intention of the sentence. The language was borrowed from the Morgenthau Commission report, he said, and given

> from whence that language comes, we are not talking about people who are soft or hard. We are looking for fairness. We are not looking for over-leniency. However, we are not looking for punitive legislation. We are looking for balance, which I think this language will give us because, remember, we are the repository of the final power ... [T]he whole focal point of this bill is for the commission to set what they believe are the appropriate guidelines ... I think it's consistent with present sentencing law, a judge sentences on what he believes is necessary to do. ... and whether you use the word "least" or "most" you don't change the nature of the sentence.[73]

This tortuous reasoning did not, however, convince those advocating the amendment to withdraw their opposition: "I think it's pretty clear that least

and most have different meanings," Assemblyman Winner said.[74] He noted
that the Liman Commission had grounded their recommendation for the least
severe sanction in concerns over prison crowding.

Disparaging such a linkage as irresponsible policy, he asked:

> Is it really our underlying intent to lock less people up and reduce our popu-
> lation through the back door of a sentencing guideline proposal that may
> result in shorter sentences for violent criminals? If that is the case, I don't
> want to support a measure like this. I was hopeful this measure was
> designed to bring fairness and equity into the system, not to result in less
> punishment for violent offenders. Code words such as "least" make me
> very suspicious, and my colleagues very nervous, with respect to the inten-
> tion of the sponsors here.[75]

The amendment to change least to most was defeated on a party-line vote,
but that did not end the debate. Assemblyman Flanagan reminded the bill's
supporters that there would be some who would question the need for another
sentencing commission. The legislature itself, he warned, was perfectly capable of establishing sentencing ranges. With these barely veiled threats lurking,
Assemblyman Flanagan suggested that all references to "most" or "least" be
deleted, and that the phrase read simply "the sanctions imposed shall be a
measure consistent with the principles..." Otherwise, he warned,

> [y]ou are going to hear about it in your next campaign. It's going to be
> stamped right on your forehead ... You are not going to be able to say, "I
> went on that one because I was going to be hard on crime" ... They are going
> to say, "Did you read it, because it says in the bill that the guidelines will be
> based on the least severe penalties, not the most, not even severe, not even
> light, but the least possible penalties." That's a very bad premise ... The only
> thing you are going to have to hang your hat on is this bill, the one you voted
> for which says you wanted the least severe penalties, that's how it's going to
> be phrased, and how it's going to be put to you, and that's how you are going
> to deserve to get it put to you. All you have to do is reflect on this, think
> about it, and just change those three words. The Governor gets his commis-
> sion, everybody who he wants to appoint gets appointed. We all get a chance
> to look at these things, but we don't submit a preconceived notion to the
> minds of the people who sit on this panel.[76]

The bill was next assailed for giving the commission too long to complete its task. In defense, Chairman Miller noted that the Morgenthau Commission recommended that the guidelines commission be given two years to
do its work. The bill already reduced the time to eighteen months. Assemblyman Miller explained the enormity of the task before the committee:

> We are telling them to give us guidelines. We have never told any commis-
> sion dealing with sentencing, and there was only one, Lehman [sic], was

not a sentencing commission. We have asked the Morgenthau Commission, and then we had a commission last year which came down with a report that everyone rejected out of hand[77] ... We think it's going to take eighteen months, it is extremely tight because what you are, in essence, doing is what they did in '67, you are redoing the entire sentencing provisions of the penal law. It took them almost four years last time.[78]

Faced with the threat of no guidelines committee, or, in the alternative, a committee with insufficient time to complete its task, Chairman Miller, after consulting with the Senate sponsors of the bill, the governor's Director of Criminal Justice, and the governor's counsel, agreed to the requested change and deleted reference to the least or most severe sanction. Although the change mollified the bill's opponents temporarily, they warned that their support of Chapter 711 should not be interpreted as support of the committee's recommendations.

Mr. Saland, who had originally proposed substituting "most severe" for "least severe", warned that a vote for 711 was not a vote for determinate sentencing:

The jury is out, there are findings that have to be made, and when those findings are made, we'll be asked to deliberate. In no way, shape or form do I embrace whatever that end product will be, and I am assuming there is no one in this House that has the clairvoyance to be able to know what they will be, and I assume further that we all must go into it with that in mind. It's interesting to see that people from as disparate political philosophies as Senator Ted Kennedy, who has written in support of this particular concept, and some very conservative people, have come out in favor of determinate sentencing, so, it can't really mean to all of us the same things that we think it means. I would just ask that you be aware of these problems, and be aware of the problem that has been written about in so many articles of the elevation of the district attorney to a level of such heights that you begin to wonder whether he, and not the court, under the determinate sentencing system, is actually the one who makes a determination of the sentences.[79]

In a recent interview, Assemblyman Gottfreid recalled the debate over the least versus the most severe sanction:

Talk about a ship turning back to port. The Flanagan amendment saying wait, didn't you all campaign that sentences should be the most restrictive? This is what the whole discussion is about. Even if it's only a study bill, it blows up in your face politically. Once anyone reads that sentence aloud, the notion of having that bill on the floor becomes instantly untenable. You could have commissions up your kazoo that would sign off in a minute on that, but the minute it comes to public and political light, its untenable. That phrase—least/most—is what happened to determinate sentencing.

The Senate Issues a Warning

Ralph Marino, then the Chairman of the Senate Committee on Crime and Correction, issued a report to his colleagues entitled *Determinate Sentencing: Danger Ahead*. The Senator claimed that the case for sentencing disparity had not been made, and that the real problem with sentencing lay in prosecutorial discretion: "It is not difficult to conclude that the person who controls the conviction charge controls the sentence, and that person is the prosecutor."[80]

Senator Marino warned that determinate sentencing would cause prison populations to spiral ever upward. Demonstrating his political acumen, the Senator predicted the response to the guidelines committee's work:

> The Legislature will not accept without debate recommendations made by a Sentencing Guidelines Commission. For the liberally inclined, sentence duration will appear too harsh; for the conservatively oriented, too lenient. Policy differences will not be reconciled for years, if at all.[81]

Chapter 711 of the Laws of 1983

Nevertheless, despite reservations in both Houses of the Legislature, Chapter 711 passed the Assembly by a vote of 134 to 6 and the Senate by a vote of 51 to 8 and was signed into law by Governor Cuomo on July 28, 1983.[82] On approving Chapter 711, Governor Cuomo cited favorably the Morgenthau and Liman Committees; no mention was made of the McQuillan Commission, which had raised serious questions about the determinate model. The governor announced that the

> concept of fairness in sentencing depends, in large measure, upon the imposition of similar penalties upon similar offenders who commit similar crimes. To remedy the problem of disparate sentences, the commissions recommended the adoption of a system of determinate sentencing. Such a system would be based upon the concept that the court, rather than the Board of Parole, should set the actual period of confinement. It would ensure that both the defendant and the public will know at time of sentence the nature and length of the sentence.[83]

Mayor Koch supports 711 The Memorandum of the Legislative Representative of the City of New York, representing Mayor Koch, exposes the law-enforcement appeal of determinate sentencing. Noting that the mayor had long supported determinate sentencing, the memorandum said that he was

> heartened that other public officials and private citizens have come to share our recognition of the considerable benefit of a determinate sentencing structure... The need for this change has become increasingly clear. At the same time that we are indicting, convicting and imprisoning more felons

than ever before, we remain saddled with a sentencing system that provides insufficient guarantees that these dangerous criminals will remain incarcerated for responsible periods.

Under determinate sentencing, the New York City memo continued,

[o]ur sentencing process will finally be honest, understandable, and certain so that the imposition of criminal sanctions may mean respect for the system, obedience of the law and safety in our neighborhoods.[84]

The Media Gives Chapter 711 Mixed Reviews

The New York Post   Following the election of Governor Cuomo in 1982, the New York Post increased the frequency of its coverage of determinate sentencing. Noting that the creation of a sentencing commission was supported by powerful state legislators from both sides of the aisles, the Post again indulged its favored perceptions when it described determinate sentencing as "designed to bring equal, and possibly tougher sentences for the same crime in all courts of the state."

In a 1982 editorial, entitled "End Fraud In Sentencing To Boost The War On Crime," the Post called the sentencing system a "failure and a fraud." The Post again urged governor-elect Cuomo to adopt determinate sentencing. Following the Morgenthau Committee's recommendations and appointing a guidelines commission would, the Post said,

lead to a major break-through for New York City in the battle against crime.... The present system of sentencing distorts the whole criminal justice process. It should be scrapped. The bipartisan support of the Legislature for doing so should encourage Cuomo to make it one of his top priorities.[85]

Under the byline "Lock 'Em Up & Throw Away Key," the *Post*'s Albany Bureau Chief noted that

[p]unishment, not rehabilitation, will be the official goal of New York's criminal-justice system under the terms of a top-secret sentencing plan, which could become the law this year... The new code, which will probably *increase* the maximum time that many inmates serve in prison, is being discussed by the Legislature's top criminal justice experts and senior aides to Gov. Cuomo.

The following day a *Post* editorial entitled "Long-Awaited Key To Sanity In The Criminal Justice System" appeared. The *Post* again announced that

[p]unishment; not rehabilitation, would be the order of the day under a top-secret sentencing plan which could become the law of New York State this year. None too soon! It's past time that we locked up violent and repeat criminal offenders—and the key along with them.

Calling Chapter 711 the "most dramatic and welcome revision of the state's sentencing provisions in twenty years," the editorial reminded its readers that such legislation

> is something *The Post* has repeatedly called for in its campaign to return sanity to the chaotic state of our criminal justice system ... It is therefore heartening that a panel of the state's top criminal justice experts are putting the finishing touches on a new code which would *increase* the maximum prison time that many inmates serve.[87]

The *Post* urged that the sentencing commission act fast: It recommended the committee be given only one year to make their recommendations.

The following month the *Post* ran an editorial criticizing Assembly Speaker Fink and Senate Majority Leader Anderson for the delay in passing a sentencing guidelines bill:

> Why should it be necessary for Cuomo to have to negotiate Fink's agreement to this legislation? Fink was a member of the Morgenthau Committee on sentencing reform established by Governor Carey. He signed the committee's recommendations for precisely what Cuomo now proposes. That was four years ago! And still they quibble!

The *Post* went on to complain about a proposal to require the guidelines committee to study the role of parole and consider prison crowding when fashioning the guidelines:

> That would be a mistake. That would merely repeat the work of the Morgenthau Committee. It is time to stop studying this problem and introduce reform. Miller [the Chairman of the Assembly Codes Committee and sponsor of Chapter 711] also wants the Legislature to be able to modify any of the commission's recommendations. That would also be a mistake. A debate in the Legislature is hardly the way to fix the sentences: the reason an independent commission is being proposed to do precisely that is to remove the argument from politics ... It is time for our legislators to stop making a charade of the urgency for court reform and to deal with the war against crime. Fink and Anderson should assure Cuomo that his proposed legislation will go through within a week, that the commission will report back within three months, that the legislation will be in place by the end of this year.[88]

Following the passage of Chapter 711, the *Post* characterized the new legislation as

> a *hard-hitting* bill ... The sweeping reform ... will dramatically change the thrust of the state's criminal justice system from rehabilitation to retribution.

The *get-tough* measure sailed through the Democratic-controlled Assembly
last week by a vote of 134–6, and Cuomo swiftly pledged to sign it. The
hard-nosed reform sets up the state Sentencing Guidelines Committee.[89]

The *Post* thus continued to place in determinate sentencing exactly what it
wanted to find.

The New York Times   The Times originally urged the new governor to push
forward with the Morgenthau Committee's plan. Yet. unlike the Post, the
Times foresaw some of the pitfalls in changing the sentencing system.

> Flawed as this [the indeterminate] system is, improving it is tricky . . . Let-
> ting a commission write the guidelines provides essential insulation from
> politics. But it also creates a problem, since legislatures are understandably
> reluctant to yield authority over sentencing. A compromise might give the
> legislature veto power over commission-written guidelines. This approach
> is worth trying. Building more certainty into the sentencing process could
> deter more crime and improve management of criminal justice at all levels.
> Most important, it may restore some level of public respect for the process
> of punishment.[90]

On May 29, 1983, just weeks before the passage of Chapter 711, the
Times, obviously aware of the contents of the negotiated bill, urged the governor to put on the brakes. While still supporting the idea of determinate sentencing, the *Times* warned that the bill should not be passed in its present
form. Unlike the *New York Post,* the editors of the *New York Times* were worried about the impact of the new system on the state's prison population. The
editorial said that

> Governor Cuomo is right to seek more uniformity in sentencing. But his
> proposed law leaves far too many loose ends . . . Such guidelines can indeed
> make sentences more uniform while also controlling the size of prison pop-
> ulations—but only if the process of writing the guidelines is insulated from
> the inevitable political assaults. Sensible guidelines are likely to be contro-
> versial . . . If the guidelines commission lacks some independence from the
> Legislature, every new crime scare will lead to longer sentences and pro-
> duce intolerable pressures on prison space. Yet the Governor's bill is dis-
> turbingly vague about how that independence would be assured. Ideally the
> Legislature, which defines crimes, should determine sentences, a power that
> in practice now rests with the parole board. But the commission also needs
> protection against line-item meddling. A sound compromise would require
> the Legislature to enact or reject the guidelines as a package, a point that
> needs to be made explicit in Mr. Cuomo's sentencing bill. His bill also
> leaves the commission with too much discretion. It sets no limit, for exam-
> ple, on the permissible range of any guidelines. A sounder approach can be
> found in Senator Kennedy's proposed federal guidelines bill: It would

require that the maximum sentence in any category not exceed the minimum by more than 25 percent . . . And on the urgent matter of prison crowding, it requires only that the commission "consider" available resources. At the least, the commission ought to be required to explain how its guidelines are shaped by considerations of prison capacity. These imprecisions result from unavoidable negotiations among powerful interests in the Legislature and the criminal justice system. But they do not bode well for a new system that depends so much on insulation from political pressure. Better proposals have been written elsewhere. New York's is not yet fit for enactment.[91]

Following the passage of Chapter 711, a *Times* editorial, entitled "The Sentencing Trap," again urged the governor to turn away from his program bill.

In the last days of the legislative session, Governor Cuomo pushed through a bill that could either ease New York's prison problem—or make it catastrophic. That uncertainty is regrettable, unnecessary and still avoidable if the Governor reconsiders his support and withholds his signature.

The editorial noted that the idea behind determinate sentencing was

[i]n theory . . . a good idea. The parole board, which functions in obscurity, has too much power. The existing system tolerates wide disparities in sentences and contributes to public confusion and lack of respect for the courts . . . The guidelines approach is usually sold as a way to get tough, to bring stern certainty to a haphazard process. Yet sentences designed to conserve prison space would have to be short. Once in place, guidelines sentences would never be reduced. Yet as they exceed the average time now served, they would quickly overload the prison system. So the path to fixed sentencing also leads to a political trap. When the Legislature votes on a sentence schedule it will either have to approve short sentences, which is unlikely, or agree to build a lot more prison cells, which the state can't afford. Promoters of fixed sentences had hoped to avoid the trap by asking an expert commission to prepare the sentences, rather than leaving them up to legislators imprisoned by their tough anti-crime oratory. But the Legislature resisted this limitation on its power and in the final hours of debate even purged the bill of language that might have encouraged lighter sentences. The result is a vaguely drafted bill that bodes ill for prisons built to hold 26,000 but now glutted with more than 30,000 inmates . . . What will happen if the Legislature falls into the sentencing trap? Aides to Mr. Cuomo promise he would veto a schedule of sentences harsh enough to destroy the prison system. But that's an easy promise now. If outrage against crime is running high when the guidelines are delivered, a veto may seem out of the question. The urgency of the prison crowding problem clearly outweighs the urgency of fixing sentences. Mr. Cuomo could do himself and the state a favor by vetoing the current bill and negotiating for a better one in the fall.[92]

Having been unsuccessful in blocking the creation of the guidelines committee, the *Times* gave the new committee some advice.

> The new idea is to make sentencing more consistent, a commendable goal. But the catch is that if fixed terms are any longer than those now actually served, they will quickly add thousands to the prison population. No one sees any political advantage in urging retention of the present sentencing system. And as legislators demand ever tougher guidelines, they ratchet up the prison population beyond any hope of its decent accommodation. This uncomfortable nuance is not well understood by the public, and that creates a heavy responsibility for the commission now being appointed by the Governor and state leaders to write the sentencing guidelines. From the beginning, it needs to make clear the relationship of sentencing and prison crowding, point out that sentences long enough to push the prison system over the brink would weaken, not strengthen criminal justice, and disavow any guideline system that would do so. Eventually, the Legislature will have to approve the commission's guidelines—and resist the temptation to make demagogic points by rejecting them as too lenient. That means the governor and the Legislature's leadership share the obligation of educating the public. As they convene the commission, they, too, ought to promise to scrap any guidelines that would aggravate prison crowding. Without such clear signals, the luck that prevented catastrophe at Ossining will run out.[93]

Conclusion

With the help of Governor Cuomo, determinate sentencing arrived on the formal agenda of the New York Legislature. The road to reform had been rocky, and we will never know if the determinate model would have survived the journey if it were not for the new governor's support. One thing is certain, however: Mario M. Cuomo's support of a sentencing guidelines committee ensured that the contradictions lurking in the determinate ideal would no longer remain hidden.

As many in the legislature had predicted while casting their affirmative votes for Chapter 711, the seemingly overwhelming support for the creation of a guidelines committee would not translate into support for determinate sentencing. As the remainder of the book will show, the passage of Chapter 711 of the Laws of 1983 was the turning point, the high-water mark for the determinate ideal in New York.

7

Sentencing Guidelines New York Style

This chapter discusses what happened when the determinate ideal, which had been cross-endorsed by law-and-order and defense advocates, was exposed to the harsh light of careful scrutiny. During its formative period, when determinacy remained but a conceptualization, its attraction to people with different ideologies, and their selective interpretations of the reform, posed few problems. Later, when the abstract was rendered specific, the fissures between the two perspectives became all too apparent. The resulting conflict was evident in the work of the New York State Committee on Sentencing Guidelines (Bellacosa-Feinberg Committee).

The difficulty of reducing disparity while retaining an appropriate degree of discretion, of balancing certainty with power, proved a constant reminder of the lack of guidance provided by the deceptively simple concept of determinate sentencing. The Morgenthau Committee and Chapter 711 had done little to explicate the contradictions inherent in the determinate model. Struggling to devise a new system, the sentencing guidelines committee continually faced the difficult task of specifying the previously unspecified, converting covert practices into overt ones, and balancing divergent ideologies.[1]

Members of the Bellacosa-Feinberg Committee, like members of any group, brought their personal ideologies with them when they attended committee meetings. Because the committee members had different world views, they also had conflicting expectations of determinacy, a concept whose contours had never been fully defined. Lacking a shared vision of determinacy, the Bellacosa-Feinberg Committee had no basis for allocating power between the various constellations of authority or for linking power with purpose. No calculus could be conjured up to determine whose definition would assert primacy over the others. The absence of a common definition and the presence of conflicting ideologies became apparent whenever the committee grappled with one of the many interrelated issues involved in fashioning a sentencing system.

Six of the fourteen members of the Bellacosa-Feinberg Committee were appointed by Governor Cuomo, six by legislative leaders, and two by then-

Chief Judge Cooke of the New York State Court of Appeals, the state's highest court. The governor selected the committee chairman, Joseph Bellacosa. When Mr. Bellacosa left the committee, Governor Cuomo appointed Kenneth Feinberg as his replacement.

Nine of the committee members generally spoke and voted in support of defense-oriented positions, four were aligned with law-enforcement positions, and one committee member varied between the two positions depending on the issue under discussion. Admittedly, these classifications are rough and far from absolute, and some committee members occasionally voiced an opinion or voted in favor of a position espoused by the opposite camp. Several committee members were skilled negotiators who frequently sought a middle ground between defense and law-enforcement positions. Despite the difficulty inherent in reducing complex human attitudes and behaviors into a simple dichotomy, these broad classifications reflect the committee members' overall orientation and provide a context for understanding the committee's work.

Governor Cuomo appointed four defense-oriented committee members. Arthur Liman, an attorney in private practice and past president of the Legal Aid Society, had served as Counsel to the McKay Commission during its investigation of the Attica Riot. Mr. Liman was a member of the Morgenthau Committee and chairman of the Liman Commission, which recommended that, in addition to adopting determinate sentencing, the governor be given emergency release powers to cope with prison crowding. The Governor also appointed Vincent O'Leary, President of the State University of New York at Albany. President O'Leary had served as a member of the Citizens Inquiry in Criminal Justice, which advocated the abolition of parole release and the adoption of shorter prison sentences.

The governor's two other appointments were Austin Gerald Lopez, an attorney specializing in criminal defense cases, and Lynn Walker, who had been counsel for the National Association for the Advancement of Colored People and was currently an attorney for the Ford Foundation. Mr. Lopez was a consistent supporter of alternatives to incarceration and lenient prison sentences, especially for younger offenders. Miss Walker consistently expressed concern for the impact of the guidelines on minority offenders and urged the committee to recommend greater use of alternatives to incarceration.

Both of the chairmen appointed by the governor were aligned with law-enforcement interests. The first, Joseph Bellacosa, was a law professor at Albany Law School when named to chair the committee. He left the committee in January 1985, before it completed its work, having been appointed Chief Administrative Judge of the state's court system; in January 1987 Judge Bellacosa was appointed an Associate Justice of the New York State Court of Appeals. When Chairman Bellacosa left the committee, Governor Cuomo appointed Kenneth Feinberg, an attorney in private practice, as his replacement. Mr. Feinberg had been an advisor to Senator Ted Kennedy when the Senator was supporting federal sentencing guidelines. Chairmen Bellacosa and Feinberg generally spoke and voted with the law-enforcement oriented members, but in their role as chairmen, they frequently sought a compromise between the two positions.

The governor also appointed Robert Morgenthau, who had chaired his own sentencing committee and served as a member of the Liman Commission. While District Attorney Morgenthau's committee had recommended the adoption of the parsimony principle, it was evident during the committee meetings that Mr. Morgenthau's definition of parsimony was drastically different than that of the defense-oriented creators of the movement for determinate sentencing.

Legislative leaders were true to form in their appointments. The then-Speaker of the Democratic Assembly, Stanley Fink, and the Democratic minority leader of the Senate, Manfred Orenstein, selected defense-oriented members. Speaker Fink appointed Basil Paterson, an attorney in private practice who had been secretary of state. Mr. Paterson repeatedly focused the committee's attention on the special problems of minority communities and the need to match prison resources with sentencing policy. Speaker Fink also appointed James Yates, then the counsel to the Assembly Codes Committee. Mr. Yates was the only member of the committee employed by the legislature; the Senate did not appoint a counterpart from their staff. Michael Smith, selected by Senator Orenstein, was executive director of the Vera Institute of Justice, an organization widely respected for its pioneering work in alternatives to incarceration.

As expected, Republican legislative leaders appointed two law-enforcement oriented members. The temporary president of the Senate, Warren Anderson, selected Judge William Mulligan, an attorney in private practice and former Appellate Division judge. Judge Mulligan frequently argued that sentences should be tough and that sentence length should not hinge on prison crowding. The Republican minority leader of the Assembly, Clarence Rappleyea, chose Clark Wemple, an attorney in private practice and former Republican Assemblyman. Mr. Wemple, like Judge Mulligan, took the position that sentences should not be linked to resources. Senator Anderson also selected Robert Coutant, a criminal court judge from an upstate county. Judge Coutant was the only committee member whom I was unable to classify as siding more consistently with one ideological camp as opposed to another. Instead, more so than any of his colleagues, Judge Coutant switched his vote between law-enforcement and defense, depending on the issue.

The chief judge of the Court of Appeals selected two defense-oriented judges. Betty Ellerin was deputy chief administrative judge for New York City; she was subsequently appointed an Appellate Division judge. Judge Ellerin ardently supported alternatives to incarceration and the repeal of the mandatory sentencing laws. Milton Williams, administrative judge of the Supreme Court in New York County, had been executive director of the McKay Commission. Judge Williams was subsequently appointed deputy chief administrative judge for New York City. Like Judge Ellerin, Judge Williams supported judicial discretion and relatively lenient sentencing.

Chapter 711 was signed into law on July 28, 1983. Appointments to the sentencing committee were not completed until October 1983. The committee met for the first time in November 1983; its last meeting was September 1985. Twenty scheduled committee meetings, including a two-day, a three-day, and a four-day meeting, were held.[2] Committee meetings were open to the public, and were heavily attended by outside observers and the press.

From the committee's very first meeting, it became apparent that everyone associated with the project held vastly different conceptions of determinate sentencing. Nowhere were the differences more noticeable than in the discussions over the role of research in the development of the guidelines grid.

Descriptive versus Prescriptive Guidelines

Sentence length and sentence type are at the center of the divide between law enforcement and defense interests. In 1979, the Morgenthau Committee recommended that the sentencing guidelines grid track current sentencing patterns to the extent possible. By the time the Bellacosa-Feinberg Committee was established, the effects of the 1973 second felony offender laws and the 1978 violent felony offender laws were being felt throughout the criminal-justice system: More offenders were being incarcerated for longer periods than ever before.[3] Tracking current sentencing practices would thus automatically translate into endorsing and perpetuating severe sentencing, a policy that naturally appealed to law-enforcement interests.

Mr. Morgenthau reaffirmed his commitment to mirroring current practices when he told his colleagues on the Bellacosa-Feinberg Committee that "the numbers chosen should be consistent with present sentencing practices, as opposed to average time served for these crimes over the past five years or so, and should not go below the ranges to which offenders are now being sentenced."[4]

Under the indeterminate system, the sentence imposed by the judge does not determine the true extent of confinement, as that decision ultimately rests with the parole board. Consequently, information about the length of current sentences could not be determined by studying sentences imposed by the court. The severity of sentencing under the indeterminate order could only be determined by researching time actually served in prison. The determinate sentencing structure that the Bellacosa-Feinberg Committee began grappling with was not compatible with the existing indeterminate sentencing structure, as elements of crimes and criminal history information would be weighed differently under the new system. Acquiring time-served information that would be compatible with the grid format would require extensive research. Yet, a major controversy erupted during the initial stages of the committee process concerning whether or not the committee would engage in a substantial research effort.

At the committee's first meeting in November 1983, Mr. Morgenthau urged the committee to begin the data-collection process at once. In spite of Mr. Morgenthau's plea, research was not begun immediately. Rather, the committee was without a full-time research director until June 1984, six months before it was scheduled to report its recommendations. Not until the end of November 1984 did the committee receive sentencing information in grid format.

In large part, the slow start-up on the research was caused by confusion over whether the committee was developing prescriptive or descriptive guidelines. Prescriptive guidelines are based on normative judgments; descriptive guidelines are based on empirical data. The choice between the two, while clear-cut in theory, proved one of the most difficult and confusing aspects of the committee's work.

The Role of Research

Chairman Bellacosa hired Marvin Zalman, chairman of the Criminal Justice Department at Wayne State University, as executive director of the committee. In January 1984 Mr. Zalman presented his view of guidelines development to the committee, telling them that the guidelines should not be based on empirical data. Mr. Zalman indicated that his own experience and the findings of the National Center for State Courts "point to the appropriateness of guidelines development as a normative rather than a descriptive process."[5] Furthermore, Mr. Zalman said, even if the committee wished to recommend descriptive guidelines, there was not enough time for data collection, which would require a minimum of two years, not the one year allotted for the committee's work.

Mr. Zalman acknowledged that there was broad support in the criminal-justice literature for descriptive guidelines, but said that "in practice, it has been found that it is impossible to describe sentencing norms with such precision that they result in sentencing guidelines."[6]

Mr. Zalman told the committee that the staff would not undertake a major research project, but would instead bring general information about felony case processing and correctional resources to the committee's attention. He cautioned the committee that it "must decide for itself to what extent such information will be useful to them in the development of sentencing guidelines."[7] While normative guidelines were being proposed on their merits, because they were ostensibly the right approach to grid development, it is clear that other factors were at work. Complicated, comprehensive research takes time, and the committee labored under a very pressing deadline to complete its work.

At the January 1984 meeting, Mr. Zalman outlined the committee's research objectives. First, the staff would analyze the potential impact of the committee's guidelines on criminal-justice resources. Second, the staff would monitor the guidelines once they were enacted into law. Gathering data to support descriptive guidelines was conspicuously missing from the executive director's recitation of objectives.[8]

Following the lead of his staff director, Chairman Bellacosa frequently reminded the committee that the guidelines were being developed normatively. He told the members that, while the research staff would analyze existing data and perhaps supplement it with data gathered on their own, descriptive information was intended to serve merely as a confirmation of the committee's normative judgment.

Under this formulation, descriptive and prescriptive guidelines would somehow merge. Blurring the distinction between the two approaches to guidelines development relieved the pressure to quickly obtain empirical sentencing data and led to uncertainty over the extent of the research needed to satisfy committee needs. The approach was also inherently contradictory. While on the one hand the committee repeatedly claimed that it was trying to have no effect on prison populations over and above the effect that would be produced by a continuation of current practice, on the other hand the committee professed itself ready to use its normative judgment to raise or lower sentences as it felt appropriate. Under this fuzzy formulation, current practices would somehow be followed even as sentences were changed to reflect subjective judgments.

In spite of the peripheral role originally ascribed to research by the committee, it soon became apparent that some form of original data collection would be necessary if the committee was ever to complete its assignment. The lack of research data was frequently used during the first months of the committee's work to justify postponing decisions, or allowing decisions previously made to be changed. The chairman repeatedly told the members that all decisions were tentative pending receipt of the research; further discussion on a particular topic was often tabled until the research arrived. Yet, when questioned about the use that the research would be put to once received, Mr. Bellacosa responded that "the research effort was not designed to give exact numbers, but designed to be used as an aid in making policy decisions." He said that because data were only confirmatory of the committee's subjective judgments "less than precise numbers would be acceptable."[9]

Mr. Bellacosa later reminded the committee that the "ultimate objective of the research project was to have information that would confirm the committee's normative judgments."[10] He said that the data would give the committee ballpark figures with which to play, and that the data would be only a guide, not a substitute for exercise of judgment. Other committee members, however, frequently said they were unwilling to make normative judgments until the research was completed. A vicious circle developed, with major decisions being postponed until the research, slow in starting and intended only as a backup to personal judgments already made, arrived.

Designing the Grid

At Mr. Zalman's urging, the committee initially considered adopting a three-dimensional, matrix approach to guidelines' construction. The committee ultimately rejected this approach when it realized that the three-dimensional matrix would be constructed to reflect the facts surrounding the crime, not the conviction offense. So-called fact-based sentencing presented several problems, especially for the lawyers on the committee. Basing the severity of the offense on the existence of factual circumstances would require extensive fact-finding at the sentencing stage, where currently fact-finding is limited. Blurring the distinction between the crime of conviction and the crime actually committed raised questions of constitutionality and fairness. Finally, the overlap between the legal definitions of crimes and the grid scoring factors could result in double counting, as the same fact could be used to determine the severity level of the offense and which of several sentencing grids were operative.

In April 1984, the committee opted instead to pursue a two-dimensional matrix, or grid, similar to that used by the Minnesota Sentencing Guidelines Commission. Offenses were arrayed along the vertical axis of the grid according to the severity of the offense, and prior record categories occupied the horizontal axis. Once the crime severity level and the prior record score were determined, the offender's sentence would be found at the intersection of the vertical and horizontal axes of the grid.

After settling in April 1984 on a sentencing guidelines grid with twelve offense seriousness levels, the committee decided that the current definitions of crimes were too encompassing to comport with the new sentencing system. To calibrate the punishment to the severity of the offense, offenses of equivalent severity must be grouped together. Under the broad sentencing ranges of the rehabilitative paradigm, crimes of varying degrees of severity could be lumped together for sentencing purposes, with the width of the sentencing ranges and the discretion of the parole board allowing for individualized treatment. Consequently, subsuming vastly different types of conduct within one crime category was not particularly troubling under the indeterminate system. Broad offense definitions presented a major dilemma under the determinate model, however, where sentencing ranges were narrowed and sentences were fixed.

The definition of robbery in the first degree illustrates the diversity of behaviors covered by one offense under New York's rehabilitative regime. In addition to including forcible theft of property, robbery in the first degree includes any of the following events: the victim receives serious physical injury, the offender is armed with a deadly weapon, a dangerous instrument is used or its immediate use is threatened, or the offender displays what appears to be a weapon. The statutory maximum sentence for a first offender convicted of robbery in the first degree is six to twenty-five years; the minimum is between one-third and one-half the maximum sentence imposed.[11] As the Bellacosa-Feinberg Committee noted in its preliminary report,

> [t]his broad range can result in grossly disparate results: Similar punishments can be given to offenders convicted of quite dissimilar crimes; or worse, an offender convicted of robbery in the first degree who caused serious physical injury during the course of the forcible taking could receive an indeterminate sentence of from two to six years while another offender, with a similar criminal record, convicted of the same crime, who was armed with a deadly weapon but did not display it, could be given a sentence of from twelve and one-half to twenty-five years in prison.[12]

The Morgenthau Committee had anticipated offense reclassification when it suggested that the sentencing commission might need to "create new sub-categories for each offense."[13] Chapter 711, in authorizing the committee to recommend "the redefinition of any crime if the current definition needs further articulation to conform to the principles of this act or the guidelines recommended by the Committee," had also foreseen the need to reclassify offenses.[14] Yet, neither the predecessor committee nor the enabling legislation fully recognized the inherent difficulty of the task.

Believing that a limited reclassification would be more favorably received by the legislature than a comprehensive reclassification, and recalling that the Bartlett Commission had taken several years to formulate its reclassification scheme, the Bellacosa-Feinberg Committee voted to limit reclassification to a few crimes, including burglary, robbery, rape, sodomy, arson, and assault. These offenses were selected because of their high volume and because their legal definitions describe conduct of significantly differing degrees of harmfulness.

The committee held a four-day retreat in June 1984, at which time the members first focused intently on the research question. At that point, the committee confronted the research ramifications of reclassifying the individual elements of certain crimes to fit in the grid format. Reclassification, while essential under a determinate system, drastically complicated the data collection effort upon which the research would depend.

Rearranging offense definitions meant that the committee's definitions would not conform to those of current law, and it was current law that determined how existing data were collected. The committee reclassified offenses primarily by rearranging statutory subsections of the offense. For example, robbery in the first degree had four subsections; the committee assigned two of the subsections to the new robbery in the first degree and two subsections to the new robbery in the second degree. Unfortunately, subsection information is not routinely recorded in the state's various data systems. There was no way of determining from available data whether offenders convicted of robbery in the first degree would be convicted under the committee's system of robbery in the first degree, placing them in one crime severity level, or robbery in the second degree, placing them in another crime severity level. The committee consequently had to conduct original, and time-consuming, research into actual case files to translate current sentencing practices into the grid format.

The research task was further muddled each time the committee change its vote about what crimes and what subsections of crimes would be reclassified. Frequent changes in the list of offenses to be reclassified and the arrangement of subsections made conforming the research with the committee's decisions an enormous challenge.

The Centrality of Research is Finally Recognized

At the committee's June 1984 retreat, University President O'Leary explained to his colleagues that the reclassification "created a fundamental problem with data collection." He said he thought it "critical to have data when the committee went back to the legislature. If the committee was unable to find such data it might be driven back to collapsing the categories of crimes, which had previously been narrowed."

Mr. Smith agreed and said "the problem was to create a data base sufficiently flexible that it would allow one to predict the effect of changes in the scheme." Chairman Bellacosa asked whether committee members "thought the lack of data was a complete block to further progress." Despite earlier denials, the chief staffer for the committee, Mr. Zalman, replied that "data gathering had been part of the game plan all along." Mr. Bellacosa said he was "very troubled" about the implications of the discussion. He said that, although Mr. Zalman had indicated that funds for research were part of the plan, he wondered whether "the effect was to temporarily stymie the committee."[15]

Later in the day Mr. Zalman told the committee that he wished to address the timing of the research. He said there "was a clear realization at the outset that the research could be done and the report prepared by January 15, but that it would be close." He noted that "the data collection had been aimed at impact assessment, not the setting of sentences." Mr. Zalman said "that while it is obviously useful to have the best information possible, even absolutely accurate time-served data would not tell the committee what sentences were appropriate." He continued that "Chapter 711, in neutral fashion, merely requires that the committee take impact into account, thereby leaving two options: A cap on prison population *à la* Minnesota, in which case the research information would be critical, or a normative approach."

Chairman Bellacosa said he thought that the committee's confidence in its own judgment would be insufficient to persuade the legislature to follow its recommendations. The chairman said he "felt the legislature would be very unhappy about the way the committee had pursued its mission if it merely reported the impact data without closely relating it to the committee's recommendations.

Mr. Zalman was obviously caught in a bind. Research takes time, and too much time had already been lost. Not surprisingly, Mr. Zalman continued to push for prescriptive guidelines, which are much less dependent on research. He replied to the chairman's concerns by saying that he "was sensitive to the needs of dealing with the legislature, but proposed that the committee pursue the course of setting sentence lengths normatively, that is, by what it considered correct."

Mr. Smith said that course was unacceptable to him, "even if it were enough to carry the day." Mr. Liman said he "agreed with Mr. Smith . . . The committee must be able to say whether the sentencing bands are consistent with current practice and whether they would have an impact on population."

Mr. Wemple said that, as a former legislator, he "believed that those who advocate change have the burden of proof." He said "the package the committee had could not be defended without empirical data, which it did not now have. If the committee did not have it, it would have to wait until it did."

Ms. Salem, who had just recently been hired as the research director, concluded the discussion with the observation that "the basic research problem set by the committee had changed."[16] Rather than simply assessing the impact of the grid on prison populations, research would now be needed to develop the numbers in the grid. The new research director was perhaps getting more than she had bargained for.

By the last day of the June 1984 retreat, it was clear that empirical research was going to be central to the committee's process. Unfortunately, a precious half-year had already been lost. Chairman Bellacosa told his colleagues that "no report should issue until research data verifying and supporting the conclusions had been obtained." He said "what was required was detailed information respecting each cell in the proposed guidelines grid, giving both actual average time served and impact on prison population."[17]

The retreat ended with a directive to the staff to begin the research project at once. Yet, while finally recognizing the importance of research to the overall success of the project, the committee still did not clearly define the purposes underlying the research effort. As late as September 1984, Peter Walsh, who by then had replaced Mr. Zalman as executive director of the staff, asked the committee to indicate their views on grid design, "including whether the staff should work within the existing statutory limits, and should the staff base its reworking on an incapacitative or just deserts model?"[18] Mr. Walsh received no reply.

The committee never formally stated whether they were developing descriptive or prescriptive guidelines, but in the later stages of the committee's work it became apparent that descriptive guidelines had won out. In the end, the numbers in the sentencing grid were set around the numbers supplied by the descriptive research, with the intent of replicating current practices, and thereafter, a few minor adjustments were made to accommodate certain members' normative views of the appropriate punishment for particular offenses. Had the committee made this decision up front, in the early days of its process, the research results would have been forthcoming sooner. Whether more timely research would have resolved the committee's basic dilemma is doubtful, however.

Resources and Sentences

According to the original plan outlined by Mr. Zalman, after the committee established the sentences in the grid, the staff would assess the impact of the grid on criminal-justice resources.[19] The committee's discussion on the impact analysis revealed a fundamental schism between defense and law-enforcement interests.

To what extent would the guidelines be geared to existing resources? The cleavage between defense and law enforcement was evident in the relative importance that each placed on matching sentences with existing resources. Members sympathetic with the defense perspective maintained that correctional resources should set the boundaries of the committee's work; they argued that it was unethical to recommend sentences that would increase the strain on available correctional resources. Law-enforcement sympathizers said that criminal-justice resources, while perhaps not irrelevant, should never be the primary consideration in selecting sentences.

At the committee's second meeting, Mr. Paterson articulated the defense position when he told the committee that it "should not lose sight of its primary objective, namely to face the question of prison and jail populations.... The committee should be committed to avoiding additional prison and jail building and realize the fiscal implications of its work."

Mr. Smith agreed with Mr. Paterson and noted the "importance of developing a plan for the evaluation of the possible impact of guidelines upon correctional resources, once the normative tasks involved in guidelines construction are completed."

Mr. Wemple spoke for the law-enforcement position. He said he disagreed with Mr. Paterson and Mr. Smith, and that he believed that "the committee should determine its goals, and that its goals do not include the need to necessarily avoid prison and jail crowding."[20]

As was true with the question of whether descriptive or prescriptive guidelines were being developed, the committee never clearly resolved the resource question. Instead, it opted for a middle ground, intending to neither increase nor decrease the new system's impact on correctional resources. Under the current indeterminate system, prison populations were expected to continue to rise. The committee therefore sought to design its grid to increase prison populations by the same amount that they were expected to increase under a continuation of the indeterminate system.

The lack of a clear decision on the relationship between resources and sentences was fueled, in part, by the committee's appraisal of the political landscape. Staff Director Walsh told the members that the negotiators of Chapter 711 had recognized that "capacity and resources must be considered by the committee, but that an express linkage of sentences and capacity would be politically unacceptable."[21]

While the obfuscation might have been expedient in dealing with the legislature, it proved vexing to the Bellacosa-Feinberg Committee. In the end, several of the committee members expressed their unwillingness to endorse a system that continued to increase prison populations, even if it were at the same rate of increase expected to be produced by the indeterminate system. Mr. Smith reflected this view when he told the committee that they had a responsibility to do something about the expected rise in prison population under either system. He said "it was terrifying to know that the state was moving at one hundred miles per hour toward a brick wall that was eighteen months away" and that "it was clear that the state was going to exceed its planned resources and that the committee would be derelict if it merely told the legislature that the guidelines would not exceed the present rate of growth in prison population, as only committee members appeared to know of the problem [the expected rise in prison populations]."[22]

Committee members generally understood that predicting the impact of the grid on prison resources was an inherently inaccurate and risky undertaking. Mr. Yates told the committee in January 1984 that he believed that Chapter 711 "contemplates that the sentencing guidelines would reflect the realities of available resources."[23] Nevertheless, by August of 1984, expressing the consensus of the committee, Mr. Yates said "it would be difficult to assess impact because a change in rules would result in a change in how participants would conduct business."

Despite the view that impact assessments would likely be inaccurate, committee members repeatedly withheld their votes on key issues until receiving the results of the impact analysis from the staff. The contradiction did not escape Mr. Smith, who said he "thought the committee was fudging too many issues." He said that "on one hand there is an acknowledgment that impact cannot be assessed, and then it is stated that the impact study will be completed in January." He said he "did not understand how it could be done; it was too risky to proceed when all that there is is a rolling agenda of hopes."[24]

Purposes of Punishment

The committee rarely confronted the purposes that its sentencing system was designed to achieve. While comments about the objectives of the criminal sanction were occasionally interjected into committee discussions, a careful consideration of the goals of the new system was never undertaken. That the committee was uncomfortable with an extended foray into the question of purpose was evident when they opposed Mr. Zalman's suggestion in December 1983 that he draft a statement of the goals of sentencing. Judge Mulligan reflected the committee's reluctance to tackle this thorny tangle when he objected to Mr. Zalman's suggestion, telling him "it would not be wise at this time to become involved in a discussion of the goals of sentencing and that views on these broad, philosophic matters would emerge in the course of the Committee's deliberations."[25] Judge Mulligan was right: The purpose behind what was being done could not be ignored.

Purpose and Prior Record

Historically, the crime-control objectives of sentencing have been used to justify imposing a more severe penalty on an offender with a prior record under the theory that those who have offended in the past are presumed more likely than those without a criminal record to offend in the future. Like their crime-control counterparts, some just-deserts proponents also believe that sentences should increase as the offender's prior record increases. They rely on a different rationale, however, arguing that offenders with prior criminal convictions are more blameworthy than first offenders. Not all retributists agree, and some maintain that prior record is irrelevant to the determination of deserved punishment.[26]

The committee's discussions of prior record frequently returned to the unresolved issue of purpose. The following account is taken from the minutes of the committee's March 1984 meeting.

Mr. Zalman introduced the prior criminal record scale and said the rationale for the design presented was a just-deserts model. He said "the present inability to produce a type-predictive model precluded the use of rehabilitation as a rationale."

Mr. O'Leary asked whether the rationale underlying the prior record rules was based on just deserts or rehabilitation. He said he believed that "use of prior criminal record is in fact an attempt to gauge dangerousness or risk masquerading as a just-deserts rationale." In recognition of the crime-control purposes underlying the construction of the prior record scale, Mr. O'Leary said "the committee might wish to look to other gauges of risk, such as drug use."

Mr. Zalman countered that "all indications show prior record is the best predictor of risk and that further study would be required to justify use of age or drug abuse as predictive factors." He suggested that "the safest course would be to rely on a just-deserts rationale with some predictive aspect."

Mr. Liman said that while he thought of age as a predictor, he did not want age to be considered in scoring prior record. He said he "would not use a status factor that is a surrogate for race or poverty, but the fact of drug use was less bothersome to him as it is a voluntary act."

Mr. O'Leary said he "wished to make the point that the committee should not pretend it is not taking account of risk."

Chairman Bellacosa said, in his opinion, "prior record does bear on both just deserts and incapacitation modes, and the committee should confront that fact."

Mr. O'Leary suggested that "as Oregon did, it would be possible to call the horizontal axis *both* prior record and prediction of risk."

Mr. Zalman said he felt it important for the committee to "level with the people and to speak the truth as clearly as possible. If part of the message is that we cannot guarantee protection, that must be said."

Mr. Morgenthau, while not getting embroiled in the philosophical quagmire, nevertheless revealed his hand when he suggested that the committee consider "the frequency of conviction within a particular timeframe, in that way picking up on the most active criminal, not merely those with the longest prior record."

Mr. Liman moved that the committee declare that the prior record axis be based solely on prior criminal record.

Mr. O'Leary said "the type of crime is also predictive, and he wished the committee to understand that the scale as presented discarded the predictive value to be gotten from that factor."

Mr. Yates said that his rationale for using prior record would be just deserts only, and he would oppose a predictive rationale for use of prior record.

The committee then unanimously voted to adopt Mr. Liman's motion to base the prior record axis exclusively on prior criminal convictions. In spite of the vote, minutes later the discussion returned to the purposes of the prior record scoring system.

Mr. O'Leary said he "thought it is the instant offense that allows one to reach back; once that instant offense is committed, it should be open to the sentencing judge to consider propensities."

Mr. Zalman asked whether a nonviolent crime should be a predicate for the longer term on a violent felony, which he characterized "incapacitative."

Mr. Smith asked why prior incarcerations should count in a just-deserts scale?" He said "if the rationale is in part prediction, you would miss a key piece" and "frequently property crimes have no predictive force for violent felonies."

Judge Ellerin wanted to know "whether the committee is aiming to include both risk and just-deserts factors."

Chairman Bellacosa said he "believed that, the committee having agreed that only prior record would be considered, it did not matter as either rationale could apply."[27]

The committee never resolved the question—and thus it remained unclear what purpose the prior record scoring system was designed to achieve. A prior record subcommittee was formed to continue to grapple with the issue, but the subcommittee merely kept the limbo status of purpose alive by reporting that "the view of the subcommittee members tended towards a just-deserts rationale with a hope that the results would also account for predictive leaning of committee members."[28]

Sequentiality

The confusion over whether the new system would serve retributive or crime-control ends, or both, was also apparent in the committee's discussion of New York's sequentiality rule. This rule, true to the rehabilitative philosophy, requires that prior offenses, and the criminal-justice system's response to those offenses, occur in a particular sequence to be counted as a predicate offense, subjecting the offender to the harsh, mandatory second felony offender laws when sentencing on the current offense.

According to New York's sequentiality rule, prior offenses do not count as predicates when sentencing for the current offense unless the offender has had the opportunity to benefit from the rehabilitative regime before committing the current offense. Offenders who are apprehended, convicted, and sentenced for a prior offense before committing the current offense are deemed to have had such an opportunity; offenders who have not been processed by the criminal-justice system are not considered subject to its rehabilitative benefits. Thus, an offender who committed a first offense, then committed a second offense, and then was convicted and sentenced for the first offense, would be treated as a first offender when sentenced for the second offense. Alternately, an offender who committed the first offense, was then apprehended and sentenced for the first offense, then committed the second offense, would be treated as a repeat offender when sentenced for the second offense. Thus, because of the sequence of crime and criminal justice processing, some repeat offenders are excluded from second felony offender treatment.

Under the rehabilitative system, with its broad range of discretion, the benefits of the sequentiality rule to recidivistic criminals are often more illusory than real. Where the sequentiality rule prohibits sentencing as a second or persistent felony offender, prior crimes can nevertheless enter into the indeterminate sentencing calculus, albeit *sub silencio*. Prior crimes can influence sentencing decisions through prosecutorial charge and sentence bargaining; judicial sentencing decisions, including the imposition of consecutive sentences; and parole release decisions. The Bellacosa-Feinberg Committee was thus once again confronted with transforming the covert practices of the rehabilitative regime into overt policy statements under the new determinate model. Since the purposes of the new sentencing system were never agreed upon, the sequentiality issue was not easily resolved.

Judge Ellerin argued that the sequentiality rule should be abandoned because it did not serve just deserts. She expressed outrage with the unwarranted advantage given some repeat offenders by the rule. If the rationale underlying the sentencing structure was retributive, with more severe penalties imposed upon those who were more blameworthy because of prior criminal acts, all convictions should count, regardless of the sequence of events, she reasoned. Just deserts requires that offenders be punished for what they did, not when they did it, she said.[29]

Other committee members were unwilling to forsake the sequentiality rule. Mr. Liman said that he favored continuing the existing law and warned that there would be great resistance to any attempt to change. He asked whether "someone who in the course of a single incident assaults five persons in a bar is to be credited with five separate felonies?" Mr. Liman said that he was most concerned with crimes committed by defendants free on bail. He argued that predicate felony treatment should be reserved for offenders who "come before a court, are charged with a crime, released on bail or recognizance, and then commit another crime before the first has been adjudicated."[30]

Without resolving the purposes behind the sequentiality rule, the committee arrived at a compromise that attempted to mix rehabilitative and retributive purposes. The committee's prior record scoring rules scored three points for each prior nonviolent felony. Under the sequentiality compromise, current law would be maintained and the rehabilitative regime would be served by scoring three points where the offender was sentenced for the prior offense before the commission of the current offense. Just deserts would be served by scoring two bonus points where the traditional sequentiality requirement was not met, that is, where the sentence on the prior offense was imposed after the commission of the current offense. Offenses occurring outside of the traditional sequential order would thus no longer be free rides, although the fare would be less.

Youthful Offenders

The committee's disagreement over purposes was also evident in discussions concerning the scoring of an offender's prior youthful offender convictions. Under existing law, for most crimes youths who were sixteen, seventeen, or eighteen years old when they committed the offenses are eligible for special, lenient treatment as youthful offenders. Substantial benefits accrue to recipients of youthful offender treatment. The conviction is vacated and replaced with a youthful offender determination; the maximum prison sentence is reduced to four years, regardless of the seriousness of the offense; and the conviction record is sealed and protected by confidentiality provisions.

Under the indeterminate structure, a prior youthful offender determination cannot be counted as a predicate offense if the youth is subsequently convicted for a felony. Defense-oriented committee members adopted a rehabilitative stance, and argued that prior youthful offender determinations should not be scored because they were intended to provide the youth with a second chance. Other members traveled the just-desert track, and argued, as did Judge Coutant, that youthful offender status "was designed to prevent an individual from being damaged by a youthful indiscretion." Judge Coutant believed that the youthful offender law "had never been intended to give an exemption for felonious conduct because of age." Defendants "who continue to commit felonies should be accountable, and that fact should be reflected in sentencing on subsequent offenses," Judge Coutant said.[31]

The committee eventually arrived at a compromise that, like the compromise over the sequentiality rule, combined just deserts with crime control. Prior youthful offender determinations that had been substituted for a nonviolent felony would not be counted against the offender at sentencing on the instant offense; prior youthful offender determinations that had been substituted for a violent felony would be scored, but only three points, not the five points normally scored for a prior violent felony conviction.

Sentence Review and Purpose

None of the Bellacosa-Feinberg Committee's recommendations invoked the rehabilitative ideal more clearly than the proposal for sentence review, a proposal that was neither required by Chapter 711 nor discussed by the Morgenthau Committee. Under the Bellacosa-Feinberg Committee's unique formulation, offenders with long prison sentences (fifteen to thirty years, depending on the offense) would be eligible for release after serving only a portion of their sentence if it was determined that they no longer presented a risk to public safety. Although never explicitly acknowledged as such by the majority of the committee, sentence review was a prototypical rehabilitative device, designed to control crime through the prediction of dangerousness.

Mr. O'Leary attempted to point out to his colleagues that, despite their protestations to the contrary, they had not abandoned prediction and rehabilitationism. He observed that the sentence review proposal showed that the committee had "not really dispensed with the concept of risk assessment, but had merely structured it in discrete increments of two years or six years, and were now facing the difficulty that it was too hard to structure risk assessment at twenty years."[32]

Mr. Wemple opposed sentence review, saying that he "thought the stated condition that the defendant no longer presents a risk to the public could be met after one or two years in some cases." In response to Mr. Wemple's objection, Mr. Smith moved to amend the sentence review proposal to "delete the language pertaining to risk."

Mr. Yates suggested that "there might be substituted language from the existing parole guidelines, which spoke of the defendant having a reasonable probability of living in a community without violating the law, thereby fudging the question of risk determination."

Mr. Smith denied that sentence review was based on a prediction of dangerousness. He said instead that he "was attempting to reach a new level of generality that connoted not the risk assessment of parole, but rather that it was impossible to know conditions twenty years hence, leaving the possibility of the system, represented by the three-judge panel, to say that society's view of what serves justice had changed."

Following a discussion of substituting an interest-of-justice test for risk assessment, Mr. O'Leary observed that "many rationales could pass under the interest-of-justice language."

Although Mr. Smith's suggestion to drop any reference to risk assessment was adopted, the issue was not so easily decided. Mr. Wemple continued to press his objection, arguing that the concept was no different from the notion of parole.

Judge Coutant said that he found "creeping into the Committee's discussions a departure from definite sentencing." He said that he was concerned that the committee was losing its bearings. If "certainty was what was wanted, the committee should adhere to that and cause rules to be applied across the board," he said.[33]

When sentence review was next discussed, Mr. Wemple asked "if a need existed for sentence review, why not keep the current system?"

Mr. Smith again supported the proposal by arguing that "notions of just deserts change, and that the committee's facially modest task of changing sentencing laws is actually a task of sentencing hundreds of thousands of people. A sentence review mechanism would permit others in the future to correct mistakes and apply the deserts standards of the future period."[34]

In spite of the controversy, the committee ultimately voted to adopt the sentence review proposal. Early release would be an option for offenders sentenced to long prison terms, "long" being defined as fifteen to thirty years, depending on the felony classification of the conviction offense. Applications for sentence review would be judged by considering the nature of the offense, prior criminal record, institutional record, release plans, deportation orders, health problems, meritorious acts, and risk of recidivism.

With the exception of the first factor (and maybe the second, depending on one's prejudices) all of the release criteria invoked crime-control purposes of punishment. The last factor, risk of recidivism, would be determined by "[w]hether there is a reasonable probability that, if the inmate is released, he or she will remain at liberty without violating the law, and whether an inmate's release is compatible with contemporary concepts of the welfare of society and will not so deprecate the seriousness of the crime as to undermine respect for the law."[35] It is hard to imagine a concept with closer ties to the rehabilitative regime than sentence review. Despite the rhetoric, the New York crafters of the determinate model were apparently not prepared to forsake the crime-control purposes of punishment. They were also unwilling, as the following discussion illustrates, to eliminate discretionary sentencing.

Discretion and Determinate Sentencing

While the advocates of the determinate ideal wrote volumes about ending or restricting judicial and parole board discretion, they had little to say about how discretion would be rearranged in the new system. Determinists failed to ask who would emerge as the powerful player once parole boards were abolished and judges were stripped of much of their discretion.

The determinate sentencing supporters all but ignored prosecutorial and prison guard discretion. On those rare occasions when they mentioned the potentially awesome power of these functionaries, the determinists merely suggested that increasing prosecutors' and prison guards' discretion was a possibility to be wary about, not a reality to plan for.

The report issued by the Morgenthau Committee is typical of the lack of attention paid to prosecutorial discretion in the development of determinacy. Rather than ask the guidelines commission to plan for the ordered allocation of discretion, the Morgenthau Committee relegated prosecutorial discretion to the list of housekeeping chores that the commission should tackle after completing guideline development. As part of its ongoing monitoring function following guidelines implementation, the Morgenthau Committee said that the guidelines commission should consider "the feasibility of developing charging and plea-bargaining guidelines to operate in tandem with a sentencing guidelines system."[36]

Discretion and Departure

Departure from the sentence grid was the most hotly contested issue faced by the committee. How would sentencing responsibility be distributed among prosecutors, defense attorneys, and judges? What criteria would justify departure sentences? While the proponents of the determinate model talked about abolishing or limiting discretion, the members of the Bellacosa-Feinberg Committee could not so easily escape the hard questions of distributing the power among the key courtroom actors.

Committee discussions about departure revolved around balancing discretion against disparity reduction. At the one extreme, unlimited departure meant generous grants of discretion. At the other extreme, prohibiting departure meant that there was no chance to individualize sentences, thus ostensibly preventing disparity. Again, positions were determined along ideological lines. Defense-oriented committee members argued in favor of expansive departure, while law-enforcement-oriented members pushed first for limited departure, and later for no departure.

Departure and sentence range   Striking the balance between discretion and disparity reduction turned, in large measure, on the width of the sentence ranges in the guidelines grid. Would judges select, for example, a definite sentence from a range of several months or several years? The wider the range, the greater the discretion to fit the sentence to the individual offender, thereby reducing the need for departure. The narrower the sentence range, the less the guidelines would accommodate the individual case, thereby increasing the need for departure.

The Morgenthau Committee had recommended narrow ranges, with a spread of no more than 15 percent between the top and bottom of the range, *e.g.,* thirty-seven to forty-two months.[37] While District Attorney Morgenthau had endorsed his committee's recommendation in 1979, his position had changed by the time he served on the Bellacosa-Feinberg Committee. Now, Mr. Morgenthau repeatedly argued in favor of wide ranges, asserting, inexplicably, that wider bands were no more likely to create disparity than narrower ones.

Mr. Morgenthau's change of heart is perhaps attributable to a growing realization that determinate sentencing would change the locus of plea negotiations from sentence bargaining to charge bargaining. Under the indeterminate system, prosecutors can avoid charge bargaining by engaging in sentence bargaining, whereby offenders are encouraged to plead guilty to the top count in the indictment in return for a relatively lenient sentence. Prosecutors, who are elected officials, can thus campaign on a "get tough" platform, pointing to their record to show that not only have they achieved a high conviction rate, but have also convicted a high proportion of defendants on the most serious count in the indictment.

Under a determinate structure with narrow sentence ranges, prosecutors could no longer avoid charge bargaining. With but a 15 percent difference between the top and bottom number in the grid cell (for example, ten years to eleven and one-half years as recommended by the Morgenthau Committee), the defendant would have little incentive to plead guilty to the offense charged. Unless prosecutors were willing to negotiate the charges, more offenders would be willing to risk conviction following trial under the determinate system than under current law, where it is well known that offenders convicted after trial often receive a more severe sentence than similarly situated defendants who are convicted by a guilty plea. Consequently, to keep caseloads manageable, cases moving through the system, and to avoid trials, prosecutors would be forced under a determinate model to negotiate charges. Thus, district attorneys could not rely on their conviction record to demonstrate to their constituents that they were tough on crime.

The New York State District Attorneys Association acknowledged their concern over the shift to charge bargaining. In August 1984 Mr. Walsh told the committee that the statewide association of district attorneys "felt that narrow sentence ranges would discourage top indictment guilty pleas and would require additional trials or force charge bargaining."[38]

Mr. Morgenthau continually pressed the committee to adopt wide sentence ranges. At one point he suggested that the maximum sentence in the range should double the minimum sentence. Mr. Bellacosa, while supporting wide ranges, responded that a maximum sentence of twice the minimum "was clearly too much."[39]

Mr. Morgenthau later proposed that departure be eliminated and, in effect, folded into a grid having very wide sentence ranges. With such wide ranges, he argued, the need for sentences outside of the grid would be obviated. So, noted Mr. Yates and Judge Ellerin, would any hope of reducing disparity.[40]

Departure and prior misdemeanor convictions   Decisions on departure and the width of the sentence range also affected the committee's prior record scoring system. Most committee members thought it appropriate for the new system to distinguish between offenders with no prior record and those with a prior record of misdemeanor convictions. Just deserts was often advanced in support of scoring previous misdemeanor convictions as part of the prior record scale under the rationale that offenders with prior misdemeanor convictions were considered more blameworthy than those with no prior convictions and thus deserved a longer sentence. Crime-control objectives were, of course, lurking under the surface of the committee's discussion about scoring prior misdemeanor convictions: Offenders with a history of criminality, regardless of whether the conviction was for a misdemeanor or felony, are often presumed more likely than first offenders to commit another crime.

Under the indeterminate system, prior misdemeanor convictions do not count as predicate offenses when sentencing on the instant offense. The broad grants of discretion inherent in the rehabilitative structure, however, give decisionmakers the flexibility to increase the sentence *de facto* to reflect prior misdemeanor convictions. Under a determinate model with narrow sentence ranges, the flexibility to fashion the sentence to reflect the offender's misdemeanor conviction history would be reduced significantly. The committee was thus again faced with moving under-the-table practices to the table top, exposing what some would prefer to leave hidden.

While believing misdemeanor scoring to be justified on theoretical grounds, the committee had trouble resolving the practical issues. Committee members familiar with the court system realized that scoring misdemeanors would create greater backlogs in an already congested system. Scoring misdemeanor convictions would require accurate criminal record histories, and it was well known that rap sheets often contained incomplete or inaccurate data on misdemeanor cases. Every defendant would likely challenge the prosecutor's submission of prior record, producing intolerable delays, it was feared.

The committee found the answer to its dilemma when Mr. Bellacosa suggested that the problem could be resolved by "eliminating formal reliance on
misdemeanors from the prior record scoring rules and re-examining the narrowness of sentence ranges." He suggested making the sentence ranges wider,
giving courtroom actors the ability "to exercise discretion in considering the
appropriate effect of prior misdemeanor convictions."[41] It thus appeared that
limiting discretion was no longer central to the committee's work.

Departure, Mandatory Sentences, and Discretion

The committee grappled with the relationship between sentence range,
departure and mandatory sentences. While it was axiomatic that the mandatory second felony and violent felony offender laws would not exist in their
old form under the new system, retaining mandatories in any fashion was
still an open question. Chairman Bellacosa cautioned the committee that
"there was a real question of how far it could depart from the political realities" of mandatory sentencing. Not everyone on the committee agreed with
the chairman.

Mr. Yates told the committee that he "did not think the purpose of the legislature in establishing the committee was to have it graft onto the existing
hodge-podge of statutory minima new minima on selected crimes, but rather
that it should start over and draw new lines on a blank tablet." While admit-
ting that the committee could not ignore the political realities, Mr. Yates urged
his colleagues not to "feel bound to simply duplicate the existing scheme."[42]

Mr. Liman agreed with Mr. Yates, saying that "the committee should lis-
ten to all comments, but not feel compelled to enhance punishment just
because it may be unpopular in some quarters not to do so." He said that the
committee should "do what it believes to be right." While he "recognized the
danger of escalation of sentences during the political process," he argued that
it was intended that the committee, as an independent body, would be somewhat removed from the political fray.[43]

Defense-inclined committee members were hostile to the existing
mandatory structure. They maintained that, since under their proposal mitigated departure sentences would be reserved for the extraordinary case,
mandatory sentences could safely be eliminated. Thus, they asserted, the
worst aspect of the mandatories—forcing incarceration on undeserving
offenders—would be avoided, and the best aspect—ensuring incarceration
for deserving offenders—would be retained.

Committee members adopting a law-enforcement stance urged the retention of the mandatory sentencing structure. They feared that mitigated departure would be routine and, without mandatories, there was nothing to prevent
a judge from imposing a non-incarcerative sentence on an offender who
deserved incarceration. Absent mandatory sentences, disparity would
increase rather than decrease, they claimed, as judges gave similarly situated

offenders dissimilar punishments—lengthy prison terms for some and non-incarcerative sanctions for others.

Mr. Morgenthau continued to press for wide sentence ranges, vowing that he could not support a system whose ranges were not wide enough to incorporate the existing mandatory sentencing structure. He warned the committee that eliminating mandatory sentences would be perceived by the legislature and the law-enforcement community as a "suicide wish."[44]

Judge Coutant assumed the defense perspective when he responded that "mandatory imprisonment for second felonies were the worst source of injustice."[45]

Judge Ellerin also indicated her opposition to the mandatory system, saying that she "preferred greater flexibility in the underlying in/out calculus."[46] She said the "mandatory second felony offender law outrages the bench and most of the legislature."

Waiver of departure   The committee generally proceeded under the assumption that departure from the guidelines grid would be reserved for the extraordinary case. The tricky task was to prevent departure from becoming routine. Clearly, most defendants would move for a mitigated departure sentence and most prosecutors would move for an aggravated departure sentence.

Chairman Bellacosa proposed a solution: The frequency of departure could be reduced by allowing the prosecutor to extract a waiver of the right to depart as part of a plea negotiation. Thus, assuming that all prosecutors would exercise the option—and there would be no reason for them not to—departures would never occur in convictions obtained by a guilty plea. Since about 90 percent of felony convictions result from a guilty plea, waiver of departure gave prosecutors another powerful weapon for their discretionary arsenal.

Ms. Walker opposed the waiver proposal, arguing that it would give additional power to the district attorney.[47] Ms. Walker was supported by Mr. Lopez, Judge Williams, and Mr. Paterson, who in the committee's final report said that the waiver "gives prosecutors, who already have great power, even more."[48] These defense-oriented members argued that in every case, including bargained pleas, the court should make an independent assessment of the appropriateness of departure, and the courts' ability to do so should not be foreclosed by a prior agreement between the defense and the prosecutor.

Departure and purpose   Formulating mitigating and aggravating departure factors impinged directly on the allocation of power and the purposes of the criminal sanction. Would discretion to impose a departure sentence be limited by highly specified departure factors, or would generalized factors be sanctioned? Would the enumerated departure factors be exhaustive, or would courtroom actors be free to argue the existence of other, non-enumerated factors?

Once again, the Bellacosa-Feinberg Committee sought a middle ground and ended up recommending both highly specific and generalized departure factors. Although the list of factors was inclusive, one mitigating factor was so general as to justify departure in almost every case.

In a system premised on just deserts, departure factors would be geared exclusively to the seriousness of the offense. Special circumstances surrounding the individual offender would be irrelevant. Although several committee members claimed that their votes on departure factors reflected a just-deserts orientation, an examination of the mitigating factors proposed by the committee reveals a heavy reliance on crime-control objectives.

None of the mitigating factors recommended by the committee dealt exclusively with the seriousness of the offense. Instead, six of the eight mitigating factors proposed by the committee focused on the defendant's culpability in the commission of the crime. Of the remaining two, one focused on the defendant's cooperation with police, and the other on virtually anything at all. This final factor used to justify a lenient sentence read "given extraordinary circumstances, the appropriate sentence range is unduly harsh, and a more lenient sentence would not deprecate the seriousness of the crime."[49] The extraordinary circumstances justifying departure could be based on either the seriousness of the offense or personal characteristics of the offender. The committee did not define extraordinary circumstances, leaving the definition to the courtroom actors. Clearly, the crime-control purposes of punishment were alive and well in the committee's policy on mitigated departure.

Several committee members argued that the adoption of the open-ended mitigating factor marked the committee's retreat from just deserts and disparity reduction. The catch-all mitigating factor would do just that, they feared: catch all.

Mr. Morgenthau complained that the open-ended factor, together with the elimination of mandatory sentences, opened "Pandora's box in a way that would permit disparities of the type existing today." He said he thought some judges would take advantage of any loophole to give extraordinarily lenient sentences. Perhaps in retaliation against the strong pro-defense nature of the open-ended mitigating factor, Mr. Morgenthau moved that the committee adopt an aggravating factor to match the catch-all mitigating factor. He offered language for an all-encompassing aggravating factor: "The presumptively correct sentence is unduly lenient given the special circumstances surrounding the instant offense or the prior offenses and a more severe sentence is necessary in order not to deprecate the seriousness of the offense." His motion failed.

Ms. Walker represented the defense view when she told the committee that "the consequences of using an open-ended provision in aggravation or mitigation were different." She said that she was "willing to give the defendant the benefit of the doubt by permitting use of such a factor in mitigation, but thought it unfair for it to be used in aggravation given the imprecise nature of the data that might be available."

Mr. O'Leary agreed with Ms. Walker, noting that he was "far less comfortable with allowing the character of the defendant to be used in aggravation." He said that he "would only allow evidence of a particular crime to be used in aggravation."[50]

Unlike the decision on the mitigating factors, the committee eventually proposed aggravating factors that focused exclusively on the harm caused by the crime, without consideration of personal characteristics of the offender. One aggravating factor, however, did allow considerable leeway for discretionary decisionmaking. It read: "The manner of commission of the crime was so extraordinarily heinous that a harsher sentence is required."[51]

How much departure? The extent of departure was the single most divisive aspect of the departure policy, directly pitting discretion against disparity. At first, the committee voted to allow 50 percent departure in either mitigation or aggravation. Later, the committee changed its vote, abandoning this 50 percent rule, and voting instead to allow unlimited departure in mitigation, retaining the 50 percent limit in aggravation.[52] In the end, the committee arrived at a compromise position, allowing unlimited departure in some grid cells and retaining the 50 percent rule in others.

In August 1984, when the 50 percent rule was still intact, Judge Williams told his colleagues that judges throughout the state were insulted by the rule, viewing it as an unwarranted intrusion on their decisionmaking power. They felt like "rubber stamps," he said.[53] Judge Williams argued that the 50 percent rule failed to provide the requisite relief in the truly needy case. In some cases, any incarceration would be unjust, he said.

Agreeing with Judge Williams, Judge Ellerin advocated unlimited departure in mitigation. She said that "a true departure policy should not permit such injustice."

Mr. Bellacosa asked Judge Ellerin if she was proposing the elimination of the 50 percent rule for all crime bands and all criminal history scores, even for murder. Judge Ellerin responded that she was, and that if "compelling mitigating factors existed, probation should be available."

In response to an objection that unlimited departure would lead to untrammeled judicial discretion, Judge Ellerin said that allowing the prosecutor to appeal a mitigated sentence would provide sufficient checks to ensure that judicial discretion was not abused. When challenged that unlimited departure undercut the legislative intent of mandatory sentencing provisions, she argued that unlimited departure would not be tantamount to repealing mandatories, but rather unlimited departure would merely permit the court "to do justice in the extraordinary case."[54]

Mr. Morgenthau, who had previously labeled unlimited departure in mitigation a "suicide wish," said that the committee had invited disparity, moved away from the concept of determinacy, and increased, not decreased, judicial discretion. He said that the elimination of all mandatory minimum sentences was "completely inconsistent" with the committee's mandate.[55]

As an alternative to unlimited departure in mitigation, the committee discussed drawing a line on the guidelines grid. Above the line, where the most serious offenses and the most extensive prior records were located, the court could depart in aggravation or mitigation by 50 percent. Below the line, home of the less serious offenses and the less serious prior records, the court would be permitted unlimited departure in mitigation and 50 percent departure in aggravation.

Another proposal was put forth to retain the 50 percent rule for the normal departure case and permit 100 percent departure in mitigation upon a higher standard, such as "the offense was an aberrant one for the offender, and was committed under extraordinary circumstances that satisfy the court that there will be no repetition, and that the release of the offender will not be a threat to the safety of the community."[56] This standard had little to do with just deserts, turning instead exclusively on crime control and prediction of dangerousness.

That so many proposals were considered by the committee reflects the significance of the departure percentage: It determined the balance of power in the courtroom. The ideological rift that had developed around the departure percentage caused Chairman Bellacosa to observe that the "central policy issue with which the committee had been struggling had been crystallized."

Judge Williams agreed, saying that "judges are clearly concerned that they will have very little discretion, and that prosecutors will tell them what to do, and judges will just be sitting there."

Mr. Smith said that he "concurred with Judge Williams on the importance of the role of the judge and of preserving judicial discretion."

Mr. Paterson said that he "did not feel that district attorneys should have any more discretion than they presently have."

Judge Coutant said that the "court, not the district attorney, should be the discretion exerciser." He said he "recognized the obvious pitfalls of abuse of discretion, but that discretion in the hands of someone was a necessity."

The question was, whose hands: the judge or the district attorney? Mr. O'Leary correctly summed up the discussion of the percentage of departure by noting "a polarization between two distinct positions: One of 'robot-like' judges or one of 'untrammeled discretion.'"[57]

A compromise percentage is reached   In an attempt to bridge the chasm between defense and law enforcement, a departure subcommittee was formed and asked to find a compromise position. The departure subcommittee recommended that the committee adopt a two-tier departure policy. At the first level, the trial court could aggravate or mitigate the sentence by 50 percent throughout the grid. At the second level, unlimited departure in mitigation would be allowed in certain grid cells. The trial judge would not, however, have the discretion to mitigate below what was allowed by the 50 percent rule. That power would rest with the Appellate Division of the Supreme Court. The trial court would first impose the sentence in conformity with the 50 percent rule; further departure would await the decision of the Appellate Division. The standard 50 percent rule would continue to apply to aggravated sentences.

With little enthusiasm, the committee endorsed the compromise position. Although most members expressed disdain for the proposal, they agreed that it was the only compromise likely to gather enough votes to pass the polarized committee.

While ultimately casting their votes for the proposal, members voiced their opposition to the two-tier approach. Ms. Walker said that it sent "the wrong message to the public and the legislature." She said "that it assumed that the trial court was incapable of handling the issues, would promote the abuse of discretion, place a burden on the Appellate Division, and cause delays in sentencing proceedings." Judge Coutant said that he "personally favored placing full discretion with the trial judge," but he realized that "the committee as a body could not accept such a proposal." Mr. Paterson said that the "judge is present during trial and observes all the evidence of special circumstances, both aggravating and mitigating." He said that "judicial decisionmaking was being diminished by the proposal." Judge Williams agreed, saying that "the power of the sitting judge was being taken away."

Mr. Morgenthau disagreed with the defense position, maintaining instead that the new proposal "would increase judicial discretion, not curtail it." Chairman Bellacosa agreed with the district attorney, saying that the "compromise was a reinforcement of judicial discretion." The Chairman reminded the others that "the first level of departure was solely within the discretion of the sentencing judge. Where the judge would depart in mitigation further than that allowed by the 50 percent rule, the proposal reinforces that decision subject only to review by the Appellate Division."

Judge Coutant disagreed with Mr. Morgenthau and Mr. Bellacosa, but said that it was "critical that a consensus be reached," even though the compromise "may not be ideal."

Judge Ellerin said that "while the departure policy developed by the subcommittee did not satisfy anyone completely, she would accept it in an attempt to reach a compromise on this most critical issue."

Chairman Bellacosa concurred, saying that while he "respected the sincerity of the differing viewpoints, the compromise would satisfy the need for consensus required for public hearings."[58]

In voting for the compromise, several committee members stated that they were endorsing it exclusively for the purpose of public comment at forthcoming public hearings, and that they were reserving the right to change their vote at a later time. Even though the two-tier approach was heavily criticized at the committee's public hearings, the committee was unwilling to change the recommendation prior to issuing its final report. Having experienced such difficulty in achieving consensus, albeit grudgingly, the committee was unwilling to renegotiate this controversial yet pivotal provision.

Prosecutorial Charging Discretion

Although aimed at only one of many aspects of prosecutorial discretion, one directive in Chapter 711 was intended to check prosecutorial power. This provision, referred to as inspect and reduce, required the committee to recommend "the establishment of a mechanism by which a court may review the sufficiency of evidence to support charges contained within an accusatory instrument [indictment]."[59] The inclusion of inspect and reduce in the enabling legislation was intended to give the court the discretion to overrule a prosecutor's charging decision in certain, limited cases. Inspect and reduce did not, however, affect the other important avenues of discretion open to prosecutors, who would still be free to engage in pre-and post-indictment bargaining.

Prosecutorial charging discretion assumes new importance under a determinate system, where the person who determines the charges determines the grid cell according to which the offender will be sentenced. While the court selects a sentence from the cell range, the district attorney has, in effect, selected the range.

Existing law   Although pivotal in delineating the perimeters of the court's sentencing function, prosecutorial charging discretion is virtually unreviewable under current New York law. Presently, a court may review the evidence presented to a grand jury and compare it to the charges contained in the indictment. If the evidence supports the charge filed by the prosecutor or any lesser included offense, the court cannot reduce the charges to conform to the evidence. Instead, it must sustain the indictment.[60] Where the court determines that the evidence presented to the grand jury does not support the charge in the indictment, but does support a lesser included offense, the court is thus powerless to reduce the indictment to charge the lesser included offense. While the court can dismiss an indictment in the interests of justice, it cannot reduce an indictment to make the charge conform to the evidence. Thus, defendants may be prosecuted on charges not warranted by the evidence.

Inspect and reduce was intended to change the balance of power between prosecutors and judges by allowing judges to reduce the indictment to conform to the evidence presented to the grand jury. Reducing the indictment would be a vehicle for ending overcharging and curbing prosecutorial abuse of discretion in the charging decision.

Inspect and reduce   Mr. Yates, who at the time worked as Counsel to the Assembly Codes Committee, explained to his colleagues on the Bellacosa-

Feinberg Committee that inspect and reduce was included in Chapter 711 at the insistence of the Assembly leadership. He said that it "was one of the most critical elements in the committee's work." He told his colleagues on the committee that "its inclusion in Chapter 711 had persuaded the Assembly leadership to go forward with the bill" and that he believed it to be "an implementation of the Constitutional mandate that one should not be prosecuted on a charge unsupported by the evidence."

Mr. Yates noted that the inspect and reduce provision assumed "new importance in a determinate sentencing system because it [determinacy] would eliminate parole discretion, and greatly limit judicial discretion, leaving the strongest discretion with the prosecutor." He said the prosecutor was "the least fair of the three, because he is not subject to review in any form. What was important is the balance of power struck, which would ultimately govern the actions of persons in the field," Mr. Yates said.

Mr. Liman agreed with Mr. Yates, noting that "the committee's actions were concentrating enormous power in the hands of the prosecutor, and that the failure to adopt an inspect and reduce provision, which was consistent with both logic and common sense, would impeach the committee's entire product." It was "the only provision likely to be considered by the committee that would have any checking effect on the prosecutor's power," he said.

Chairman Bellacosa agreed, saying that he thought the "adoption of an inspect and reduce provision was a partial answer to a large constituency, the Judiciary, which was very concerned about the erosion of its discretion."[61]

Robert Silbering, an aide to Mr. Morgenthau, expressed the law-enforcement view. Not surprisingly, given the amount of power that prosecutors would relinquish, Mr. Morgenthau's spokesman argued against inspect and reduce. He warned the committee that implementation of the proposal would result in substantial delay in the system. Prosecutors would no doubt make a second attempt to make the indictment stand, and "virtually every case reduced would be represented to a Grand Jury." Despite this warning, the committee voted to include an inspect and reduce provision in its final recommendations.

Prison guards: the forgotten decisionmakers   The creators and expanders of determinate sentencing seemed unaware that they were shifting discretion from parole boards to prison guards. Like prosecutorial discretion, prison-guard discretion was treated by most writers supporting determinate sentencing as something to be wary of, not something to plan for.[62]

Like other determinate advocates, the Morgenthau Committee failed to address prison-guard power. Good-time credits were necessary to control prisoners, the Morgenthau Committee said. While they warned that prison-guard discretion should be no greater than that needed for prison discipline, recommending a 20 percent good-time policy, they neglected to explain how the new good-time system would be designed, how discretion would be balanced with disparity reduction, and how new procedures would be implemented in the prison bureaucracy. The Bellacosa-Feinberg Committee, however, could not so easily escape those forgotten decisionmakers.

Heightened importance of good time   Under the rehabilitative regime, prison inmates earn good-time credits of up to one-third off their maximum sentence. Minimum terms are not reduced by good-time credits.[63] Inmates released on the basis of good-time credits, known as conditional releasees, are supervised in the community by parole officers. Most inmates, however, are paroled before their conditional-release date. Most prisoners never reap the benefits of good time—that is, good-time credits do not shorten the time that they are incarcerated.

In stripping the parole board of its release discretion, determinacy gives prison guards much of the power that had previously been exercised by the parole board. With the abolition of parole release, good time becomes the sole variable affecting release prior to the expiration of the definite sentence. Good time and prison guards' sentencing power assume new significance when an inmate's disciplinary record is the only thing affecting early release. Determinacy makes prison guards the final sentencing arbiter in the same way that the rehabilitative system makes the parole board the ultimate sentencing decisionmaker. The primary difference between the two release modes is that the parole board's decisionmaking is structured by parole guidelines, whereas no parallel structure exists for restricting prison-guard discretion. Thus, in removing the already limited power from the parole board, determinate sentencing would result in virtually unlimited power being given to prison guards and administrators, people not necessarily well schooled in making sentencing decisions.

Had the creators and expanders of determinacy been more diligent in fleshing out their model, the committee might have come to the table better prepared to deal with the complex question of prison-guard power. The following discussion briefly overviews a few of the major difficulties faced by the sentencing committee in fashioning a good-time policy.

Good-time percentage   The current law allows inmates to earn one-third off their maximum sentence for good behavior in prison. Good-time policies under the present sentencing structure do not affect the initial release date of most inmates, and are thus of little guidance to those fashioning a determinate model. Nevertheless, several committee members argued that the current 33 1/3 percent good-time allowance should be retained, if only to avoid the perception that the committee was taking something away from inmates. Others disagreed with continuing the current allowance, noting that there was no comparison between the two systems. After much debate, and without much to guide it, the committee ultimately adopted a 25 percent good-time allowance.

Vesting good time   Under the rehabilitative model, if the parole board refused to release an inmate serving, for example, a maximum sentence of twelve years, the inmate would be conditionally released after serving eight years, provided the inmate earned all available good time. If the same inmate was found guilty of certain rule infractions, known as Tier III violations, during the last day of the eighth year, all earned good time could be forfeited. If the inmate continued to misbehave and if good time continued to be revoked between the eight and twelfth year, the inmate could theoretically serve the entire twelve-year sentence in prison.

Vesting of good time—that is, once earned, good time cannot later be taken away—is conceptually consistent with determinate sentencing theory. Vesting limits the discretion of correctional personnel by progressively shortening the time period during the inmate's sentence over which prison administrators exercise control, thereby increasing the certainty of the sentence. The Bellacosa-Feinberg Committee originally voted in favor of vesting.

In spite of its vote, the committee continued to debate vesting. Prison authorities warned the committee that if good time vested there would be little incentive for good behavior during the inmate's last year in prison. Consistent with its middle-of-the-road approach, the committee ultimately changed its vote and tried to protect lost good time while simultaneously providing an incentive for good behavior during the inmate's last year in prison. The committee recommended that good time vest, except during the inmate's last year in prison, during which previously vested good time could be lost. While sounding like a compromise, this proposal was clearly nonsense as, no matter what the sentence, every inmate has to serve a last year. Previously vested good time would thus always be subject to prison-guard control, thus belying any claim that discretion was controlled.

Restoring lost good time   Consistent with the rehabilitative system, prison officials currently have the power to restore lost good time. The committee originally voted to abolish restoration of good time that had previously been taken away.

The committee ultimately acquiesced to the criticism leveled against their restoration recommendation, saying in its final report that, "[w]hile the Committee continues to believe that it is important to underscore the seriousness of the loss of good time, it was persuaded that the potential for restoration is a necessary incentive for good behavior for inmates who have lost good time."[64] Thus, in addition to taking away previously earned good time, correctional authorities could give back time previously taken away. So much for limiting prison-guard power.

The Committee Submits Its Report

The Bellacosa-Feinberg Committee was charged by Chapter 711 of the Laws of 1983 with rendering its recommendations by January 15, 1985. The committee was unable to meet its deadline, and in December 1984 Chairman

Bellacosa requested and received a three-month extension. The committee issued a preliminary report on January 15, 1985, held public hearings in February 1985, and issued its final report on March 29, 1985.

The committee's second chairman, Kenneth R. Feinberg, presented his version of the committee process in the foreword of the final report. Mr. Feinberg wrote that "[t]he committee usually reached agreement on a particular issue after the give-and-take of spirited debate. But unanimity on each and every issue is, of course, impossible. A subject as controversial as criminal sentencing reform is guaranteed to provoke differing views on specific issues."

Chairman Feinberg went on to say that "when it came to the most fundamental issues underlying the committee's legislative mandate, there was overwhelming committee support" for four recommendations.

1. The need to develop a determinate sentencing system to replace the uncertainty and the unfairness of existing law.
2. The need to consolidate the sentencing function and place it in the hands of the most visible component of the criminal-justice system, the sentencing court. Parole release must be phased out.
3. The need for the availability of appellate review of sentence by both the defendant and the people to assure consistency in the application of the sentencing guidelines.
4. The need for continued committee monitoring of the proposed sentencing reforms to gauge the impact of the new system on New York State's increasing prison population.[65]

Chairman Feinberg's account does not do justice to the committee process. Rather than reaching agreement "after the give-and-take of spirited debate," the Bellacosa-Feinberg Committee failed to reach consensus on most vital issues. Rather, the committee imploded under the weight of strident internal opposition, with its final report riven with dissents from eight of its fourteen members.

Messrs. Paterson, Williams, and Lopez and Ms. Walker joined together in proffering the defense dissent. Ms. Walker and Mr. Paterson joined with Mr. Smith in a separate dissent, which included a less severe sentencing grid. Messrs. Morgenthau, Mulligan, and Wemple, representing the law-enforcement position, combined their several dissents, also proposing their own sentencing grid. The dissents were laced throughout the report, often occupying more space on a given topic than the plurality opinion. Not only did the dissents render the final report incomprehensible in parts, they also opened to question Chairman Feinberg's claim that the committee had reached agreement on the need for determinate sentencing, especially since four members joined in a dissent challenging the wisdom of abolishing the rehabilitative sentencing system.[66]

After all the discussion, after all the years of forward movement, it was now clear that the essence of the determinate ideal was as clouded with ambiguity in 1985 as it had been in the early 1970s. The four areas of supposed agreement mentioned by Chairman Feinberg were less than impressive. The wisdom of ending parole release was never questioned seriously by the committee or by any other advocate of determinate sentencing. The need for certainty in sentencing remained but a vague abstraction. The other two areas of agreement—giving prosecutors the right to appeal lenient sentences and monitoring the guidelines after implementation—were hardly sufficient to define the new system. While repeating the rhetoric of the early advocates of the determinate ideal, it was apparent that the Bellacosa-Feinberg Committee was no closer than its long line of predecessors to agreeing how these lofty ideals could be implemented in the day-to-day realities of the criminal-sentencing system.

8

The Fall of the Determinate Ideal

Long before the report was published, it was evident that the Bellacosa-Feinberg Committee's recommendations would face stiff resistance. The public response to the committee's proposals mirrored the positions taken by the committee members—defense interests disliked the system for one set of reasons, while law enforcement were opposed for another. That former supporters of determinacy would respond negatively to the recommendations of the sentencing committee is not surprising: The clash between the promise and the reality of the determinate ideal, begun so long ago, was now patently evident. Once a concrete proposal was put forward for resolution, proponents of determinacy could no longer hide their differences behind the thick rhetorical underbrush.

Public Hearings

Instead of issuing a final report on January 15, 1985, as directed by Chapter 711, on that date the committee issued a preliminary report, which served as the basis for public comment at public hearings. Before voting in favor of the preliminary report, most members said that their vote for the report was not a vote in support of its contents; rather, their vote signaled only that they agreed to issue the report for the purpose of receiving public comment at public hearings. Committee members said that they reserved the right to change their vote on any issue before agreeing to support a final report.

Nevertheless, in spite of the widespread disagreement among committee members with the preliminary report, and in spite of the testimony received at public hearings, the preliminary and the final reports were strikingly similar. Only three substantive recommendations were changed between the issuance of the two reports.[1] While these changes were not inconsequential, they did not disturb the basic character of the committee's recommendations. Therefore, it seems reasonable to assume that the comments received on the preliminary report are adequate proxies for the comments that would have been received had hearings been held on the final report. Given the similarity of the final and preliminary report, it is doubtful that many witnesses would have substantially altered their testimony between the two reports.

Witnesses' Response

The same methodology was used for determining the position of the witnesses at the Bellacosa-Feinberg hearings as was used for determining the positions of the witnesses at the Morgenthau and Senate and Assembly Codes Committee's hearings.[2] Transcripts from the hearings were read to determine whether the witnesses favored determinate sentencing and whether they could be categorized by ideological position.

The Bellacosa-Feinberg Committee held five days of public hearings in February 1985, during which eighty-seven witnesses testified.[3] Ideological positions could be determined for eighty-five (98 percent) of the eighty-seven respondents, of which sixty-two (73 percent) were categorized as defense oriented and twenty-three (27 percent) as law-enforcement oriented. The 1985 witnesses' ideological views were almost identical to those expressed by witnesses at the 1978 and 1979 hearings on determinate sentencing.

Data on witnesses' preference for determinate sentencing, however, was not as easily obtained for the 1985 group as it had been for the 1978/79 group. Where it had been possible to determine the positions of 97 percent of the witnesses in 1978/79, positions on determinate sentencing could be determined for only 41 percent of the 1985 witnesses.

Why were over half of the 1985 witnesses' position on determinate sentencing not scorable? The answer is clear: These witnesses confronted a different dynamic than the 1978/79 witnesses. Instead of dealing in vague abstractions, these witnesses were responding to specific proposals. Not willing to spend the limited time allocated for testimony discussing the theoretical merits or demerits of determinacy, the witnesses testifying before the Bellacosa-Feinberg Committee launched immediately into a full scale assault on the committee's recommendations. Only two of the eighty-seven witnesses approved of the overall thrust of the committee's report, although they too had objections to specific recommendations. The remaining eighty-five witnesses could find little to commend in the committee's version of the determinate ideal.

The following table presents the findings for the thirty-six witnesses whose position on both determinate sentencing and ideological affiliation could be determined.

Sentencing Guidelines Committee Hearings (1985)

Ideology	Witnesses' Position on Determinate Sentencing		
	Favored	*Opposed*	*Total*
Defense	12 (63%)	7 (37%)	19 (100%)
Law Enforcement	14 (82%)	3 (18%)	17 (100%)
Total	26 (72%)	10 (28%)	36 (100%)

The next table compares the position on determinate sentencing between the 1985 and the 1978/79 witnesses.

All Hearings

Witnesses' Position on Determinate Sentencing

Ideology	1978 & 1979		1985	
	Favored	*Opposed*	*Favored*	*Opposed*
Defense	61%	39%	63%	37%
Law Enforcement	71%	29%	82%	18%

Thus, in spite of the heavy criticism that witnesses leveled against the Bellacosa-Feinberg Committee's report, the support for the concept of determinacy was not diminished among these thirty-six witnesses. On the contrary, determinacy seemed to be gaining adherents, especially among the law-enforcement community. This observation is inherently suspect, however, given that preference for determinacy could not be scored for 58.6 percent of the witnesses.

Regardless of their position on the viability of the determinate model, witnesses at the Bellacosa-Feinberg Committee's public hearings reacted negatively to most aspects of the committee's proposal. Similar to the pattern observed among members of the sentencing committee, witnesses' testimony evidenced a distinct pattern between defense and law-enforcement perspectives, however.

Witnesses representing defense interests urged abolishing all limits on departure in mitigation; witnesses espousing law-enforcement views warned against allowing more than 50 percent departure in mitigation. Defense witnesses said that the trial judge needed unlimited departure in mitigation to do justice in the individual case; law enforcement witnesses argued for constraining judicial discretion to impose lenient sentences. The Attorney General, Robert Abrams, and New York City Mayor Koch called for 25 percent departure at the trial level and no departure at the appellate level. The District Attorneys Association urged that the committee eliminate all departure that would result in a sentence less than the current mandatory minimum sentence.

Several defense witnesses would require the court to ascertain in every case if mitigating circumstances existed; one law-enforcement witness suggested that all mitigating factors be eliminated. The catch-all mitigating factor, that the "presumptively correct sentence is unduly harsh given extraordinary circumstances, and a more lenient sentence would not deprecate the seriousness of the crime,"[4] was heavily criticized by law-enforcement-oriented witnesses. The state attorney general complained that this mitigating factor was vague and susceptible to varying interpretations; the president of the District Attorneys Association agreed, noting that the factor was fatally flawed because it was not limited to the circumstances surrounding the current offense. They both warned that an open-ended factor would result in frequent departure hearings, crushing an already overburdened judiciary and encouraging the growth of the very discretion that determinacy was intended to shrink.

Both defense and law-enforcement witnesses complained about the prior record scoring system, but for different reasons. Defense witnesses were concerned with the impact of the scoring system on prison crowding. They feared that too many offenders would be in the high and extreme prior record categories, receiving very long prison sentences. Under the indeterminate model, the court decides whether to sentence a person with three or more prior convictions as a persistent nonviolent felony offender; offenders who could be sentenced as persistent nonviolent felony offenders are frequently sentenced as second nonviolent felony offenders, and given shorter sentences than if they were sentenced as persistent nonviolent felony offenders. Under the committee's proposal, each predicate felony would be scored, and prior record would not be subject to plea bargaining. Thus, the defense claimed, the committee's recommendations would potentially result in offenders with more than one prior conviction serving vastly longer prison terms than they serve under current law, thereby driving up prison populations.

Law-enforcement witnesses were not as concerned about prison resources, but they complained that scoring each prior felony would strain court resources. Defendants, they claimed, could be expected to routinely challenge the prosecutor's submission of prior record, thereby increasing the number of hearings required in each case. New York City Mayor Koch warned that extra hearings would cause delay, which would result in offenders spending more time in local jails, thereby shifting the responsibility for housing these offenders from the state to the localities.[5]

Law enforcement criticized the committee for rejecting misdemeanor scoring. The committee had abandoned scoring prior misdemeanors for several reasons, including the practical problems of obtaining good data on prior misdemeanor convictions. The president of the District Attorneys Association and the attorney general cautioned that prosecutors would stop accepting misdemeanor pleas to felony charges if misdemeanors were not scored. They suggested that the practical problems of data quality could be solved by giving prosecutors the discretion to charge only those prior misdemeanors that they could verify. Defense witnesses were not so eager to give the prosecutor the power to determine prior record.

The committee's treatment of the sequentiality rule was attacked by defense witnesses, who argued that the compromise of awarding two bonus points for crimes not covered by the sequence rule should be eliminated. Giving offenders two points if they were sentenced on the prior felony before being sentenced on the instant felony, regardless of the sequence of commission of the two felonies, would aggravate prosecutorial abuse, the defense asserted. Prosecutors would seek multiple indictments in closely related offenses to boost the offenders' score, they claimed. It was noted that defendants often plead guilty on the same day to several indictments in exchange for a lesser sentence, even if they are not guilty of one or more of the crimes charged; therefore, these witnesses argued, prior convictions were often an unreliable basis for enhancing punishment.

Witnesses testifying from the law-enforcement perspective also disliked the committee's treatment of sequentiality. They argued that all offenders should be punished for what they did, not for when they did it. They urged the committee to recommend abolishing the sequentiality rule of current law and to fully score all prior convictions.

Witnesses representing law enforcement argued that a prior youthful offender adjudication should be scored the same as a prior criminal conviction: three points for a nonviolent felony, five for a violent felony. Defense-oriented witnesses argued that prior youthful offender adjudications should not be scored under any circumstances.

Defense witnesses claimed that the committee had merely shifted discretion from the court to the prosecutor, and that the court's discretion within the guidelines range was illusory if the prosecutor selected the grid cell. Summing up the defense position on prosecutorial discretion, one witness testified that he believed that "much of this almost gratuitous transfer of power is due to political pressures and the untested assumption that prosecutorial power, particularly in the area of sanctioning, is somehow related to crime control and services to crime victims." The witness concluded that "it will take more than prosecutorial "get tough" assertions . . . to prove to us that giving more power to the already strongest of the parties in the adversarial system has a provable or desirable relationship to the key issue, and that is doing justice."[6]

As expected, the inspect and reduce proposal was bitterly opposed by law-enforcement interests and applauded by defense interests. In addition to reducing the indictment to conform to the evidence presented to the grand jury, defense witnesses suggested that the judge be given the authority to reduce the indictment in the interests of justice. Several defense witnesses suggested allowing the court to prevent the prosecutor from resubmitting a reduced indictment to another grand jury.

Prison administrators complained about virtually all aspects of the committee's proposals. They objected to the committee's proposed 25 percent good-time allowance, incorporating the rules for violations of good time into statute, vesting, limiting the loss of good time to forty-five days per incident, transferring the administration of good time to the Division of Parole, requiring that disciplinary hearings commence within seven days from the date of the incident if the offender is in pre-hearing confinement, allowing inmate advisers at disciplinary hearings, and abolishing restoration of good time.[7]

Mayor Koch's Testimony

The fundamental schism between law enforcement and defense perspectives was evident in New York City Mayor Edward Koch's testimony before the committee. Mayor Koch began his testimony by launching a full-scale assault on the committee's proposal, which he claimed was "dead in the water, and if it isn't, it ought to be." The mayor described himself as a staunch supporter of determinate sentencing, claiming that it "reduces the disparity inherent in the present system and provides the certainty of punishment, which I believe is the cornerstone of a just and effective criminal justice policy." The mayor was not prepared to forsake crime-control purposes, however, saying that "the whole purpose here is to address crime."[8] Excerpts from a revealing repartee between the mayor and committee member Basil Paterson follows.

MR. PATERSON: It would seem in good conscience, and sound governance, that the legislature would first move towards increasing prison capacity [before allowing another wholesale release as occurred at Riker's Island jail].[9]

MAYOR KOCH: In the legislature . . . I believe that there are two forces operating. I think that you have those who believe in rehabilitation, that it works, and that alternative sentences work. I don't believe in any of that. I believe that jail works. I believe that people who go to jail have less tendency to commit another crime than someone who is in an alternative sentencing program who has committed a comparable crime and hasn't gone to jail. That is a philosophy, and I don't want to argue good or bad, evil or good; it is a philosophy which is my philosophy . . . If this committee believes, as I hope it does, that there should be tougher admonitions and sentencing, then it should not be constrained on the basis of resources. What it should say is these are the resources, and we are recommending to the State Legislature we want you to do A, which is sentencing, and all the other stuff that goes into it, and we want to tell you now that you cannot do A unless you do B, and B means that if you can't get a bond issue, then take it out of current revenue.

The proposal is a useful first step, a basis for discussion, but I have grave concern about a number of its provisions. I am especially chagrined at your failure to address the potential fiscal and resource impacts of the proposals on local correction and probation departments. I also do not support your decisions which alter the current laws of mandatory incarceration for violent felons or recidivists, and [object to] the gutting of the present mandatory jail provisions of the gun laws, and the decision to remove certain violent predatory behavior from the mandatory jail provisions of current law, your proposal for 100 percent departure in mitigation.

EXECUTIVE DIRECTOR WALSH: Mr. Mayor, given the cost of construction of cells at a hundred thousand plus, as a matter of social utility, would you accept that there are any limitations on the number of prison cells that should be constructed to house the population?

MAYOR KOCH: None... What good does it do to provide for every other social service that people want, if they fear, correctly, that they can't walk the streets and ride the subways or be safe in their own homes? What good would anything else be? What I am saying is, you cannot substitute, you cannot say the hell with it, crime is going to be with us, and we just have to accept it because we don't have the resources to deal with it. If it means changing our priorities, if it means saying that the number one priority, as opposed to all other priorities, is dealing with personal protection of our citizenry...

The two top priorities for us are education and law enforcement... I want to tell you that if I had to deal with only one, if I had to make a choice, it would be to punish the criminal. Is it because you just want revenge? No, people are fed up, absolutely fed up, and this isn't something new...

MR. PATERSON: You made an interesting comment, that if given the opportunity you would use the unlimited resources for building more jails.

MAYOR KOCH: Yes.

MR. PATERSON: I suppose Mr. Conboy and Mr. Haughey [the criminal-justice advisors accompanying the mayor] would confirm the fact that if we were looking for the single greatest common denominator in Riker's Island, you would find it is functional illiteracy. It would seem to me that if we are going to talk about crime, without any panaceas, we would at least want to make sure that the people who are coming through the school system in New York City would leave that school system with at least the skills to enable them to hold some jobs, and it is clear, and you know it, you have been to Riker's Island, that many of those youngsters, they come in for a petty crime, and you make the point, or somebody made the point... that some of them are receiving life terms, thirty days at a time, committing petty crime after petty crime, in, out, with no way to earn a living or support themselves or their dependents, if such is the case.

MAYOR KOCH: That is another question of philosophical approach to this. Some people say that people commit crimes because of poverty, or because of lack of education. I don't believe it.

MR. PATERSON: I'm not contending that, I am saying that it is quite clear, and there is no question about the logic of it, that if a person is living in this society, without even the most basic skills to work in a supermarket, that that person, being a human being, with a mind...

MAYOR KOCH: Is going to do what?

MR. PATERSON   Is going to find some way to survive. You and I will certainly condemn them going out and taking our wallets or trying to rip off something.

MAYOR KOCH: But you are saying exactly what I say I don't believe. You are saying that because people don't have an education, or are poor, that they are going to turn to crime, which is what you are saying. I don't believe that.

MR. PATERSON: I am saying quite categorically that... you cannot eliminate the economic aspects of crime... [T]here is no question that if we are turning out the youngsters that we do from our school system because of an alleged lack of resources, if they are not given the minimal skills, we are going to have an increase in crime.

MAYOR KOCH: Can I disagree with you, and let me tell you why?

MR. PATERSON: We often do, but absolutely.

MAYOR KOCH: Let me tell you why. Most poor people don't commit crimes. There is a very small number of poor people who do commit crimes. I believe most people who are uneducated don't commit crimes, a very small percentage of those who are uneducated commit crimes. I will tell you why I think people commit crimes. I am not talking about in every case, but nobody goes out and commits a crime because they are hungry today. It is baloney. Nobody goes out and commits a crime because there is not bread on the table, I don't accept that because this society, as bad as it is, you don't have to go hungry, you just don't. There are soup kitchens, they are not nice, but you don't have to go hungry. So why do people overwhelmingly commit crimes? Because you have better odds not getting caught than you do at the race track.[10]

The Political Response

The Bellacosa-Feinberg Committee issued its final report and recommendations on March 29, 1985. A few days later, Governor Cuomo announced that he was pleased that the committee had issued its report, although he did not immediately endorse the committee's recommendations.[11] The Governor's Criminal Justice Director, Lawrence T. Kurlander, released a statement congratulating the committee for "their extraordinary efforts in completing this complex task in a timely manner." Director Kurlander said that "[t]he report represents an important first step in our continuing effort to develop an improved system of criminal sentencing for the citizens of New York... Now that the report is in, we can begin to work together with the Legislature to make this desperately needed and long-sought reform of our sentencing laws."[12]

Two weeks later, on May 8, 1985, the governor submitted a program bill that was nearly identical to the bill proposed in the sentencing committee's final report.[13] In submitting the bill, the governor announced that

> [t]he real deterrent to crime is found not in draconian punishment or circumventing due process, but in the certainty of swift, sure justice. Determinate sentencing is a major element in restoring that certainty to New York's criminal justice system. The Committee on Sentencing Guidelines has produced a report that reflects a consensus for changing the felony sentencing laws in New York State. I commend the Committee for its efforts and submit the product of its deliberations to the Legislature with my endorsement.[14]

Defense Responds: The Black and Puerto Rican Caucus

Both sides of the political spectrum challenged the determinate sentencing bill; each offered its own prescription for change. The defense position was best represented by the Black and Puerto Rican Legislative Caucus, made up of Democratic minority members of the Assembly and Senate. The caucus opposed the governor's bill for failing to confront the roots of crime—unemployment, housing, and the disproportionate incarceration of minorities. Not satisfied with criticizing the committee's product, the caucus submitted its own sentencing bill on May 31, 1985.[15] The bill was a paragon of the rehabilitative ideal.

The caucus began by endorsing crime control and recommending that judges have broad sentencing discretion. According to the caucus's bill, the

> purpose of sentencing and its legal objective is public protection... It is hereby declared to be the public policy of this state that sentencing not be based upon revenge or retribution, and that incarceration, when used, should be used as a last resort. All sentences should be the least restrictive infringement on personal liberty necessary to protect the public safety.

Public protection—the objective of the criminal sanction for caucus members—included:

> a) making people safe from harm, injury or loss; b) the prevention of offenses through the creative application of nonviolent sanctions applied to offenders; c) the economic, social and psychological restoration of victims by the creative application of non-incarcerative sanctions upon offenders; d) the economic, social and psychological restoration of offenders by the creative application of non-incarcerative sanctions; e) the promotion of

social harmony; f) the reconciliation of offender with victim; g) the reconciliation of offender with community; and the establishment of peace between the offender and victim.[16]

The caucus reversed the traditional hierarchy of punishment by authorizing numerous non-prison dispositions. The statutes covering sentences of probation, conditional discharge, and unconditional discharge, would be amended to include twenty-four non-incarcerative dispositions, including dismissal, unconditional discharge, five types of suspended sentences, fines, ten levels of conditional discharge, three levels of probation, and three levels of intensive probation. The court was required to impose a non-incarcerative sentence in every case unless it concluded that "no less restrictive sentence fashioned and applied to an individual offender will adequately protect the public safety."[17]

Within the twenty-four non-incarcerative options, the court would select the least restrictive alternative unless a more restrictive alternative was necessary for public protection. Thus, the court would first consider whether to dismiss a case; if dismissal was not appropriate, the court would then consider whether to impose an unconditional discharge; if that sanction was considered insufficient, a conditional discharge would be considered, and so on.

Like the non-incarcerative sentences, the incarcerative sentences recommended by the caucus ranged on a continuum from least to most restrictive. Thirteen forms of incarcerative sentences were specified in the bill: intermittent imprisonment, partial confinement, six types of jail sentences (*e.g.,* jail combined with a fine or a form of parole), and five types of prison sentences.[18] After satisfying itself that a non-incarcerative sentence would not adequately protect the public, the court would impose the least restrictive incarcerative sentence that would provide the requisite safety.

The caucus's bill included indeterminate as well as determinate prison sentences. The court could impose an indeterminate sentence

> if such a sentence will, in the opinion of the court, protect the public safety more adequately than the imposition of a definite sentence. In any case where either a definite or indeterminate sentence is deemed adequate to protect public safety, the court shall impose an indeterminate sentence if such a sentence will, in the opinion of the court, constitute a less restrictive sentence than a definite sentence.[19]

The maximum term of an indeterminate sentence for any felony would be five years; the minimum term would be at least six months, but could not exceed one-third of the maximum term imposed. Definite sentences would be selected from a wide statutory range. The sentence for class A felonies could not exceed twenty years; class B felonies could not exceed ten years; class C felonies, three years; class D felonies, two years; and class E felonies, one year. These were maximum sentences; the court could sentence the offender anywhere within the range. Thus, there was nothing to prevent the court from imposing a one year sentence on a murderer (or dismissing the case or granting an unconditional discharge).

The caucus' determinate sentences were not entirely determinate, however. An inmate serving a determinate sentence could apply for early release. Upon reviewing the inmate's application, the parole authorities could ask the sentencing court for a hearing on early release. The inmate would have the right to be present at the hearing and be represented by counsel.[20] In deciding whether to apply to the court for an inmate's early release, the parole authorities would consider

> (i) the institutional record of the prospective releasee, including program goals and accomplishments, academic achievements, vocational education, training and work assignments, vocational and educational aptitude, therapy and interpersonal relationships with staff and inmates; (ii) performance, if any, as a participant in a temporary release program; (iii) release plans, including community resources, employment, education, and training and support services available to the prospective releasee and the level of his motivation to undertake such activities or develop such resources after release; and (iv) any deportation proceeding.[21]

The caucus was quite explicit about the crime-control rationale underlying its early release proposal. Although the Bellacosa-Feinberg Committee made no such acknowledgment, its sentence review proposal was strikingly similar to the early-release proposal put forward by the caucus, the difference being that the former limited early release to long-term offenders while the latter proposed the escape mechanism for all prisoners.

Law Enforcement Responds

Law-enforcement interests attacked the committee's report with vigor. On June 17, 1985 the Law Enforcement Council, an umbrella group that included Mayor Koch's criminal-justice coordinator, the Attorney General, the Citizens Crime Commission, the Association of Sheriffs, the Association of Police Chiefs, and the District Attorneys Association, held a news conference in Albany to denounce the bill. Kenneth Conboy, the then-New York City criminal-justice coordinator, told reporters "we're doing everything we can to stop this."[22]

Members of the Law Enforcement Council spent the day of June 17, 1985 in Albany lobbying legislators, urging them to defeat the bill. They distributed a position paper prepared by the District Attorneys Association, which claimed that the determinate sentencing bill has

> a number of features that favor the criminal and threaten the safety and well being of the law-abiding public. Our primary concerns are that the proposal

will drastically reduce present sentences, and have a dramatic and unwarranted impact on local jail populations . . . The proposed legislation would significantly undercut, and in many cases totally eliminate, existing mandatory sentences. With downward departure taken into account, the grid lowers mandatory sentences for literally every felony crime in New York . . . Even worse, the reductions are most pronounced in the predicate felony categories involving "career criminals". . . . Drug offenders, and particularly those who possess and deal large quantities of drugs, would benefit most by the proposed legislation . . . The fact that sentences for a few crimes are raised under the grid does not justify the reductions in the overwhelming majority of others . . . New York's mandatory sentences have served to ensure the certainty of punishment, which is an important factor in deterring crime. And the evidence clearly shows that such sentences have resulted in significant reductions in serious crime . . . We are not persuaded by the fact that the bill expressly states that departure should occur infrequently. For experience tells us that courts—and particularly those operating under enormous caseloads—will exercise that option routinely. For example, in other situations where the New York legislature has sought to fashion a narrow escape hatch for exceptional cases, very significant numbers of defendants have succeeded in escaping. New York's "tough" gun law is one example, where the majority of defendants are the beneficiaries of a mitigating provision almost identical to that found in the departure rules.

The District Attorneys Association memorandum continued:

For many offenses where state prison sentences are now mandatory, the bill would permit sentences to local jails . . . As a result, the prospect exists—frightening to say the least—that one third, or even one half, of those now sentenced to state prison might be rerouted to local institutions. The consequences of such a massive shift in population cannot be overstated. Our local institutions are already seriously overcrowded, and in any event were not designed to accommodate large numbers of sentenced violent felons. In addition, adding state inmates to local jails will undoubtedly cause judges to impose alternative sentences on offenders who, while perhaps not violent, nevertheless deserve to go to jail. The problem is exacerbated even further by the potential impact on local jails of the proposal's contemplated departure and scoring hearings, which will delay many sentences.

The memorandum zeroed in on what law enforcement saw as the report's fatal flaw:

This bill purports to be guided, at least in part, by the premise that scarce prison resources should be reserved for the most serious offenders. Nevertheless, it also reduces the permissible maximum terms of imprisonment imposed in many serious cases . . . The problem stems from the methodology employed in constructing the grid, which seeks to limit opportunities for disparity by the use of narrow sentence ranges. Contrary to the view of the sentencing committee, however, narrow sentence ranges will not reduce opportunities for disparity. Four other states have narrow sentences ranges similar to those proposed in [the bill]. In two states, Minnesota and California, disparity has not been limited because plea bargaining, departure, and manipulation of the rules are common. . . . In the third state, Colorado, the narrowness of the bands has resulted in a public outcry because sufficient punishment for serious offenders is precluded. In the fourth state, Washington, determinate sentencing is too new for any conclusions to be drawn.

The district attorneys criticized the abandonment of misdemeanor scoring:

Although the offender's prior criminal history is one of the two most important factors to be considered in determining the appropriate sentence—the severity of the offense being the other—the rules by which one's prior record is scored fail to take into account the offender's full history. Most disturbing in this respect is the bill's failure to attach any weight to the offender's prior misdemeanor record . . . Indeed, the term "career criminal" oftentimes more aptly describes the lifestyle of the habitual misdemeanant than it does that of the offender with a single prior felony conviction . . . The proposed determinate sentencing bill will significantly erode public confidence in our criminal-justice system, and will breed contempt among its strongest supporters, the law-abiding public.[23]

The Committee Gets Sued

The criticism advanced by members of the Law Enforcement Council focused heavily on the impact of the guidelines on local jails. In a memorandum released at the Council's Albany press conference, New York City's Criminal Justice Coordinator complained that the bill "would significantly expand the number of felons who qualify for local jail sentences. As a result, the impact upon local jails will be devastating . . . Indeed, conditions may develop which would resemble those that led to the prisoner release of November 1983."

The Law Enforcement Council's memorandum included a statement by Peter Kehoe, Executive Director of the Sheriff's Association, who claimed that the "guidelines would shift as many as 4,300 prisoners from the State prisons to the local jails. We are already struggling with an unfair burden of state-ready inmates. Our local correctional systems would collapse under this new burden."[24]

Law-enforcement interests did more than complain, however. On the same day that the Law Enforcement Council held its press conference in Albany, a law suit was filed against the committee. Mayor Koch, joined by county executives from Nassau, Suffolk, Orange, and Westchester counties, the New York State Association of Counties, and the New York State Sheriff's Association, filed the unprecedented suit in State Supreme Court in Manhattan challenging the committee's report for failing to include a statement of the estimated impact of the guidelines on local jail resources.[25] The suit asked the court to vacate the report and require the committee to prepare an in-depth analysis of the impact of its proposal on local jail resources.

The lawsuit was largely symbolic: Local governments cannot stop action by the legislature. On June 19, 1985 the suit was dismissed by the Supreme Court as not justiciable. The court noted that the suit raised a political, not a judicial, question. The court commented, however, that there "is no gainsaying that Petitioners have a real and serious concern as to the impact on local criminal-justice resources, especially correction and jail facilities, if and when the proposed determinate sentencing legislation is enacted."[26]

The Media

Chapter Six presented highlights of the media's coverage of the early and middle phases of the movement for determinate sentencing. The discussion below focuses on accounts by the *New York Post* and the *New York Times* during the later stages, when the meaning underlying the vague concepts of the ideal had been rendered into specific policy proposals.

The New York Post

The *New York Post* followed the Bellacosa-Feinberg Committee's progress closely. As had been true during the earlier, formative period, the *New York Post* continued to imbue the determinate ideal with its own preferred meaning.

The *Post* reported on October 1, 1984 that the Bellacosa-Feinberg Committee was

> wracked by ideological warfare . . . Determinate sentences, authorized by the legislature last year, are meant to make sure that criminals serve a fixed prison sentence, with no chance for a parole. But liberals and judges on the 14-member panel are fighting tooth and nail to permit judges to circumvent the fixed sentence requirements in special cases. But determined law-and-order advocates fear such a move would defeat the whole purpose of the law.[27]

On October 5, 1984, under the heading "If Other States Impose Fixed Sentences, Why Not N.Y.?", the *Post* carried an editorial claiming that the committee was "straying far from its task." Calling the present system of sentencing a "fraud and a failure," the *Post* warned that it had taken the legislature more than five years to decide to

> scrap this flawed system and opt for determinate sentences. Are we now confronting a major rearguard on the very committee of experts appointed

to recommend the guidelines for a more accountable system—a system in which the parole board would be abolished and judges would impose fixed sentences subject only to appeal to the Appellate Division? Certainly, this is what the committee's proceedings tend to suggest.

The *Post* editorial noted that the committee had voted at the last meeting to allow unlimited departure in mitigation. This, the *Post* reported, "would negate the whole concept of determinate sentencing."

The *Post* went on to complain that the committee was going beyond its mandate, wasting time rewriting the penal law when "[i]t had been asked to do only one thing—recommend specific sentences for specific crimes." The *Post* argued that the committee should not engage in a reclassification of offenses, conduct an impact assessment, plan for monitoring the guidelines, or recommend alternatives to incarceration.[28]

The editorial concluded:

> The committee's work has all the elements of a disaster in the making. Even if it reports by Jan. 15 the legislature surely will have no recourse—as things are going—but to throw out the report and fix its own guidelines. That is what it should have done more than a year ago. If California, Colorado, Connecticut, Illinois, Indiana, Maine, Minnesota, New Mexico, North Carolina and Washington can impose fixed sentences on their criminals, why can't New York?[29]

Following the issuance of the committee's preliminary report, in an editorial entitled "Compromise Is the Last Way to Deal with Criminals," the *Post* criticized both the departure policy and the sentence review proposal.

> On the one hand, Gov. Cuomo's blue-ribbon commission on sentencing reform recommends tough—and very specific—prison terms for convicted felons. On the other, it recommends permitting judges to reduce those sentences by as much as 50 percent. On the one hand, the commission recommends that parole—and the state parole board—be abolished. On the other, it recommends that very long sentences be reviewed after 15 years—with an eye toward early release.
>
> Something odd is going on here. Ordinary people call it sleight-of-hand. Politicians think of it as compromise, that process whereby both philosophical and practical questions are resolved in rough agreement. The public interest demands that there be no compromise on sentence reform . . . There is simply too much leeway in the system being recommended by the commission. What sense is there in mandating a tough sentence and then permitting a judge to reduce it by as much as half? That kind of discretion is exactly what is wrong with the present system. What sense is there in mandating a long sentence and then permitting an unaccountable and politically appointed board to set it aside after 15 years? None.[30]

In an editorial covering the exchange at the public hearings between Basil Paterson and Mayor Koch, the *Post* noted that

> Fixed sentences were not invented to keep prison expenditures down. Koch rightly attacked that distortion. They were meant to mandate more severe sentences. And with good reason. Every American knows that a man is innocent until proven guilty. The problem is that some judges seem to believe a man is innocent even *after* he has been proven guilty.[31]

On March 23, 1985, in an editorial entitled "The Argument for Fixed Sentences is Overwhelming," the *Post* quoted Melvin Miller as saying that the odds that the bill would pass were "at best 50-50—and that's being generous."

Rewriting history, the *Post* presented its own version of the creation of determinate sentencing:

> Cuomo's support for fixed sentencing was prompted by public rage at the "turn-table justice" system in which criminals are convicted, serve a fraction of their sentence, are released on parole and promptly commit more crimes— inspired partly by contempt for the leniency with which they are treated.
>
> So the case for fixed determinate sentencing is strong. It would prevent judges setting negligible sentences for serious crimes. It would protect the public from dangerous criminals by keeping them in prison for longer periods. The prospect of longer sentences, which could not be shortened by parole, would increase deterrence. And, together, these changes would reassure the public.
>
> The general idea of fixed sentencing is one thing; the proposal that seems to be emerging from the committee is another. Fixed sentences, after all, are meant to be fixed. But the committee wants to give the judges discretion to vary from its "guidelines" by 50 percent either way. Discretion of any amount is doubtful. Discretion on the scale of 50 percent either way robs determinate sentencing of any real meaning.[32]

Following the issuance of the committee's final report, under the heading "Now it's Up to the Governor to Rescue Sentencing Reform," a *Post* editorial claimed that "[i]t's usually considered common sense not to throw the baby out with the bathwater. The principle of determinate sentencing is the baby and the report of the New York Committee on Sentencing Guidelines is the bathwater." The editorial called the committee's ranges "ridiculously wide."[33]

The editorial claimed that, with the additional leeway provided by 50 percent departure,

> the committee has not proposed determinate sentencing at all. It has simply laid down a set of guidelines so broad that any judge, no matter how lenient, could live comfortably within them. One absurd result of this supposedly tough reform is that sentences could theoretically be imposed for

certain crimes that are actually lower than the present minimum. There are, admittedly, some sensible proposals. The parole board would be abolished and the maximum amount of time off for good behavior would be reduced from one-third to one-quarter of the sentence—though it should probably be something like 15 percent. But the central idea of fixed sentences has vanished. As a result a bizarre coalition has formed in Albany. There are those who dislike the report's leniency, like Republican Ronald Stafford, chairman of the powerful Senate Codes Committee. And those who have always wanted to strangle the baby of determinate sentencing, like Assemblyman Melvin Miller, the influential Brooklyn Democrat who chairs the Assembly Codes Committee. This puts the entire principle of determinate sentencing at risk. The baby is drowning in the bathwater.

If Mario Cuomo is to remain true to his campaign support for fixed sentences, he cannot allow this to happen. Let him contact those members of the committee, like Manhattan DA Robert Morgenthau, who resisted the weakening of the determinate principle. Let him explore such ideas as Morgenthau's suggestion that a sentence might be varied 50 percent up—but not down. Let him assemble his own package of reforms. Let him take this fight to the people. He will have the people on his side.[34]

On April 12, 1985 the Post quoted the then-U.S. attorney general for the Southern District of New York, Rudolph Giuliani, as saying that the committee's proposal would make New York the "crime capital of the nation." Speaking at the *Post*'s Crime Busters Forum, Giuliani commented that "one of the things that could happen is that criminals in other states would decide that New York is the place to come and commit crimes." He said that the proposal would "reduce substantially the amount of time that people now spend in prison."

The *Post* quoted Senator Ralph Marino as saying that Giuliani's attack "means the proposal is dead."[35] Senator Marino was right.

The New York Times

Like the *Post,* the *New York Times* reported that the Bellacosa-Feinberg Committee was

> sharply divided, and the dispute threatens to block any action on the issue by the State Legislature. The committee is divided over how much authority judges should have to set aside predetermined sentences, an issue that has created a split between the state's judiciary and law-enforcement officials.
>
> The judges, led by Judge Betty Weinberg Ellerin, a committee member and the chief administrative judge for New York City, say judges are not "robots" and should have the authority to set aside fixed sentences in "extraordinary circumstances." Prosecutors, led by another committee member, Robert M. Morgenthau, the Manhattan District Attorney, say that such authority would nullify mandatory imprisonment laws and jeopardize public confidence. Mr. Morgenthau called Judge Ellerin's position a "death

wish" that would make it difficult for the plan to get through the Legislature. Governor Cuomo, Attorney General Robert Abrams and the State District Attorneys Association have warned the committee not to be "too soft."[36] ... Legislative aides said that without a consensus on the committee and support of the law enforcement community, the legislature would be unlikely to take any action on the sensitive issue.[37]

On November 10, 1984, in an editorial entitled "Bogged Down Over Sentencing," the *Times* noted that, while determinate sentencing was advertised as "simple," it was far from that, as the sentencing committee had found out. The editorial claimed that the committee was "struggling with the technical problems and has become deeply divided. Unless it surmounts the conflict, flat sentencing would be better abandoned."

The *Times* began what would become a familiar refrain: Determinate sentencing was not worth the price of prison overcrowding.

> Research to determine whether the sentences being considered will overwhelm the prison system has proved much more difficult than anticipated. And open warfare has erupted between judges who want to retain discretion to reduce sentences and prosecutors who want it limited. These and other issues might easily be compromised, but each side seems afraid of being associated with a report judged either too lenient or too harsh.

The editorial suggested extending the committee's deadline until April 1985. "More rational sentencing is desirable, but not worth destroying the prison system or tinkering too much with the balance of power between judges and prosecutors. If flat sentencing can't be introduced properly, it shouldn't be tried at all," the *Times* said.[38]

Following the issuance of the sentencing guidelines committee's preliminary report, the *Times* continued to express concern about the impact of the guidelines on prison resources. In a January 22, 1985 editorial, it noted that

> the new system would clearly proclaim punishment as the purpose of prisons, and the punishments would be determined in court, where judges and prosecutors are visibly accountable, not years later in obscure parole hearings. The end of parole releases, however, would create a new problem: loss of control over the total number of prisoners. As prisons fill up, parole boards now become more generous and relieve the crowding. And even so, the state's prisons remain overcrowded."
>
> The commission wants its sentence chart to create a prison population of no more than 40,000, the state's capacity when current expansions are completed. But the use of its grid chart might produce many more prisoners. For in analyzing current practice, the commission ignored felons who were not sent to prison. And it may have understated the criminal records of those who were. It thus may be greatly underestimating the lengths of sentences to be derived from its chart.[39]

Why worry that criminals might be sent away for longer terms? Because of the expense. It is costing New York $635 million to add just 8,600 new cell spaces. Even a slight miscalculation in the proposed chart could add tens of thousands of new prisoners. Once the grid is approved, it's unlikely the legislature would ever reduce sentences. Proceeding on the basis of doubtful estimates could mean having to choose one day between spending hundreds of millions more for prisons or releasing convicts under court order.

The sentencing chart would be a useful reform if the commission's estimates of future prison populations can be verified with confidence. The reform is desirable, but not at any cost.[40]

Like the *Post,* the *New York Times* covered the exchange at the committee's public hearings between Basil Paterson and Mayor Koch. Unlike the *Post,* which sided with the mayor, the *Times* supported Paterson. Reminding readers that the mayor had previously said that education was the "highest priority of my administration," the *Times* questioned whether the Mayor's comments signaled that he would renege on his promises for educational initiatives, such as public schools for four year olds and more help for potential dropouts:

How is Mr. Koch going to secure money for pre-kindergarten programs if he insists on giving priority to $100,000 prison cells? Financing both is the price of life in a civilized city. New Yorkers should never be asked to choose between them.[41]

Following the issuance of the sentencing committee's final report, the *New York Times* again reported that the committee was "sharply divided." Committee Chairman Kenneth Feinberg told the *Times* that the proposal

would constitute a major change in New York's sentencing laws. The unanimous decision of this committee is that New York State switch from this existing hybrid system of sentencing—some of it indeterminate, some of it mandatory—to a system of sentencing that to me is a major step forward.

The *Times* was not convinced:

Despite Mr. Feinberg's assertion of unanimity, the committee was riven with disagreement over the effects of a new system on the state's minorities, over whether the proposed sentences were adequate and what would be the impact on the state's prison population.

The *Times* noted that

the committee's report encountered a lukewarm reception from many quarters and no outright support . . . The report itself was laced with acid dissents, the four minority members of the committee were particularly acerbic, writing that "it is intolerable for the state to consider implementing a plan to reduce disparities in sentencing without paying equal attention to the implementation of strategies to reduce the overrepresentation of minorities, a marked disparity in the composition of its correctional facilities."

An April 8, 1985 a *Times* editorial questioned whether determinate sentencing should be used for crime-control purposes. Noting that fixed sentences made sense to people angry at crime, the *Times* doubted that they were "worth the likely price: the expensive expansion of an already-swollen prison population." The *Times* traced the genesis of determinate sentencing to concerns about disparate sentences for similar crimes.[42]

Only recently has it [determinate sentencing] been promoted as a way to make the streets safer. It can do that, however, only if the fixed sentences, in addition to being fixed, are much longer than those now served. Using fixed sentencing for crime control thus has powerful implications for the prison population. The commission, while unanimously supporting the need for simpler, more comprehensible sentencing, could not agree on how to achieve it.

Despite months of debate to produce a schedule of sentencing that would punish adequately without swamping the prisons, some members wound up disavowing it as too lenient. Concern for the prison population, they say, ought not to be so influential. An opposing faction argues that even the proposed schedule would increase the prison population from 34,000 to 48,000 in five years—10,000 more than will be accommodated even after the current $635 million prison expansion. Another 10,000 cells would cost nearly $2 billion to build and operate over five years. That kind of money could pay for more than 10,000 new police officers or restore the long-neglected lower courts, measures that could have a more direct, decisive effect on public safety.Is it desirable to lock up billions more dollars in prisons? The real question is not how to sentence, but how to get the most crime control for the money.[43]

So much for just deserts.

The following month, the *Times* reported that, by submitting a bill incorporating virtually all of the committee's recommendations, the governor had made determinate sentencing "the centerpiece of his criminal-justice agenda."

Key lawmakers were reported as saying that there was little chance of passage, despite the governor's strong support. Melvin Miller, the then-chairman of the Assembly Codes Committee, said "It's going to be kind of tough. Everybody tells me they can't find three people in favor of the bill. I keep getting counterproposals on every side of every issue in the bill, which means it's going to be very difficult to build a consensus."

On May 28, 1985, in an editorial titled "Tell the Truth About Punishment," the *Times* put aside its concerns about prison overcrowding and declared itself in support of the Governor's sentencing bill.

The proposal inspires much controversy. Critics call it too lenient because it eliminates mandatory sentences. The restriction on judges may be illusory because they would be able to deviate from prescribed sentences by 50 percent. Other critics worry that the prison population will soar as legislators rush to ratchet sentences upward.

The leniency argument is unpersuasive. Eliminating mandatory sentences is hardly likely to reduce the number of criminals sent to prison. It will just change the mix, and probably for the better... The worries about prison population are more serious. The Governor proposes to answer them by giving the sentencing commission continuing power to revise the chart subject to the Legislature's veto.

The committee's proposal apparently satisfied the *Times'* concern about the impact of the grid on prison populations.

Outweighing any objections, in any case, is the big benefit of truth in sentencing. With the chart, the extent of punishment would be clear at the time a sentence is imposed. The broad discretion of the parole board would no longer be a factor. The criminal justice system's crumbling credibility needs such a repair.[44]

On June 14, 1985, with the legislature close to adjournment, the *Times* observed that the governor was "pressing harder for his criminal sentencing package than many legislators expected." Mayor Koch was reported to have "sent a letter to all 211 legislators saying the proposal would overcrowd local jails." The push by the governor had

touched off a strong opposition campaign. "The Governor's put it on the leaders' list," James A. Yates, Counsel to the Assembly Codes Committee, said referring to the short agenda of items that Mr. Cuomo wants the Senate and Assembly leaders to resolve before the legislative session ends.

'We want it,' said Mr. Cuomo's criminal justice coordinator, Lawrence T. Kurlander. Stanley Fink, the Assembly speaker, supports the Governor. There has been no formal word from the Senate.

The *Times* went on to report that

law-enforcement officials, who had shared the legislators' belief that the plan was unlikely to be pressed this year, decided recently that Mr. Cuomo would try to have it enacted and met privately in New York City to plan an organized push against it here Monday. They have criticized the plan as too soft on criminals.[45]

With but a few days remaining in the legislative session, the *Times* ran an editorial entitled "New York's Unfinished Business; Still Time for Truth in Sentencing." The editorial hit hard at law enforcement, noting that the bill "remains barely alive in the legislature, having been abandoned by district attorneys. Their defection is based on reasons of narrow interest that ought not to prevail."

The *Times* said that, while district attorneys were initially supportive of determinate sentencing, they

> now object to provisions that preserve some discretion for judges. The chart would supplant the mandatory sentences now in effect for some offenses, and judges could deviate from the chart sentences by 50 percent, provided they state sound reasons.
>
> What's wrong with that? In terms of public safety, nothing. Eliminating mandatory sentences will most likely reduce imprisonment of those convicted of nonviolent crimes and free more cells for violent criminals. Limited and justified deviation from the chart would permit sensible flexibility in special circumstances. The chart would not reduce the number of offenders sent to prison; on the contrary, a major concern is that it may add to the already severe overcrowding.
>
> The prosecutors' objections seem based on an unworthy desire to hoard the sentencing function. Retaining mandatory sentences and working from a more rigid chart would drastically reduce the discretion of the sentencing judge and shift it to the district attorney who selects the charges on which defendant are prosecuted. That parochial concern is no reason to hold up this effort to promote greater truth in sentencing.[46]

Four days later, the *Times* noted that

> Despite much opposition, a plan remains alive for determinate criminal sentences, supplanting the system in which a judge sets a range and a parole board decides when an inmate gets out. Mr. Crotty [then counsel to the governor, subsequently secretary to the governor] called the plan "the strangest issue of the session." There has been widespread opposition, and little organized support, "but it just keeps inching along," he said.

Determinacy Fails

The Senate Responds

Even without the heavy volley of opposition discharged by defense and law-enforcement cannons, it was generally acknowledged that the Democratic governor's sentencing bill would have to surmount major obstacles to gain passage by the Republican-controlled Senate. In 1983 Ralph Marino, then the Chairman of the Senate Committee on Crime and Correction, had warned his colleagues that he was opposed to the formation of a guidelines committee, and that he challenged the assumptions underlying the determinate ideal.[47]

It was generally recognized from the outset that the Senate's endorsement of Chapter 711 was not an endorsement of the committee's product or even an endorsement of determinate sentencing. James Cantwell, then counsel to the Senate Codes Committee, and Jerimiah McKenna, then counsel to the Senate Committee on Crime and Correction, told this author in separate interviews that the Senate considered Chapter 711 a study bill. According to this view, the Bellacosa-Feinberg Committee would study sentencing, provide the legislature with data and recommendations, and the Senate would then decide whether it wanted to abandon the current system. Consequently, senators who supported indeterminacy and opposed determinate sentencing voted for the bill, as did senators who favored determinacy.

Given the internal resistance to the bill, passage in the Senate would have been possible only if external sources pressured the Senate to act. Had law enforcement, the natural ally of the Republican-controlled Senate, fought in support of the bill, it is possible that Senate resistance could have been overcome. In the face of seemingly universal opposition, however, it is not surprising that the the Senate refused to act on the bill. Indeed, there was no indication that any senator was actively supporting the bill, and Senate representatives refused to negotiate the bill with the governor's staff.

The Assembly Responds

Observers might have expected the Democratic-controlled Assembly to support the Democratic governor's bill. And Assembly Speaker Stanley Fink and Codes Chairman Melvin Miller did endorse the bill.[48] Aside from Governor Cuomo and his aides, however, Speaker Fink and Chairman Miller were virtually alone in their support of the bill.

Speaker Fink attempted to persuade his colleagues to support the bill. They refused.[49] Adopting the defense perspective, many in the Assembly saw the sentences as too tough, alternatives to incarceration as too few, and adverse impact on minorities as too great. Many of these concerns were reflected in the sentencing bill introduced by the Black and Puerto Rican Caucus.

Assembly representatives, like their Senate counterparts, were unwilling to negotiate the bill with the governor's staff. Melvin Miller and James Yates claimed that negotiation would be inappropriate because the sentencing committee had already engaged in sufficient compromises; further negotiations would make the bill, which they believed was already too severe, untenable.

The sentencing bill was not reported out of the Senate or Assembly Codes Committees during the 1985 regular legislative session. During the legislature's summer adjournment, the governor's staff continued to seek support for the bill. Attempts were made to get representatives from the Assembly and Senate to discuss the bill over the summer, in the hopes of having a compromise proposal ready for legislative action in the fall. Both

Houses refused to negotiate, with the Assembly continuing to claim that it was not willing to compromise further, and the Senate saying that it was not willing to consider the bill absent significant changes. Determinacy fared no better in 1986. Faced with certain defeat, the Governor decided not to reintroduce the determinate sentencing bill in later legislative sessions.

Attitudes of New York Legislators

A 1985 survey of New York State legislators provides interesting insights into their attitudes about determinacy.[50] The survey suggests that legislators, like other decisionmakers, do not share a common definition of determinacy.

A bare majority of the survey respondents (55 percent) favored determinate sentencing, with 26 percent opposed, and 19 percent neutral.[51] Forty-eight percent of the legislators who described themselves as liberals favored determinate sentencing; 43 percent of those who saw themselves as conservatives favored the reform; and 69 percent of self-labeled middle-of-the-roaders liked determinate sentencing.[52] The findings of the study on legislators' attitudes mirrors the fundamental theme discussed throughout this book: That roughly the same proportion of legislators from both sides of the ideological aisles favored a policy of determinate sentencing indicates that the lawmakers, like other New Yorkers, read their own preferred meaning into the policy issue.

Legislative support for determinacy may have been more illusory than real. Although 55 percent of the legislators said that they supported determinate sentencing, most survey respondents opposed the essential components of determinacy: 69 percent favored forced treatment of offenders, and 86 percent supported early release from prison for offenders who were rehabilitated.[53] Furthermore, only 24 percent favored abolition of the parole board, the fundamental feature of determinate sentencing.[54] Nor did the legislators agree with the philosophical underpinnings of determinacy: When asked about the primary purpose of punishment, 43 percent cited deterrence, 37 percent named incapacitation, 15 percent cited rehabilitation, and only 5 percent listed retribution.[55]

Interviews

James Yates described the reaction to the committee's report:

> There were so many different views of it. That was exactly what I wanted. I wanted people to quit saying "Yes, we like this thing called reform." I wanted them to say "'Here it is, do I like it or don't I?" So there were a lot of sharply different opinions. The Speaker looked at it and said, "You know, this is better than present law. It serves the law-and-order interests while at the same time does accomplish something good and what the heck,

let's do it." Mel [Miller] looked at it and immediately he had the Law Enforcement Council coming in and saying, "This is the worst thing ever, don't do it." And Mel looked at it and said, "You know, you must have had a pretty good compromise."

On our side [Assembly] there was a lot of discussion about whether we should pass the bill or try to hold up and wait to work out an agreement with the Senate rather than just pass the bill ourselves. Criminal justice is the kind of thing that in politics you can be so exploited by either side and each side knows that they can be vulnerable to tomorrow's charge. There's no end to how much you can beat the drums on crime. People therefore tend to be more responsible on both sides of the aisle. While it's true that out in the public forum they'll have a tough stand on crime, [it is different] in the real decisionmaking process... The more important thing is not what you say on the hustings, but what you really do here when you make decisions. We tend not to try and use tactical nuclear arms in the hopes that they won't become strategic. And so we tend not to do things like pass one-House bills [knowing that the bill would not pass the other House] on big crime issues, as a general rule, because we know that then there's no end to it once you start doing that. We try and work out an agreement first.

John Poklemba, then counsel to the director of criminal justice, and subsequently the director of criminal justice and chief criminal justice advisor to the governor:

Chapter 711 was a mistake. It would have been better to do what they did in the federal system, where a commission is appointed to do guidelines that will go into effect unless rejected by the Senate. Chapter 711 called for yet another commission making the same recommendation.

When asked why the governor's program bill was not submitted until five weeks after the issuance of the committee's report, Mr. Poklemba explained:

We realized with Chapter 711 that we would have to negotiate a bill that would pass the legislature. Everyone was offering amendments. It therefore made no sense to indicate what our position would be. There was no interest in the legislature in moving the bill, and there was strong opposition everywhere. We took the committee's bill because it was the best option available. We continued to ask the legislature to sit down and negotiate. They refused—both sides. Jim Yates said that he had already made all the compromises they were going to make. The Senate took the law-enforcement view, saying that the bill reduced mandatories, the sentences were too lenient, and the reclassification of offenses was wrong.

Miller and Fink were for it. Fink lobbied his members...No one wanted a one-House bill. Even if they could have got it out of Codes, or even if the Assembly could have passed it, it was not worth it because there was no way that it would pass the Senate.

When asked about the future of the bill, Mr. Poklemba responded that determinate sentencing was "dead." He said that

> none of the opponents have indicated a willingness to change positions. In the present atmosphere of prison overcrowding, we have to be very careful in tinkering with sentencing provisions. If the law-enforcement objections are met, the Assembly would not pass it. The bottom line is that it is too tough for the Assembly.

Matthew Crosson, former assistant counsel to Governor Cuomo and subsequently chief administrator for the Office of Court Administration, when asked if a different product by the committee might have produced different results, responded:

> The product mattered a great deal. The ultimate product would have in any event been caught between the two poles—conservative and liberal. But if it had come out being associated with law-and-order it would have passed. The Caucus [Black and Puerto Rican Democratic Caucus] would only have twenty-five votes. For example, the rumor that they were eliminating the second felony offender law made all of the difference in the world.

Mr. Crosson recalled the December 20, 1984 meeting of the Bellacosa-Feinberg Committee, during which the committee voted to reduce some of the sentences in the proposed guidelines grid, adopting instead more alternative and jail sentences:

> They never recovered from that. The jail population problem was generated by the same set of decisions. Law enforcement fixed on eliminating the second felony offender law and reducing penalties for drugs. The Republicans fixed on jails.
> Fink really tried—private meetings; it was not for lack of effort. The people just did not like it. The Democratic Caucus said no. It never stood a chance with law enforcement. Morgenthau was frustrated and annoyed. He would have made other concessions, like absorbing inspect and reduce. He had said OK to the C grid.[56] It could have been sold. Twenty-five percent departure would have been OK. One hundred percent departure drove them [law enforcement] crazy.
> The political implications and the prison populations have to be addressed simultaneously. The legislature cannot abdicate their responsibility for sentencing—they can't say the committee did it—their constituents would hang them...Not only are there political problems to overcome, but the empirical problems: It has been a terrible experience in other states.
> It was doable. The further it moved away from law enforcement, it was doomed. Absent their support, active pushing for it, there was no chance. Law enforcement had to say to the legislature "Please do it, we need it." They had to push to overcome skepticism in the legislature.

Said James Cantwell:

The reaction to the bill is interesting. Some thought it lowered penalties; others felt it raised them ... The Senate had wanted the committee to propose a structure that would provide for the enactment of existing law overall. Not a reduction or an increase in penalties.

The bill was not passed in the Assembly because they did not have 76 votes. The Assembly was not willing to negotiate, claiming that the negotiation had been done by the committee ... Everyone was opposed. There was no political percentage in trying to get it passed.

Arthur Liman said:

When Governor Cuomo became Governor, he made the decision that he was going to get through a commission, but I ... suspect that Governor Cuomo has now realized that the commission's recommendations are in the first place politically divisive and are being attacked on the right and on the left, and second, I suspect he realizes that the formulae did not necessarily mean that we'll end up with more just sentences. He sees that there have been tradeoffs and I'm not certain whether Governor Cuomo is prepared to make this a stand or fall issue for his administration. And unless someone is prepared to do that, it won't happen because you could get almost unity of all groups against this kind of a plan.

People don't care about disparity so much any more and the argument for this is disparity. They care about whether or not you're going to take an offense where people now go to prison and you're either going to put them in local jail at local expense or you're going to let them out in the streets.

Guidelines, once they're promulgated, reveal that they are not everything that everybody wanted them to be. They're either too severe for some people or they are too lenient for others. Also, the process loses some of its mystery. If guideline commissions could sit like the priests in old inner sanctums and just come out with their wisdom, then the public might conclude they had a reason for doing what they do. But we [Bellacosa-Feinberg Committee] did ours under the sunshine, and anyone who observed it could see that we had no special claim to expertise. What we tried to do was to find what the norm of sentencing was today and then to adhere to it, and there were tradeoffs, compromises, and we functioned as a legislature of lawyers. That is all we were, and because we were not elected, we did not have to be demagogues. We had our constituencies, brought all of the ideologies to this that you'd expect in a legislature, and so it lost the kind of reverence that mystery can breathe ...

I think that this commission did a superb job. It think it did have a fair balance of flexibility and consistency in its provisions. I think that one of the reasons that it is politically controversial is because achieving that balance will satisfy no one ... Criminal justice has an attraction to the status quo, and unless the Governor, Anderson, and Fink make a pact that it is not perfect, but let's get it through, it is not going to happen. I don't know how much political capital the Governor wants to spend. And I don't fault him for this. The Governor—it's like chips in a poker game. You have a certain number of them, and he has to deal with the economy, the environment, tax equity, school financing, public works, and when he starts doling out his chips—and do you want to use them on this? He cannot get reelected Governor by supporting this program. This is at best neutral and probably it is a liability.

Assemblyman Richard Gottfried, long-time opponent of determinate sentencing had this to say:

> Criminal-justice issues come in fads. The Kennedy legislation and Chapter 711 were the highpoints for determinate sentencing. It was again popular last year as resurgence of interest because of the specific bill. There is still a danger that it could be enacted, but last year may have had the opposite effect of putting nails in the coffin because people finally saw a bill and all were aghast with what they saw...
>
> Fink tried to have the Assembly pass it. This is the only instance I can remember where the Speaker did not get his way...He wanted the Assembly to pass it but almost no one else wanted to do it. So many people inside and outside of the legislature were beating up on the bill that it became senseless.

Lawrence T. Kurlander summed up the fate of determinate sentencing in New York: "Everybody was for determinate sentencing in concept, but when the reality became apparent, the entire western world rebelled."

9

Conclusion: The Rhetoric and the Reality

A fundamental theme permeated this book: A major schism exists between the rhetoric and the reality of the determinate ideal. Support for this proposition was pursued on two fronts. First, I examined the purported purposes of punishment served by the determinate model and the way in which sentencing authority was allocated. Second, I explored determinacy's unique attraction to people with vastly different world views. Both lines of analysis supported the hypothesis that what you see is not what you get, that the advocates of the determinate ideal made many bold claims that could never come to fruition.

Hidden Purpose, Shifting Power

What happens when a sentencing model is ostensibly rooted in retribution and discretion is eliminated or restricted? Will policymakers stop trying to control crime through sentencing? Will discretion disappear?

Throughout the book, it was demonstrated that, despite protestations to the contrary, crime-control purposes of punishment and wide-ranging discretion were omnipresent in the determinate model. In sharp contrast to the rhetoric put forward by the proponents of the new reform, policymakers charged with operationalizing the determinate ideal did not accept retribution as the exclusive, or even as the primary purpose of punishment, nor were they able to avoid the tough decisions inherent in distributing power among criminal justice functionaries.

Purpose and Power in New York

Efforts to implement the determinate ideal were destined to face stiff challenges in New York, where policymakers had long been accustomed to viewing the criminal sanction as a way to control crime and discretionary decisionmaking as an inevitable corollary of that pursuit. From the late 1800s to the early 1970s, the rehabilitative philosophy, which was based on crime-control purposes and discretionary decisionmaking, dominated sentencing policy in New York State.

Encouraged by the work of the American Law Institute's Model Penal Code, New York, along with more than thirty other states, undertook the statutory modernization of its criminal code during the 1960s. As was true in the other states, crime-control purposes of punishment and discretionary decisionmaking suffered few serious challenges from the code revisionists on the Bartlett Commission.

The members of the Bartlett Commission agreed on the purposes of punishment and the allocation of sentencing authority. Utilitarian objectives— rehabilitation, incapacitation, and deterrence—were heralded as the *raison d'etre* for the sentencing system; retributive purposes were relegated to a boundary-setting role.

Reasoning that the objectives of the sentencing system and the allocation of sentencing authority were ineluctably interwoven, the Bartlett Commission laid out a clear plan for linking purpose with power. The legislature would serve the retributive function by establishing sentencing limits for broad classes of criminal conduct. After setting the perimeters, the legislature would delegate control over sentence length to the courts, corrections, and parole, "each to its proper purpose and, within its special sphere of competence, to individualize the sentence."[1] Believing that the desired objectives would only be met if the system was sufficiently flexible and treatment individualized, the Bartlett Commission rejected mandatory incarceration, mandatory minimum sentences, mandatory recidivist laws, and mandatory consecutive sentences.

While the Bartlett Commission was concerned with the statutory modernization of the rehabilitative paradigm, the McGinnis-Oswald Committee sought to implement the tenets of the rehabilitative order into the day-to-day practice of the criminal-justice bureaucracy. The New York legislature was receptive to the recommendations of the McQuinnis-Oswald Committee and began the process of reorganizing the state's criminal-justice bureaucracy in accordance with the actual function performed by each department.

But just as the McGinnis-Oswald Committee was delivering its blueprint for the modernization of the rehabilitative sentencing system, a new antithesis ascended to challenge the reigning paradigm. The indictment against the rehabilitative ideal centered on the purposes of punishment and the allocation of sentencing authority. The challengers claimed that rehabilitationists' pursuit of crime control was a folly and a fraud, and that its generous grants of discretion were antithetical to the rule of law. The newly emerging theory held that offenders were not sick, and they did not require treatment; further, even if they were sick, the criminal justice system was incapable of administering the requisite cure. Incapacitation was a myth. Crimes were not prevented by removing some offenders from society; even if some crimes could be prevented, the price was too high for a democracy to pay, the new breed of reformers said.

Individualization of justice (the euphemism for discretion), the preeminent cornerstone of the rehabilitative system, was declared to be *"prima facie* at war with such concepts . . . as equality, objectivity, and consistency in the law."[2] The consequences of individualization were clear to the reformers: It was but a short leap from discretion to disparity to discrimination. The indeterminate system's basis in expertise, deferred decisionmaking, and parole release was assailed.

The antithesis was quickly transformed into the concept of determinate sentencing. Following the direction suggested by the counts in the indictment against the rehabilitative ideal, proponents of the new model stressed retribution and restrained power.

Endorsed by the Morgenthau Committee, the New York version of determinacy ignored prosecutorial discretion, attempted to tightly constrain judicial discretion, and sought to eliminate parole release discretion. Although the Morgenthau Committee recognized the theoretical validity of the crime-control objective of incapacitation, it claimed that

> our present lack of knowledge severely limits the role that incapacitation can play as a purpose of sentencing . . . Our belief that criminal sanctions should be calibrated to both the seriousness of the offense *and* the prior criminal record of the offender is thus premised more on considerations of justice than crime control. Repeat offenders merit additional punishment because of their sustained unwillingness to abide by the law. If increased penalties for recidivists also have some marginal utility for crime control, we regard this as a subsidiary benefit, rather than a primary purpose, of our sentencing laws.[3]

When testifying at legislative hearings on determinate sentencing, District Attorney Morgenthau candidly admitted that, despite his committee's protestations to the contrary, crime control would inevitably be prominent in the new system. Asked whether determinate sentencing was meant to reduce crime through incapacitation, Mr. Morgenthau replied that it was, and that "we try to get into that by looking at the prior criminal record, because if somebody committed a lot of crimes in a short period of time, it is predicted that they will do it again. That certainly would be cranked into the sentencing system."[4]

Next came the Liman and McQuillan Commissions. While the former repeated the anti-rehabilitationists' rejection of crime-control purposes and discretion, the latter did not, and it can be viewed as a bid at containing the spread of the determinate ideal. Unwilling to accept retribution as the primary purpose of punishment, the members of the McQuillan Commission supported utilitarian sentencing objectives and linked the purposes of punishment with the allocation of sentencing authority. In sharp contrast with the widespread disillusionment with discretion evident in other quarters, the

McQuillan Commission demonstrated little suspicion of the misuse of power and endorsed a policy based on prediction of dangerousness.

When finally the determinate ideal was exposed to the harsh light of explicit policy, the hard questions of the allocation of sentencing authority and the purposes of the criminal sanction could not be escaped. Whether discussing the offense severity scale, prior record scoring, sentence ranges, departure, good time, parole release and supervision, or any of the other interrelated features of their sentencing model, the members of the Bellacosa-Feinberg Committee, the blue-ribbon panel charged with operationalizing the vague concepts of determinacy, were consistently confronted with balancing individualized justice against structured decisionmaking and controlling crime through a retributive mask.

Attracting Strange Bedfellows

This book sought to further expose the gulf between the rhetoric and the reality of the determinate paradigm by examining how the new reform came to appeal to divergent audiences. By casting the benefits to be derived from determinate sentencing in vague terms, its proponents were able to garner support from virtually every corner. When the abstract concepts underlying the amorphous proposals were transformed into specific policies, however, it was apparent why the opposing camps rebelled, finding little to support in the new sentencing model.

How could an ideal with so much promise, with so many supporters, so quickly be cast adrift? The book emphasized the ramifications for public policy of transforming complex ideas into simplistic concepts.

The liberal ideologues who lashed out at the rehabilitative sentencing model hoped to introduce the rule of law into the sentencing system and end arbitrary and capricious decisionmaking. They wanted to make the sentencing system better, to infuse it with fairness, equity, and justice. Believing that the nation's reliance on incarceration was misplaced, the early proponents of the determinate ideal trumpeted the parsimony principle, advocating shorter prison sentences and extended use of alternatives to incarceration. Viewing the parole board as the embodiment of what was wrong with the rehabilitative regime and concerned with the plight of inmates, these early reformers wanted to abolish parole release and the concomitant uncertainty about sentence length.

To attract a larger audience and to win the approval of policymakers, the resort to rhetoric was used to spread the message of determinacy. In so doing, it was easy to avoid specifics; instead, the issue was couched in terms of general social values and vague abstractions.

Expanding determinacy to attract a larger following had many unforeseen consequences, however. The early supporters of determinacy quickly lost control over the substance of the new reform. While generalizing and simplifying the message attracted people with different ideological agendas, it also attracted people with different conceptions of appropriate sentencing policy. As more people jumped on the determinate bandwagon, the liberal reformers' ability to shape policy decisions diminished. Other, more conservative groups began to influence policymakers, convincing them that their definitions and solutions were preferable to those of the originators of the determinate ideal.

The Rise and Fall of the Determinate Ideal in New York

This book examined what happened when the liberal thesis of determinacy was expanded in New York State. By the end of the 1970s, the New York legislature had abandoned much of the rehabilitative sentencing structure, having in 1973 and 1978 reintroduced mandatory sentencing for drug offenders, violent felony offenders, recidivists, and juvenile criminals. Thus, the liberal ideal was thrust into a political environment dominated by get-tough, law-and-order enthusiasts.

Not all politicians are allied with law-enforcement positions, of course, and the New York Legislature reacted to a defense refrain when it enacted the Parole Reform Act of 1977. The Attica prison riot of 1971 had served as the catalyst for the attack on parole release. The McKay Commission, formed in the wake of the bloody riot, reported that discretionary release was "by far the greatest source of inmate anxiety and frustration."[5] New York's parole system was further taken to task by the defense-oriented Citizens' Committee on Parole and Criminal Justice, which found parole release "oppressive and arbitrary" and beyond repair.[6] Spurred by a left-leaning staff report of the Assembly Codes Committee, the Parole Reform Act of 1977 mandated the use of written guidelines in making parole release decisions.

Parole guidelines were an attempt to address the problem of disparity through administrative rule-making. Had the Parole Reform Act of 1977 not been enacted, the policy issue of determinate sentencing might have emerged on New York policymakers' agenda earlier and more forcibly; had policymakers been satisfied with parole guidelines, determinate sentencing might never have attracted such widespread attention.

Despite the introduction of parole guidelines, release decisionmaking remained under attack. Dissatisfied with the direction of reform, some policymakers sought a different solution to disparity. Inspired by sentencing movements in California and the federal system, prominent New Yorkers embraced the determinate ideal.

The Morgenthau Committee, chaired by the New York City District Attorney, Robert M. Morgenthau, crystallized interest in determinate sentencing in New York. While the report of District Attorney Morgenthau's committee read like a liberal manifesto, the system that was being recommended was painted in broad brush strokes. Its component parts were vague and inherently ambiguous, allowing people with differing world-views to read their own preferred meaning into the new reform. That determinate sentencing meant different things to different people was not particularly troubling while the new model remained largely unspecified. Later, when the contradictions could no longer be camouflaged, determinate sentencing would flounder—an untethered abstraction, loose from its moorings.

Interest groups played a major role in New York's movement for determinate sentencing. The public hearings held by the Morgenthau Committee and by the Senate and Assembly Joint Codes Committee illuminated what would be determinate sentencing's fatal flaw: It offered something for everyone, attracting support from opposing ideological camps. The majority of witnesses from both sides of the political aisle supported determinate sentencing: 62 percent of the defense-oriented and 71 percent of the law enforcement-oriented witnesses testified that determinacy would be a much-needed reform. That the new model was so well received by both the left and the right underscored the confusion and ambiguity surrounding determinate sentencing. Was it a liberal or a conservative reform? Some district attorneys liked it; others did not. Some defense attorneys liked it; some did not. Cutting clearly across all the traditional ideological lines, the antithesis was largely undefined, allowing people to draw their own mental images of the proposed new order.

The media also played an influential role. Determinate sentencing received widespread coverage from the state's newspapers. Newspaper editors, like members of interest groups, selectively interpreted determinacy. The *New York Post,* which traditionally appeals to a law-and-order readership, repeatedly demonstrated that people packaged the message of determinate sentencing for themselves. The *Post* claimed that the Morgenthau Committee had called for tough, severe sentences. In truth, the Morgenthau report had all the trappings of a liberal thesis, calling for the least severe sanction and extended use of alternatives to incarceration. Perhaps the *Post* was responding to the occupation of the committee's chairman, rather than the rhetoric of the report.

Governor Carey, while continuing to talk about the need for eradicating disparity and endorsing the Morgenthau Committee's recommendations, failed to appoint a commission to formulate sentencing guidelines. Instead, in 1981 the governor established two more study commissions.

The Liman Commission's recommendations paralleled those of the Morgenthau Committee. Supporters of determinate sentencing were surely dismayed, however, when they saw the McQuillan Commission's blueprint for change. In a report permeated with the trappings of the rehabilitative ideal, the McQuillan Commission advocated a dual-track sentencing system, which was widely viewed as a confusing hybrid. The McQuillan Commission served as a buffer against the expansion of determinate sentencing—a bid at containment that would diffuse support and confuse supporters.

The series of commissions appointed to study New York's sentencing system were intended by some to postpone, perhaps forever, the day of reckoning. With each commission, policymakers bought additional time while giving the appearance of "doing something" about reforming sentencing.

One can only speculate on the fate of the determinate ideal in New York had Mario M. Cuomo not been elected governor in 1982. Without the staunch support of the new governor, the movement for determinate sentencing might have been effectively quashed by the McQuillan Commission's report and by legislative suspicion and concern over the negative impact of the reform on prison crowding.

With the active support of the new governor, the legislature passed Chapter 711 of the Laws of 1983, creating the Bellacosa-Feinberg Committee. Despite casting their votes in favor of Chapter 711, many legislators were suspicious about determinate sentencing. The warning issued by the then-chairman of the Senate Crime and Correction Committee, Ralph Marino, made clear that legislative passage of the product of the guidelines committee was far from certain.What was certain was that legislative support for Chapter 711 would not automatically translate into support for determinate sentencing. Many legislators, especially those in the Republican-controlled Senate, viewed Chapter 711 as mandating yet another study committee, not as the step immediately prior to implementation of determinate sentencing. For some, Chapter 711 was seen as a way of postponing, perhaps indefinitely, a fundamental change in the sentencing system. Indeed, in some respects, the passage of Chapter 711 symbolized another, albeit convoluted, bid at containing the expansion of determinate sentencing.

The Bellacosa-Feinberg Committee confronted seemingly intractable problems as it sought to operationalize the amorphous concepts underlying the determinate ideal. The difficulty encountered in balancing uniformity and equity against individualization and case-by-case decisionmaking proved a constant reminder of the lack of guidance provided by the early proponents of the determinate ideal.

While the divergence between the promise and the reality of determinacy had not been overly apparent, and hence not problematic, when the movement was in its formative stages, once the effort to write the code began, the differences became all too obvious. Faced with conflicting expectations of determinacy, the guidelines committee had no basis for allocating power between the various constellations of authority or for linking power with purpose.

Who would decide whose definition would assert primacy over the others? Without a chart, cast adrift in complexity, the Bellacosa-Feinberg Committee was forced to proceed rudderless from one complex issue to another, each time being forced to navigate through the same murky seas. In the end, the committee agreed to disagree, with eight of its fourteen members filing dissenting opinions, which were peppered throughout the committee's final report.

Long before the Bellacosa-Feinberg Committee finished its work, it was evident that its proposal would face stiff resistance. Only two of the eighty-seven witnesses testifying at the committee's public hearings approved the overall thrust of the report, although they too voiced objections to the specific recommendations. The remaining eight-five witnesses could find little to commend in the committee's operationalization of the determinate ideal. Defense-oriented witnesses claimed that the sentences were too tough; law-enforcement-oriented witnesses thought that they were not tough enough.

The response was no different once the committee's divided recommendations were published. No one was satisfied. That former supporters of determinate sentencing would object to the recommendations of the sentencing committee was not surprising. The clash between the rhetoric and the reality of the determinate ideal was by then patently evident.

Defense interests submitted their own sentencing bill, introduced by the Black and Puerto Rican Caucus, made up of Democratic members of the Assembly and Senate. Law enforcement also attacked the determinate sentencing bill with vigor, seeking to limit judicial discretion by tightening departure and to increase prosecutorial discretion by widening the sentence ranges.[7]

The Republican-controlled Senate opposed the governor's sentencing bill, as did the Democratic Assembly. Passage of the bill in the Senate would have been possible only if the bill were supported strongly by law enforcement. It was not, and the guidelines bill languished in the Senate Codes Committee.

While Assembly Democrats might normally have been expected to support the Democratic governor's bill, they too objected, claiming that the sentencing bill was too tough, that it provided insufficient alternatives to incarceration, and that it would have an adverse affect on minorities. In the end, the seemingly universal opposition kept the determinate sentencing bill from reaching the floor of the Assembly or Senate, having died in the respective Codes Committees.

Linking the Themes

This book exposed the schism between the promise and the reality of the determinate ideal by examining two phenomena. First, I discussed the distribution of power and the purposes of punishment in the determinate model. Second, I followed the path from abstract to concrete, and explored the consequences of attracting support from widely divergent ideological groups. These two themes are inexorably linked. The explanation for the rise and fall of the determinate model in New York is found, in part, in its failure to recognize the inevitability of the exercise of discretion at all points in the criminal-justice system and its refusal to take a hard look at the purposes undergirding the imposition of the criminal sanction. Had the proponents of the determinate ideal carefully considered the role of prosecutorial and prison-guard discretion, had they clearly balanced judicial discretion against dispari-ty reduction, had they recognized the legitimacy and necessity of trying to control crime through sentencing, they would perhaps have decided to for-sake their conceptual ideal and seek instead a theoretical model more in har-mony with the reality of the criminal-justice system.

How is Determinacy Doing?

The determinate ideal failed in New York State, but it ostensibly succeeded in other jurisdictions. What has happened in the states that have adopted determinate sentencing systems? Has discretion been reduced or merely realigned? Has retributive justice prevailed, or have the old crime-control purposes of punishment resurfaced?

The full impact of determinacy has not been fully evaluated yet. In some states, the reform is too new to assess its impact; in others, a lack of critical research makes it difficult to judge the practical outcome of the reform move-ment. The following overview is by no means exhaustive, but it is suggestive.

Discretion is apparently alive and well in Indiana. Rather than removing discretion, researchers found that the new system simply moved it. Prosecu-tors, through charge and sentencing bargaining, and prison guards, through good-time decisions, have become the sentencing powers in Indiana.[8]

The results from Minnesota are less clear. The Minnesota sentencing commission has issued several research reports, most of which have been quite positive. Judges are said to be following the guidelines closely. The original indications were that imprisonment patterns had changed in the intended direction, with more violent and fewer property offenders being incarcerated. Disparity was reported to have been reduced.[9]

Compliance with the guidelines is high in Minnesota, but this does not necessarily mean that the system is working as intended. Rather, recent research indicates that prosecutorial discretion is dominating sentencing decisions in Minnesota.[10] Prosecutors are circumventing the system and thwarting the intent of the guidelines.

It should be no surprise that prosecutors have learned to manipulate the system, changing their plea bargaining practices to ensure the results they want. Rather than first deciding on the offense to be charged and selecting an appropriate grid cell, prosecutors choose the sentence they want, and there-after enter into the charge or sentence bargain that yields the desired result.

Minnesota prosecutors have also manipulated the sentencing system by increasing the number of charges filed in each case. If offenders are convict-ed simultaneously of multiple offenses, prior record scores can increase, with the result that imprisonment is more likely, even for property offenses. The drafters of the Minnesota guidelines wanted to reserve prison space for violent felons, but they failed to anticipate that prosecutors would build up prior record scores, with the result that more nonviolent, property offenders would be sent to prison.[11]

While the Minnesota guidelines may have initially changed imprisonment trends in the desired direction, the patterns now appear to be shifting towards the pre-guidelines days. Research indicates that compliance with the guidelines has dropped, departure is on the rise, and prison rates for certain property offenders have almost reached their former levels.[12]

Washington's experience with determinacy is new and thus difficult to evaluate. The limited research that does exist suggests that the guidelines are being followed closely. One study found that departure sentences made up just 3 percent of sentences in the study period.[13] It is likely, however, that future researchers will uncover untoward results.

Pennsylvania's guidelines are hard to evaluate. The extreme width of the sentencing ranges in the grid allow for vast sentencing discrepancy even without departure sentences. Nevertheless, departures are common, and the guidelines system does not appear to provide much guidance to Pennsylvania's judiciary.[14]

Not surprisingly, the research on California suggests that prosecutors have become much more powerful under the new system. Sentencing bargaining has increased considerably. By controlling the number of charges filed and by moving for a variety of sentence enhancements, prosecutors in practice control sentencing outcomes in California.[15] A more detailed summary of the California experience follows.

A Comparative Perspective

Comparing the evolution of the determinate ideal in California and New York provides a different perspective on the movement for determinate sentencing.

California and New York are similar in several significant respects. Both have large urban populations, both have large minority populations, and both have large prison populations. Remarkable parallels exist between legislative sentencing initiatives in California, a determinate sentencing state, and legislative sentencing initiatives in New York, an indeterminate sentencing state. During the same period, both states repeatedly revised their sentencing structures; both states' revisions were aimed at increasing the severity of the criminal sanction through mandatory imprisonment statutes; and both states experienced substantial increases in prison populations as a result.

The two states represent polar extremes, however, in the evolution of the determinate ideal. Determinate sentencing matured rapidly in California, whereas it followed a long and tortuous path in New York. While policymakers in both states were influenced by the rhetoric of the liberal creators, in California the movement for determinate sentencing began in earnest in 1974 and culminated in 1976 with the passage of the Uniform Determinate Sentence Law, whereas in New York interest in determinate sentencing crystallized in 1979 with the issuance of the Morgenthau Committee's report but, as of this writing in 1990, the movement for determinate sentencing in New York appears lost. Thus, the experience in the two states are counterpoints, one a "failure," the other a "success."

Understanding the Different Outcomes

That California adopted determinate sentencing and New York did not can be understood, in part, by examining four fundamental differences between the development of determinacy in the two states. Most notable among these differences was the virtually unfettered sentencing discretion exercised by the Adult Authority, California's paroling agency, prior to the enactment of determinate sentencing. Having rejected the American Law Institute's Model Penal Code approach, California carried the rehabilitative ideal to its logical extreme. Judges merely sentenced the offender to the term prescribed by law, which generally was zero to life or five years to life. The Adult Authority determined the actual prison sentence and the length of the parole supervision term. Its sentencing discretion was absolute, unregulated by statute, administrative rules, or case law. Thus, determinate sentencing supporters in California confronted a parole board with enormous sentencing power. Attackers of California's rehabilitative regime could legitimately decry its standardless decisionmaking.

Determinate sentencing advocates in New York confronted a different dynamic. The New York legislature had restricted the Parole Board's discretion within the context of the indeterminate sentencing structure. In adopting the Model Penal Code's sentencing categorizations, New York had reduced the length of the maximum prison terms, thereby providing limits on parole discretion. Since 1973, the board had operated in an environment of legislatively-set mandatory sentencing provisions, including mandatory incarceration, mandatory minimum sentences, mandatory plea bargaining, and mandatory consecutive sentence provisions. The Parole Reform Act of 1977, which required the board to use written guidelines in making its release decision, provided further checks on the parole's discretion. Since 1980, again to curtail the board's discretion, courts have been required to set the minimum term of imprisonment for all offenders.

The second fundamental difference between the two states centers on the role of the judiciary. California's Supreme Court and Court of Appeals assumed a pivotal role in the adoption of determinate sentencing. In deciding *In Re Lynch* and *In Re Foss*, the California Supreme Court chipped away at the rehabilitative ideal by establishing a proportionality test for sentence length under the indeterminate sentence. *In Re Rodriquez* further undercut the rehabilitative bastions by attacking the term-setting power of the Adult

Authority. *In Re Stanley* invalidated a directive by the chairman of the Adult Authority calling for early time-fixes based on the seriousness of the offense and the offender's prior criminal record.[16] In quashing the parole authority's bid at containing the spread of determinacy, *Stanley* acted as a catalyst, convincing California Governor Edmund Brown, Jr. that legislative action was necessary. The Determinate Sentence Law was passed by both Houses of the California legislature shortly after the *Stanley* decision was handed down.

New York's judiciary, unlike its California counterpart, has not seriously challenged the rehabilitative regime. New York's highest court, the Court of Appeals, is statutorily precluded from reviewing sentences unless the intermediate appellate court decision was illegal or rested exclusively on questions of law or upon the law and "such facts, which but for the determination of law, would not have led to reversal or modification." The state's highest court cannot reduce a sentence in the interests of justice.[17] A sentence is legal if it is within statutorily prescribed limits.[18] Thus limited, the New York State Court of Appeals has not raised serious challenges to the rehabilitative sentencing structure.

New York's four Appellate Divisions are statutorily authorized to review and reduce sentences that are harsh or excessive.[19] The prosecutor cannot, however, appeal a sentence as too lenient. It is well established in case law that the imposition of a sentence is within the discretion of the trial court. The Appellate Divisions consequently do not interfere with the exercise of the court's sentencing discretion unless there is a clear abuse of discretion, or extraordinary circumstances justify a lesser sentence in the interests of justice.[20]

Third, the opposite outcomes in the two states can be understood by considering the role of determinate sentencing's proponents. While determinate sentencing owes its passage in California to a bizarre coalition of liberal and conservative supporters, determinate sentencing's demise in New York can be traced to a bizarre coalition of liberal and conservative proponents turned opponents.

The Prisoners Union and other liberal groups in California supported determinate sentencing because of its perceived equity and fairness; law enforcement was attracted to the certainty of punishment, especially for violent and repeat offenders. In New York, people from differing ideological persuasions favored the concept of creating a sentencing commission to develop sentencing guidelines. Once the code was set down, however, both sides rebelled. Liberals were convinced that the sentences were too tough, conservatives that they were not tough enough.

Finally, the different outcomes are attributable to the negative reviews received about determinate sentencing in the 1980s. When Californians adopted determinate sentencing, they were pioneers. By 1985, when the New York Legislature considered the question, a wealth of experience from other states was available, much of which suggested that determinate sentencing was associated with sharp rises in prison populations.[21]

Crime Control and Discretion Live On

The New York sentencing commission was not alone in its inability to avoid crime-control purposes of punishment and forsake discretion. The breadth of the discretion inherent in California's version of determinate sentencing is impressive. Although mandatory sentencing provisions have increased in recent years, the most fundamental decision—whether to incarcerate the offender—continues to be left to courtroom actors in many instances. The aggravating and mitigating factors that make up the California system are so general as to justify virtually any sentencing outcome. Charging discretion is unstructured, and prosecutors decide whether to charge enhancements or aggravating factors. Courts retain the discretion to impose enhancements or departure factors once they have been proved by the prosecutor.

Crime-control purposes of punishment are thriving, despite the overt statement in the California Determinate Sentencing Law "that the purpose of imprisonment for crime is punishment." For example, California courts are instructed to consider dangerousness when deciding whether to incarcerate an offender; being a danger to society is an aggravating factor that courts are encouraged to consider. The California experience reinforces the theme that guided this book. Regardless of the philosophy of the sentencing model, authority and responsibility must be allocated among criminal-justice practitioners. Failing to provide for the rational exercise of discretion will not make discretion disappear, although it may force it underground.

I contend that rather than seeking to dismantle discretion, sentencing models should provide for the just and ordered allocation of sentencing authority. The consequences of failing to do so are antithetical to the very promise undergirding the determinate ideal. Standardless and hidden decisionmaking flourishes when covert practices remain hidden.

Nor can sentencing systems divorce themselves from the pursuit of crime control. Even where utilitarian purposes are obfuscated by the rhetoric of determinacy, decisionmakers seek to control crime through the imposition of the criminal sanction. Like ignoring the reality of discretionary decisionmaking, ignoring crime-control purposes virtually guarantees an intolerable divergence between the expressed goals and the real policy of the sentencing system.

The theory undergirding determinate sentencing is intuitively appealing: Like offenders should receive like punishment, discretion should be guided by the rule of law, equity, justice, and truth should prevail. But theories, no matter how grand and intellectually satisfying, do not always translate into sound public policy. As this book has shown, turning a blind eye on the allocation of sentencing discretion and the crime-control purposes of punishment does not bode well for public policy.

Paradigm Shifts

The history of sentencing reform in New York State reveals an oscillating pattern: from discretionary sentences, to determinate sentences, to discretionary sentences, to an unsuccessful attempt to return to determinate sentences. This history of paradigm shifts suggests that sentencing policy bears a heavy and unrealistic burden. Unable to cure the ills of the criminal-justice system, incapable of confronting the broader inequities that have always been present in American society, the sentencing system is often attacked as a failure.

The determinate ideal arose as a reaction, a backlash against the perceived evil of the reigning paradigm. While the theoretical underpinnings of determinacy attracted a large following, in practice the determinate ideal has not lived up to the dreams or the promises of its creators.

History teaches that the sentencing pendulum will swing again in the future. Like a dialectic searching for synthesis, sentencing policy in New York and elsewhere around the nation will continue to undergo challenge and change.

APPENDIX I
PUBLIC HEARINGS ON
DETERMINATE SENTENCING

The following decision rules were developed for determining whether witnesses testifying at public hearings on determinate sentencing would be categorized as affiliated with defense or law-enforcement interests.

Professional Affiliation: A witness testifying on behalf of an organization known to take an ideological position aligned with defense or law-enforcement interests was assigned to the respective group on the basis of the witnesses' affiliation. For example, representatives of Prisoners' Legal Services, NAACP, and the American Civil Liberties Union were assigned to the defense category; district attorneys and police were assigned to the law-enforcement category.[1]

In many instances, it was not possible to identify the witnesses' ideological position from knowledge of their professional affiliation. For example, judges, professors, and bar association members could not be placed in a category on the basis of their professional affiliation. In such cases, witnesses would not be identified with an ideological position unless their testimony could also be coded on at least two of the following dimensions.

Alternative v. Incarcerative Sentences: Defense-oriented witnesses would recommend extended use of alternatives to incarceration, while law-enforcement witnesses would urge that the present incarcerative policy be perpetuated or extended.

Mandatory v. Discretionary Sentences: Defense interests would favor a variety of sentencing options and oppose the continuation or extension of mandatory statutes. Law-enforcement advocates would urge the continuation or expansion of mandatory sentencing.

Least Severe v. More Severe Sentences: Defense-oriented witnesses would argue that the sentence should be the least drastic consistent with public safety. Law-enforcement witnesses would contend that severe sentences are necessary.

Short v. Long Sentences: When a prison sentence was imposed, the groups would diverge, in the expected direction, on the length of the incarcerative term.

Equity v. Certainty: Defense witnesses would be attracted to equity and

187

fairness; law enforcement to certainty of punishment.

   Incarceration Fails v. Incarceration Succeeds: Defense groups would view incarceration as counterproductive. To law-enforcement groups, incarceration would be seen as the primary crime-control strategy.

APPENDIX II
INTERVIEWS

The following people graciously agreed to be interviewed for this study. I am grateful for their candor and insights. The professional affiliations noted are those of the interviewee at the time of his involvement with sentencing policy; many of the respondents subsequently assumed new professional responsibilities.

Richard Bartlett, chairman of the Bartlett Commission

James Cantwell, counsel to the Senate Codes Committee

Matthew Crosson, assistant counsel to Governor Cuomo

Scott Fein, assistant counsel to both Governors Carey and Cuomo

Senator Emanuel Gold, member of the Morgenthau Committee and deputy minority leader of the Senate

Assemblyman Richard Gottfried, Chairman of the Assembly Codes Committee, 1977–78, and long-time opponent of determinate sentencing

Edward Hammock, former chairman of the Board of Parole and director of the Division of Parole

Lawrence T. Kurlander, director of Criminal Justice and commissioner of the Division of Criminal Justice Services

Arthur Liman, counsel to the McKay Commission, member of the Morgenthau and Bellacosa-Feinberg Committees, chairman of the Liman Commission

Jerimiah McKenna, counsel to the Senate Committee on Crime and Corrections

Peter McQuillan, staff member of the Bartlett Commission, chairman of the McQuillan Commission

John Poklemba, counsel to the director of Criminal Justice and the Division of Criminal Justice Services

Peter Preiser, sentencing architect for the Bartlett Commission and executive director of the McQuinnis-Oswald Committee, currently a professor at Albany Law School and a consultant to the New York State Senate

Howard Shapiro, assistant counsel to Governor Rockefeller

Clarence Sundrum, assistant counsel to Governor Carey

James Yates, counsel to the Assembly Codes Committee and member of the Bellacosa-Feinberg Committee.

APPENDIX III
CHAPTER 711 OF THE LAWS OF 1983

Committee Composition

Chapter 711 established a fourteen-member committee, with appointments made by each branch of government. The chief judge of the Court of Appeals would appoint two criminal court judges. The governor would have six appointments: one defense attorney, one prosecutor, one non-lawyer with a probation background, one person with a background in sentencing policy and quantitative research, and two members of the bar. The legislature would have six appointments, each a member of the state bar: The temporary president of the Senate and the speaker of the Assembly would each appoint two members, and the minority leaders of the Senate and Assembly would each appoint one member.

The governor would designate one of the appointees as chairman; the temporary president of the Senate and the speaker of the Assembly would each select one appointee to be associate chairmen. No senator or member of the Assembly would be eligible for membership. Members would receive no compensation for their services.

Committee Mandate

Chapter 711 provided the Bellacosa-Feinberg Committee with but a sketch of its assignment. The pertinent sections of the enabling legislation are presented in full below.

Section 2. Principles of Sentencing The committee on sentencing guidelines shall premise the guidelines upon the following principles:

1. Similar crimes committed under similar circumstances by similar offenders should receive similar sanctions. The severity of criminal sanctions should be directly related to the seriousness of the offense and the offender's prior criminal record.
2. The sanction imposed should be a measure consistent with the principles of sentencing set forth herein.[1]
3. Sanctions of incarceration shall be established when:
   a. confinement is appropriate to protect society by restraining a

defendant who has a history of conviction for serious criminal conduct;

b. confinement is appropriate to justly punish a defendant or to avoid deprecating the seriousness of the offense;

c. confinement is appropriate to provide an effective deterrent to others likely to commit similar offenses; or

d. measures less restrictive than confinement have been applied frequently or recently to a defendant and have been unsuccessful.

4. In formulating sentencing guidelines the committee shall consider availability of probation resources, resources of the division of parole, and resources of any other alternative to detention or incarceration as well as prison resources and local jail resources.

Section 3. Powers and Duties of Committee

1. The committee shall transmit sentencing guidelines and recommend statutory amendments required for their implementation to the governor and legislature on January fifteenth, nineteen hundred eighty-five. Such guidelines shall have no force and effect unless enacted into law. The guidelines shall prescribe non-incarcerative and incarcerative sentences which shall be imposed upon conviction of a crime.

a. The guidelines shall conform to the principles of sentencing established by this act.

b. Sentences of incarceration, when required by the terms of the guidelines so established, shall be definite sentences. The length of incarceration to be served by a defendant under a definite sentence shall be the period of time imposed by the sentencing court, less good time.

c. Sentencing guidelines shall specify the non-incarcerative sentence or incarcerative sentencing range which is presumptively appropriate for each offense, based upon the seriousness of the offense and the prior criminal history of the offender. The guidelines shall further provide for specified aggravating and mitigating circumstances which may be taken into account by a sentencing court and a procedural mechanism for determining sentences for purposes of deviating from the presumptively appropriate sentences to the extent authorized by the guidelines.

2. The committee shall monitor the operation of the sentencing guidelines and if appropriate recommend modification of the guidelines. The committee shall transmit a report to the governor and the legislature every two years on the operation of the guidelines and recommend modification, if any, of the guidelines.

3. Duties of the committee. The committee shall recommend all necessary or appropriate amendments to the penal law, the criminal proce-

dure law, the correction law and the executive law necessary for implementing the guidelines which shall include:

a. the repeal of all provisions of law inconsistent with this act or the guidelines established by the committee, and recommending conforming amendments where appropriate;

b. the redefinition of any crime if the current definition needs further articulation to conform to the principles of this act or the guidelines recommended by the committee;

c. the establishment of a mechanism for time allowances for good behavior for incarcerated inmates;

d. the establishment of a mechanism for the division of parole to compute and apply time allowances for good behavior;

e. the provision of a statement of the estimated effect of the guidelines on judicial, prosecution and defense resources, prison population, jail population, probation and parole services;

f. the establishment of a mechanism by which the court may review the sufficiency of evidence to support charges contained within an accusatory instrument; and

g. the establishment of a procedure for appellate review by either party to ensure proper operation of the guidelines.

REFERENCES

Adams, Stuart S. "Evaluating Correctional Treatments." *Criminal Justice and Behavior* 4 (1977):323–340.

Advisory Commission on Criminal Sanctions. *Report of the Advisory Commission on Criminal Sanctions,* Parts I, II and III. New York: Advisory Commission on Criminal Sactions, 1982.

Allen, Francis A. *The Borderland of Criminal Justice: Essays in Law and Criminology.* Chicago: University of Chicago Press, 1964.

———. *The Decline of the Rehabilitative Ideal: Penal Policy and Social Purpose.* New Haven: Yale University Press, 1981 .

American Friends Service Committee. *Struggle for Justice.* New York: Hill and Wang, 1971.

American Law Institute. *Official Draft of the Model Penal Code.* Philadelphia: American Law Institute, 1962.

Beccaria, Cesare. *On Crime and Punishment.* London: J. Almon, 1776.

Blumstein, Alfred; Jacqueline Cohen; Susan E. Martin; and Michael H. Tonry, eds. *Research on Sentencing: The Search for Reform Volume I.* Washington, D.C.: National Academy Press, 1983.

Bureau of Justice Statistics. *Report to the Nation on Crime and Justice: The Data.* Washington, D.C.: U.S. Department of Justice, 1983.

———. *Setting Prison Terms.* Washington D.C.: U.S. Department of Justice, 1983.

California Board of Prison Terms. *Sentencing Patterns under the Determinate Sentencing Law.* Sacramento: Youth and Adult Correctional Agency, 1983.

Casper, Jonathan D.; David Brereton; and David Neal. "The California Determinate Sentence Law." *Criminal Law Bulletin* 19 (September–October 1983): 405–433.

———. *The Implementation of the California Determinate Sentencing Law.* Washington, D.C.: U.S. Department of Justice, 1982.

Cassou, April K., and Brian Taugher. "Determinate Sentencing in California: The New Numbers Game." *Pacific Law Journal* 9 (January 1978).

Citizens' Inquiry on Parole and Criminal Justice *Report on New York Parole.* New York: Citizens' Inquiry on Parole and Criminal Justice, Inc., 1974.

———. *Prison Without Walls: Report on New York Parole.* New York: Praeger, 1975.

City of New York. *Mayor's Survey of the Criminal Justice System.* New York: 1981.

Clear, Todd; John Hewitt; and Robert Regoli. "Discretion and the Determinate Sentence: Its Distribution, Control and Effect on Time Served." *Crime and Delinquency* 24 (1978).

Cobb, Roger W., and Charles D. Elder. *Participation in American Politics: The Dynamics of Agenda-Building*. Boston: Allen and Bacon, Inc., 1972.

Codes Committee of the New York State Assembly (Staff Report). *Paul Said "But I Was Free Born": A Report on Parole Reform*. Albany: Codes Committee of the New York State Assembly, 1976.

Committee for the Study of Incarceration. *Doing Justice*. New York: Hill and Wang, 1975.

Cuomo, Governor Mario M. (Remarks) *Governor's Conference on Law Enforcement*. Latham, N.Y., October 10, 1984.

District Attorneys' Association. *Memorandum in Opposition to A. 7127 Determinate Sentencing*. New York State District Attorneys' Association. June 11, 1985.

Duffee, David E. *Corrections: Practice and Policy*. New York: Random House, 1989.

Epstein, Edward J. "The Great Rockefeller Power Machine." *New York Magazine* (November 24, 1975): 71.

Executive Advisory Commission on the Administration of Justice. *Recommendations to Governor Hugh L. Carey Regarding Prison Overcrowding*. New York: Executive Advisory Commission on the Administration of Justice, 1982.

———. *Recommendations to the Governor Regarding the Administration of the Criminal Justice System*. New York: Executive Adviory Commission of the Administration of Justice, 1982.

Executive Advisory Committee on Sentencing (Morgenthau Committee). *Crime and Punishment in New York: An Inquiry into Sentencing and the Criminal Justice System*. New York: Executive Advisory Committee on Sentencing, 1979.

———. *Crime and Punishment in New York: An Inquiry into Sentencing and the Criminal Justice System. Appendix*. New York: Executive Advisory Committee on Sentencing, 1979.

Feeley, Malcolm. *Court Reform on Trial*. New York: Basic Books, 1983.

Flanagan, Timothy J. and Edmund F. McGarrell. *Attitudes of New York Legislators Toward Crime and Criminal Justice: A Report of the State Legislator Survey—1985*. Albany: The Hindelang Criminal Justice Research Center, State University of New York Albany, 1986.

Fletcher, George. "The Recidivist Premium." *Criminal Justice Ethics* 54 (Summer–Fall 1982): 54–59.

Frankel, Marvin. *Criminal Sentences: Law Without Order*. New York: Hill and Wang, 1972.

Gamson, William A. *The Strategy of Social Protest*. Homewood, Ill.: Dorsey Press, 1975.

George, B. J., Jr. "A Comparative Analysis of the New Penal Laws of New York and Michigan." *Buffalo Law Review* 2 (1968): 233–250.

Goebel, J., and T. R. Naughton. *Law Enforcement in Colonial New York* (1944), p. 702, cited by New York State Executive Advisory Committee on Sentencing, *Crime and Punishment in New York*. New York: New York State Executive Advisory Committee on Sentencing, 1979: 158.

Goodstein, Lynne; John R. Hepburn; John H. Kramer; and Doris L. MacKenzie. *Determinate Sentencing and the Correctional Process: A Study of the Implementation and Impact of Sentencing Reform in Three States—Executive Summary.* Washington, D.C.: United States Government Printing Office, 1984.

Gordon, Walter L. III. *Crime and California Law: The California Experience 1960–1975.* Gaithersburg, Md.: Associated Faculty Press, 1981.

Governor's Panel on Juvenile Violence (Cahill Commission). *Report to the Governor.* Albany: Panel on Juvenile Violence, 1976.

Governor's Special Committee on Criminal Offenders (McGinnis-Oswald Committee). *Preliminary Report of the Governor's Special Committee on Criminal Offenders.* New York: State of New York, 1968.

Hart, H. L. A. "Prolegomenon to the Principles of Punishment." In *Sentencing:* 7–22. Hyman Gross and Andrew von Hirsch, eds. New York: Oxford University Press, 1981.

Howard, Dick. *Determinate Sentencing in California.* Lexington, Ky.: Council of State Goverments, 1978.

Jacobs, James B. "Sentencing by Prison Personnel: Good Time." *UCLA Law Review* 30 (December 1982): 217–270.

Koch, Edward I. *Mayor's Survey of Criminal Justice.* New York, 1981.

Kramer, John H. et al. *Assessing the Impact of Determinate Sentencing and Parole Abolition in Maine.* University Park, Pa.: Pennsylvania State University, Institute for Human Development, 1978.

Kramer, John H.; John P. McClosky; and Nancy J. Kurtz. *Sentencing Reform: The Pennsylvania Commission on Sentencing.* Paper presented at the 1982 annual meeting of the Academy of Criminal Justice Sciences, Louisville, Kentucky.

Lagoy, Stephen; Frederick A. Hussey; and John H. Kramer. "A Comparative Assessment of Determinate Sentencing in the Four Pioneer States." *Crime and Delinquency* 24 (1978): 385–400.

Law Enforcement Council. *New York State Law Enforcement Council Criticizes Determinate Sentencing Bill.* New York State Law Enforcement Council. June 17, 1985.

Legislative Commission on Expenditure Review. *State Prison Release Programs.* Albany: Legislative Commission on Expenditure Review, 1984.

Levine, Howard A. "The New York Penal Law: A Prosecutor's Evaluation." *Buffalo Law Review* 18 (1968): 269–283.

Lewis, Orlando F. *The Development of American Prisons and Prison Customs, 1776–1845.* Albany: Prison Association of New York, 1922.

Lindsey, Edward. "Historical Sketch of the Indeterminate Sentence and Parole System." *Journal of Criminal Law and Criminology* (May 1925):21.

Lipton, Douglas; Robert Martinson; and Judith Wilks. *The Effectiveness of Correctional Treatment: A Survey of Treatment Evaluation Studies.* New York: Praeger, 1975.

Marino, Ralph. *Determinate Sentencing: Danger Ahead.* Albany: New York State Senate Committee on Crime and Correction, 1983.

Martinson, Robert. "What Works? Questions and Answers About Prison Reform."
    The Public Interest 35 (1974): 22–54.
McGarrell, Edmund F. *Changes in New York's Juvenile Corrections System.* Rocke-
    feller Institute Working Papers, No. 22. Albany: The Nelson A. Rocke-
    feller Institute of Government, 1985.
————. "The Role of the Media in Juvenile Justice Policymaking: The New York
    Case." Paper presented at the annual meeting of the American Society
    of Criminology, San Diego, California, 1985.
McKinney's New York Session Laws. Volumes from 1960–1985. St. Paul, Minn.:
    West Publishing Company.
McKinney's Consolidated Laws of New York. Volumes from 1960–1985. St. Paul,
    Minn.: West Publishing Company.
Messinger, Sheldon, and Phillip Johnson. "California's Determinate Sentencing
    Statute: History and Issues." In *Determinate Sentencing: Reform or
    Regression?* Washington, D.C.: Government Printing Office, 1977:
    13–58.
Messinger, Sheldon; Andrew Von Hirsch; and Richard F. Sparks. *A Report on Strate-
    gies of Determinate Sentencing.* Washington, D.C.: The National Insti-
    tute of Justice, 1984.
Miller, Alden D.; Lloyd E. Ohlin; and Robert B. Coates. *A Theory of Social Reform:
    Correction   Change   Processes   in   Two   States.* Cambridge,
    Mass.:Ballinger, 1977.
————. "Evaluating Correctional Systems under Normalcy and Change." In *Hand-
    book of Criminal Justice Evaluation.* Edited by Malcolm W. Klein and
    Katherine S. Teilman. Beverly Hills, Calif.: Sage, 1980.
Minneosota Sentencing Guidelines Commission. *The Impact of the Minnesota Sen-
    tencing Guidelines: Three-Year Evaluations.* St. Paul, Minn.: Minnesota
    Sentencing Guidelines Commission, 1984.
————. *Preliminary Report on the Development and Impact of the Minnesota Sen-
    tencing Guidelines.* St. Paul, Minn.: Minnesota Sentencing Guidelines
    Commission, 1982.
Mitford, Jessica. *Kind and Usual Punishment: The Prison Business.* New York:
    Alfred A. Knopf, 1973.
Morris, Norval. *The Future of Imprisonment.* Chicago: University of Chicago Press,
    1974.
Murrah, Alfred P. and Sol Rubin. "Penal Reform and the Model Sentencing Act."
    Columbia Law Review 65 (1965): 1167–1183.
New York State Assembly and Senate Joint Codes Committee Hearings on Determi-
    nate Sentencing, 1979.
New York State Committee on Sentencing Guidelines. *Determinate Sentencing: A
    Preliminary Proposal for Public Comment.* Albany: New York State
    Committee on Sentencing Guidelines, 1985.
————. *Determinate Sentencing: Report and Recommendations.* Albany: New York
    State Committee on Sentencing Guidelines, 1985.
————. *Minutes of the Monthly Meetings.* November 1983–September 1985. Albany:
    New York State Committee on Sentencing Guidelines, 1985.

New York State Department of Correctional Services. *Trends in Time Served by the Under-Custody Population: 1975–1986.* Albany, Department of Correctional Services, 1986.

New York State Law Enforcement Council. *New York State Law Enforcement Council Criticizes Determinate Sentencing Bill.* June 17, 1985.

New York State Special Commission on Attica. *Attica: The Official Report of the New York State Commission on Attica.* New York: Bantam Books, 1972.

New York Temporary Commission on Revision of the Penal Law and Criminal Code (Bartlett Commission). *Commission Staff Notes.* Brooklyn: Edward Thompson Co., 1964.

——. *Interim Report of the State of New York Temporary Committee on Revision of the Penal Law and Criminal Code.* Leg. Doc. 8, 1963.

——. *Interim Report of the State of New York Temporary Committee on Revision of the Penal Law and Criminal Code.* Leg. Doc. 41, 1962.

——. *Proposed New York Penal Law.* Brooklyn: Edward Thompson Co., 1964.

——. *Third Interim Report of the State of New York Temporary Commission on Revisions of the Penal Law and Criminal Code.* Leg. Doc. 14, 1964.

O'Leary, Vincent et al. "Policies Toward Crime and the Criminal Justice System. " In *Rockefeller In Retrospect: The Governor's New York Legacy,* Gerald Benjamin and T. Norman Hurd, eds. Albany: The Nelson A. Rockefeller Institute of Government, 1984.

Palmer, Ted. "Martinson Revisited." *Crime and Delinquency* 4 (1975).

Persico, Joseph E. *The Imperial Rockefeller.* New York: Simon and Schuster, 1982.

Phillips, H. J. "Final Report of the Maine Sentencing Commission." A report submitted to the 111th Maine Legislature. Augusta, Ga.: 1984.

President's Commission on Law Enforcement and the Administration of Justice. *The Challenge of Crime in a Free Society.* Washington, D.C.: U.S. Government Printing Office, 1967.

Rockefeller, Nelson A. *Public Papers of Nelson A. Rockefeller, Fifty-Third Governor of the State of New York.* Albany: New York State, 1973.

Rothman, David J. *Conscience and Convenience: The Asylum and its Alternatives in Progressive America.* Boston: Little, Brown and Company, 1980.

——. "Decarcerating Prisoners and Patients." *Civil Liberties Review* 1 (1980): 130–147.

——. *The Discovery of the Asylum: Social Order and Disorder in the New Republic.* Boston: Little, Brown and Company, 1971.

——. "Sentencing Reform in Historical Perspective." *Crime and Delinquency* (October 1983): 631–647.

Schwartz, Herman. "Criminal Law Revision Through a Legislative Commission: The New York Experience—An Interview with Richard Bartlett." *Buffalo Law Review* 18 (1968): 213–232.

Schwartz, Herman and Skolnick, Jerome. "Drafting a New Penal Law for New York: An Interview with Richard Denzer." *Buffalo Law Review* 18 (1968):251–268.

Shane-DuBow, Sandra; Alice P. Brown; and Erik Olsen. *Sentencing Reform in the United States: History, Content, and Effect.* Washington, D.C.: U.S. Department of Justice, 1985.

Silberman, Charles. *Criminal Violence, Criminal Justice* New York: Random House, 1978.

Singer, Richard G. *Just Deserts: Sentencing Based on Equity and Deserts.* Cambridge, Mass.: Ballinger Publishing Company, 1979.

Special Commission on Attica. *Attica: The Official Report of the New York State Special Commission on Attica.* New York: Bantam Books, 1972.

State of New York in Assembly, Extraordinary Session. *Unrevised Reporter.* Albany: New York State Assembly, July 19, 1978.

Travis III, Lawrence F. "Recent Sentencing Reforms in the United States: An Examination of Change in the Justice Process." Ph.D. dissertation, State University of New York at Albany, School of Criminal Justice, 1982.

Travis III, Lawrence F. and Vincent O'Leary. *Changes in Sentencing and Parole Decision Making: 1976–78.* Washington, D.C.: National Parole Institutes and Parole Policy Seminars, 1979.

Underwood, James E. and William J. Daniels, *Governor Rockefeller In New York: The Apex of Pragmatic Liberalism in the United States.* Westport, Conn.:Greenwood Press, 1982.

U.S. Congress. House. *Comprehensive Crime Control Act of 1984.* H.J. Res. 648, P.L. #98–473, October 12, 1984.

Van Den Haag, Ernest. *Punishing Criminals.* New York: Basic Books, 1975.

Von Hirsch, Andrew. "Constructing Guidelines for Sentencing: The Critical Choices for the Minnesota Sentencing Guidelines Commission." *Hamline Law Review* 5 (June 1982): 164–215

———. "Desert and Previous Convictions in Sentencing." *Minnesota Law Review* 65 (1981): 591–634.

———. *Doing Justice.* New York: Hill and Wang, 1976.

———. "The New Indiana Sentencing Code: Is It Indeterminate Sentencing?" In *An Anatomy of Criminal Justice: A Systems Overview.* Edited by Cleon Foust and D. R. Webster. Lexington, Mass.: D. C. Heath, 1980.

———. "Recent Trends in American Criminal Sentencing Theory." The Maryland Law Review 42 (1983):6–36.

———. "Selective Incapacitation: Some Questions About Research Design and Equity." *New York University Review of Law and Social Change* 12 (1984): 11–53.

———. "The Ethics of Selective Incapacitation: Observations on the Contemporary Debate." *Crime and Delinquency* 30 (April 1984): 175–194.

Von Hirsch, Andrew; Kay A. Knapp; and Michael Tonry. *The Sentencing Commission and its Guidelines.* Mass.: Northeastern University Press, 1987.

Von Hirsch, Andrew and Mueller, Julia M. "California's Determinate Sentencing Law: An Analysis of its Structure." *Criminal and Civil Confinement* 10 (1984): 253–300.

Warren, Marguerite Q. "Correctional Treatment and Coercion: The Differential Effectiveness Perspective." *Criminal Justice Behavior* 4 (1977): 355.

Warren, Roland L. *Social Change and Human Purpose: Toward Understanding and Action.* Chicago: Rand McNally College, 1977.

Washington Sentencing Commission. *Report to the Legislature: January 1, 1986.* Olympia, Wash.: Washington Sentencing Commission, 1986.

Wechsler, Herbert. "Codification of Criminal Law in the United States: The Model Penal Code." *Columbia Law Review* 68 (1968): 1425–1456.

Wilkens, Leslie T. *The Principles of Guidelines for Sentencing: Methodological and Philosophical Issues in Their Development.* Washington, D.C.: National Institute of Justice, 1981.

Wilson, James Q. *Thinking About Crime.* New York: Bantam Books, 1975.

Zimring, Franklin E. "Sentencing Reform in the States: Lessons from the 1970s." In *Reform and Punishment: Essays on Criminal Sentencing,* Michael Tonry and Franklin E. Zimring. eds. Chicago: University of Chicago Press, 1983.

NOTES

Chapter 1

1. Francis A. Allen termed the collective expression of these ideals as "rehabilitationism" and characterized advocates of the model as "rehabilitationists." Francis A. Allen, *The Decline of the Rehabilitative Ideal: Penal Policy and Social Purpose* (New Haven: Yale University Press, 1981).

2. A distinction must be made between striving to control crime and controlling crime. The question is simple: Will criminal-justice functionaries continue to pursue crime control, no matter how elusive the chase?

Chapter 2

1. Orlando F. Lewis, *The Development of American Prisons and Prison Customs, 1776–1845* (Albany, New York: Prison Association of New York, 1922); David J. Rothman, *The Discovery of the Asylum: Social Order and Disorder in the New Republic* (Boston: Little, Brown and Company, 1971).

2. J. Goebel and T. R. Naughton, *Law Enforcement in Colonial New York* (1944), p. 702, as reported in The Executive Advisory Committee on Sentencing, *Crime and Punishment in New York* (New York: The Executive Advisory Committee on Sentencing, 1979), p. 158.

3. Cesare Beccaria, *On Crime and Punishment* (London: J. Almon, 1776).

4. Rothman, *The Discovery of the Asylum.*

5. David J. Rothman, "Sentencing Reform in Historical Perspective," *Crime and Delinquency* (October 1983): 633.

6. Rothman, *The Discovery of the Asylum,* p. 79.

7. Alfred Blumstein et al., eds., *Research on Sentencing: The Search for Reform,* Vol. 1 (Washington, D.C.: National Academy Press, 1983), p. 9.

8. Rothman, *The Discovery of the Asylum.*

9. Rothman, "Sentencing Reform in Historical Perspective," p. 636.

10. David J. Rothman, *Conscience and Convenience: The Asylum and its Alternatives in Progressive America* (Boston: Little, Brown and Company, 1980).

11. Edward Lindsey, "Historical Sketch of the Indeterminate Sentence and Parole System," *Journal of Criminal Law and Criminology* (May 1925), p. 21, as reported in Lawrence Travis III and Vincent O'Leary, *Changes in Sentencing and Parole Decision Making:1976–78* (Washington, D.C.: National Parole Institutes and Parole Policy Seminars, 1979), p. 5; also reported in Malcolm Feeley, *Court Reform on Trial* (New York: Basic Books, 1983), p. 25.

12. N.Y. Laws, Chapter 260 of the Laws of 1901.

13. N.Y. Laws, Chapter 737 of the Laws of 1907.

14. Lindsey, pp. 9–126, as reported in Feeley, p. 234.

15. Herbert Wechsler, "Codification of Criminal Law in the United States: The Model Penal Code," *Columbia Law Review* 62 (1968): 1427.

16. Alfred P. Murrah and Sol Rubin, "Penal Reform and the Model Sentencing Act," *Columbia Law Review* 65 (1965): 1167.

17. President's Commission on Law Enforcement and Administration of Justice, *The Challenge of Crime in a Free Society* (Washington, D.C.: U.S. Government Printing Office, 1967), p. 126.

18. Wechsler, p. 1433.

19. American Law Institute, *Official Draft of the Model Penal Code,* Comment on Section 6.06 and 6.07, (Philadelphia: American Law Institute, 1962).

20. Wechsler, p. 1434.

21. B. J. George, Jr., "A Comparative Analysis of the New Penal Laws of New York and Michigan," *Buffalo Law Review* 2 (1968): 233.

22. Ibid; Walter L. Gordon III, *Crime and California Law: The California Experience 1960–1975* (Gaithersburg, Md.: Associated Faculty Press, 1981), p. 5. Speaking at a 1985 symposium at the Nelson A. Rockefeller College of Public Affairs and Public Policy, Herbert Wechsler, chief reporter of the American Law Institute's Model Penal Code and member of the Bartlett Commission, said that of all the states that had revised their criminal codes, New York had followed the Model Penal Code design most closely.

23. Herman Schwartz, "Criminal Law Revision Through a Legislative Commission: The New York Experience—An Interview with Richard Bartlett," *Buffalo Law Review* 18 (1968–69): 213.

24. N.Y. Laws, Chapters 1030 and 1031 of the Laws of 1965.

25. N.Y. Laws, Chapter 680 Laws of 1881.

26. New York Temporary Commission on Revision of the Penal Law and Criminal Code, *Interim Report* (1962), p. 8.

27. Howard A. Levine,"The New York Penal Law: A Prosecutor's Evaluation," *Buffalo Law Review* 18 (1968): 271.

28. New York Temporary Commission on Revision of the Penal Law and Criminal Code, *Third Interim Report of the State of New York Temporary Commission on Revisions of the Penal Law and Criminal Code*, Leg. Doc. No. 14 (1964), p. 16.

29. New York Temporary Commission on Revision of the Penal Law and Criminal Code, *Interim Report* (1962), p. 9.

30. Schwartz, p. 214.

31. New York Temporary Commission on Revision of the Penal Law and Criminal Code, *Interim Report of the State of New York Temporary Commission on Revision of the Penal Law and Criminal Code*, Leg. Doc. No. 8 (1963), p. 27.

32. Ibid. No. 41 (1962), p. 10.

33. Ibid. Proposed New York Penal Law (Brooklyn: Edward Thompson Co., 1964), p. v.

34. Ibid.

35. The New York commission also recommended three misdemeanor categories and one category for violations.

36. *1967 Penal Law*, section 1.05 (5).

37. The Temporary Commission on Revision of the Penal Law and Criminal Code, *Commission Staff Notes* (Brooklyn: Edward Thompson Co., 1964), p. 275.

38. Ibid., p. 272.

39. Ibid., p. 276.

40. Ibid., p. 277.

41. New York Temporary Commission on Revision of the Penal Law and Criminal Code, *Commission Staff Notes*, p. 299.

42. Ibid., p. 280.

43. Ibid., p. 282.

44. Class A felonies were punished by a mandatory maximum sentence of life imprisonment; class B felonies were punishable by up to twenty-five years; class C felonies by up to fifteen years; class D felonies by up to seven years; and class E felonies by up to four years.

45. NYTC, *Commission Staff Notes*, p. 278.

46. N.Y. Penal Law, Section 65.00 (3).

47. Ibid., p. 284.

48. N.Y. Penal Law, Section 70.10(1)(b)(c).

49. NYTC, *Commission Staff Notes*, p. 285.

50. N.Y. Penal Law, section 2190.

51. NYTC, *Commission Staff Notes*, p. 291.

52. Ibid.

53. Herman Schwartz and Jerome Skolnick, "Drafting a New Penal Law for New York: An Interview with Richard Denzer," *Buffalo Law Review* 18 (1968), p. 256.

54. Schwartz, p. 226.

55. McKinney's 1965 Session Laws of New York, *Governor's Memorandum* (St. Paul, Minn.: West Publishing, 1965), p. 2102.

56. Ibid., p. 11.

57. Governor's Special Committee on Criminal Offenders, *Preliminary Report of the Governor's Special Committee on Criminal Offenders* (New York: State of New York, 1968), p. 56, note.

58. Ibid., p. 102.

59. Ibid., p. 38.

60. Ibid., p. 40.

61. Ibid.

62. Ibid., p. 41.

63. Ibid., p. 48.

64. Persons not convicted of a crime, however, could not be housed in facilities with persons convicted of a crime, although the latter group could be housed with the former.

65. Governor's Special Committee on Criminal Offenders, *Preliminary Report of the Governor's Special Committee on Criminal Offenders*, p. 37.

66. Ibid., p. 51.

67. Ibid., p. 37.

68. Ibid., p. 54.

69. McKinney's 1970 New York Session Laws, *Governor's Memoranda*, p. 3101.

70. The Division of Parole had been part of the executive branch of government from its inception in 1931 until the 1970 merger.

71. McKinney's 1970 New York Session Laws, *State Executive Department Memorandum*, p. 2943.

72. Ibid., *Governor's Memoranda*, p. 3101.

73. Ibid.

74. Ibid., *State Executive Department Memoranda*, p. 2944.

Chapter 3

1. David J. Rothman, *The Discovery of the Asylum: Social Order and Disorder in the New Republic* (Boston: Little, Brown and Company, 1971).

2. David J. Rothman, "Sentencing Reforms in Historical Perspective," *Crime and Delinquency* (October 1983): 643.

3. 389 U.S. 128 (1967).

4. 408 U.S. 471 (1972).

5. 411 U.S. 778 (1973).

6. 418 U.S. 539 (1974).

7. 383 U.S. 107 (1966).

8. 422 U.S. 563 (1975).

9. 383 U.S. 541 (1966).

10. 387 U.S. 1 (1966).

11. 397 U.S. 358 (1969).

12. Jessica Mitford, *Kind and Usual Punishment: The Prison Business* (New York: Alfred A. Knopf, 1973).

13. Francis A. Allen, *The Borderland of Criminal Justice: Essays in Law and Criminology* (Chicago: University of Chicago Press, 1964), p. 29.

14. Ibid., pp. 33–34.

15. Francis A. Allen, *The Decline of the Rehabilitative Ideal: Penal Policy and Social Purpose* (New Haven: Yale University Press, 1981), p. 16.

16. Marvin Frankel, *Criminal Sentences: Law Without Order* (New York: Hill and Wang, 1972), p. 89.

17. Norval Morris, *The Future of Imprisonment* (Chicago: University of Chicago Press, 1974), p. 17.

18. American Friends Service Committee, *Struggle for Justice* (New York: Hill and Wang, 1971), p. 9.

19. Ibid., p. 40.

20. Morris, p. 16.

21. American Friends Service Committee, p. 42.

22. Ibid., p. 13.

23. Committee for the Study of Incarceration, *Doing Justice* (New York: Hill and Wang, 1975), p. xxxviii.

24. Frankel, p. 92.

25. Ibid., p. 91.

26. Douglas Lipton, Robert Martinson, and Judith Wilks, *The Effectiveness of Correctional Treatment: A Survey of Treatment Evaluation Studies* (New York: Praeger, 1975).

27. Robert Martinson, "What Works? Questions and Answers About Prison Reform," *The Public Interest* 35 (1974): 25. For a rebuttal to Martinson, see Ted Palmer, "Martinson Revisited," *Journal of Research in Crime and Delinquincy* 12: 133–152. See also Stuart S. Adams, "Evaluating Correctional Treatments," *Criminal Justice and Behavior* 4 (1977): 323–340; Marguerite Q. Warren, "Correctional Treatment and Coercion: The Differential Effectiveness Perspective," *Criminal Justice Behavior* 4 (1977): 355.

28. Of course, the false-positive issue is rarely confronted: Incarcerated offenders cannot easily demonstrate their law-abiding nature.

29. Morris, p. 72.

30. Frankel, p. 93.

31. Committee for the Study of Incarceration, p. xxxii.

32. Frankel, p. 10.

33. Ibid., p. 5.

34. American Friends Service Committee, p. 45.

35. Frankel, p. 38.

36. Ibid., p. 21.

37. American Friends Service Committee, p. 31.

38. David J. Rothman, *Conscience and Convenience: The Asylum and its Alternatives in Progressive America* (Boston: Little, Brown and Company, 1980), p. 7.

39. American Friends Service Committee, p. 29.

40. Frankel, p. 56.

41. American Friends Service Committee, p. 91.

42. Frankel, p. 49.

43. Morris, p. 35.

44. Morris, p. 26.

45. Francis A. Allen, *The Borderland of Criminal Justice, p. 35–41;* David J. Rothman, "Decarcerating Prisoners and Patients," *Civil Liberties Review* 1:8 (1980); American Friends Service Committee.

46. Committee for the Study of Incarceration, p. xxxiv.

47. Ernest van den Haag, *Punishing Criminals,* (New York: Basic Books, 1975). James Q. Wilson, *Thinking About Crime* (New York: Bantam Books, 1975).

48. Given the abysmally low clearance rate for most crimes, such certainty is illusory. Determinate sentencing does not affect the certainty of arrest, prosecution, conviction, or prison sentence. The only thing that is certain about determinate sentencing is that, if the offender is sentenced to prison, the amount of time spent incarcerated will be known in advance, with the exception of credits for good behavior in prison.

49. American Friends Service Committee, p. 153.

50. Franklin Zimring, "Sentencing Reform in the States: Lessons from the 1970s," in *Reform and Punishment: Essays on Criminal Sentencing,* Michael Tonry and Franklin E. Zimring, eds. (Chicago: University of Chicago Press, 1983), p. 120.

51. Frankel, p. 93.

52. Ibid., p. 113–114.

53. Ibid., p. 119.

54. Morris, p. 83.

55. Ibid., p. 36.

56. Ibid., p. 35.

57. The report was written by the Committee's Executive Director, Andrew Von Hirsch, who later became one of the most prolific advocates of determinate sentencing.

58. The Committee for the Study of Incarceration argued that both the rationale for and the distribution of punishment should conform to retributive requirements. In so urging, they rejected the formulation advanced by the well-known theorist H. L. A. Hart, who had distinguished between the reason for the punishment and the distribution of the punishment. Hart had argued that deterrence was the rationale for sentencing and that retributive goals should shape the distribution decision—that is, only the blameworthy would be punished. H. L. A. Hart, "Prolegomenon to the Principles of Punishment" in *Sentencing,* Hyman Gross and Andrew von Hirsch, eds. (New York: Oxford University Press, 1981): pp. 7–22.

59. The Committee for the Study of Incarceration, p. xvii.

60. Ibid., p. 6.

61. Ibid., pp. 83, 133.

62. Ibid., p. 116.

63. Ibid., pp. 105, 106, 116, 135.

64. New York State Special Commission on Attica, *Attica: The Official Report of the New York State Commission on Attica* (New York: Bantam Books, 1972), p. xi.

65. Ibid., p. xi.

66. Ibid., p. xii.

67. Ibid., p. 91.

68. Ibid., p. xviii.

69. Ibid., p. xix.

70. Citizens' Inquiry on Parole and Criminal Justice, *Prison Without Walls: Report on New York Parole* (New York: Praeger, 1975), p. xix, 178.

71. Ibid., p. xx.

72. Ibid., p. 178.

73. As is often the dynamic in these types of groups, the Citizens' Inquiry's 1974 report was substantially more radical than its 1975 final report, upon which the above discussion is based. Citizens' Inquiry on Parole and Criminal Justice, *Report on New York Parole* (New York: Citizens' Inquiry on Parole and Criminal Justice, 1974).

74. Ibid., p. 179.

Chapter 4

1. Franklin E. Zimring,"Sentencing Reform in the States: Lessons from the 1970s" in *Reform and Punishment: Essays on Criminal Sentencing,* Michael Tonry and Franklin E. Zimring, eds. (Chicago: University of Chicago Press, 1983), p. 101.

2. Sandra Shane-DuBow, Alice P. Brown, and Erik Olsen, *Sentencing Reform in the United States: History, Content, and Effect* (Washington, D.C.: U.S. Department of Justice, 1985), p. 279.

3. For example, two 1983 reports issued by the Bureau of Justice Statistics gave widely varying counts of the national status of determinacy. One listed twenty-five determinate sentencing states; the other listed nine. Bureau of Justice Statistics, *Report to the Nation on Crime and Justice: The Data* (Washington, D.C: U.S. Department of Justice, 1983); Bureau of Justice Statistics, *Setting Prison Terms* (Washington, D.C.: U.S. Department of Justice, 1983). Shane-DuBow, Brown, and Olsen, list fifteen determinate sentencing states, including Ohio, which had minimum and maximum sentences and parole release.

4. On November 1, 1989, a new sentencing structure went into effect in Oregon. Parole release has been abolished and a sentencing guidelines system based on the Minnesota model has been adopted.

5. John H. Kramer et al., *Assessing the Impact of Determinate Sentencing and Parole Abolition in Maine.* (University Park, Pa.: Pennsylvania State University, Institute for Human Development, 1978); David E. Duffee, *Corrections: Practice and Policy,* (New York: Random House, 1989), p. 137.

6. H. J. Phillips, "Final Report of the Maine Sentencing Commission," A report submitted to the 111th Maine Legislature. Augusta: 1984.

7. Andrew von Hirsch, Kay A. Knapp, and Michael Tonry, *The Sentencing Commission and its Guidelines* (Mass.: Northeastern University Press, 1987), p. 21

8. Ibid., p. 5. Also see Andrew von Hirsch, "The New Indiana Sentencing Code: Is It Indeterminate Sentencing?" in *An Anatomy of Criminal Justice: A Systems Overview*, Cleon Foust and D. R. Webster, eds. (Lexington, Mass.: D. C. Heath, 1980), pp. 143–56; Lynne Goodstein et al., *Determinate Sentencing and the Correctional Process: A Study of the Implementation and Impact of Sentencing Reform in Three States—Executive Summary*. (Washington, D.C.: United States Government Printing Office, 1984), pp. 19–22; and Stephen Lagoy, Frederick A. Hussey and John H. Kramer, "A Comparative Assessment of Determinate Sentencing in the Four Pioneer States," *Crime And Delinquency* 24 (1978): 385–400.

9. Von Hirsch, Knapp, and Tonry, p. 24.

10. Leslie T. Wilkens, *The Principles of Guidelines for Sentencing: Methodological and Philosophical Issues in Their Development*, (Washington, D.C.: National Institute of Justice, 1981).

11. State v. Evans, 311 N.W.2d 481 (Minn.: 1981).

12. State v. Hagen, 317 N.W.2d 701 (Minn. 1982); State v. King, 337 N.W.2d 674 (Minn.: 1983).

13. Von Hirsch, Knapp, and Tonry, p. 58.

14. Ibid., p. 35.

15. John H. Kramer, John P. McClosky and Nancy J. Kurtz, *Sentencing Reform: The Pennsylvania Commission on Sentencing*. Paper presented at the 1982 annual meeting of the Academy of Criminal Justice Sciences, Louisville, Kentucky in 1982.

16. Comprehensive Crime Control Act of 1984, H.J. Res. 648, P.L. #98–473, signed by President Reagan on October 12, 1984.

17. Messinger and Johnson, p. 15.

18. Ibid., p. 16.

19. Walter L. Gordon, *Crime and California Law: The California Experience 1960–1975* (Gaithersburg, Md.: Associated Faculty Press, 1981).

20. There is little disagreement on the sequence or interpretation of events in the extant literature on determinate sentencing in California. See, for example, Sheldon L. Messinger and Phillip E. Johnson, "California's Determinate Sentencing Statute: History and Issues," *Determinate Sentencing: Reform or Regression?* (Washington, D.C.: U.S. Department of Justice, 1978), pp. 13–58; Andrew von Hirsch and Julia M. Mueller, "California's Determinate Sentencing Law: An Analysis of its Structure," *Criminal and Civil Confinement* 10 (Summer 1984): 253–300; Dick Howard, *Determinate Sentencing in California* (Lexington, Ky.: Council of State Governments, 1978); April Kestell Cassou and Brian Taugher, "Determinate Sentencing in California: The New Numbers Game," *Pacific Law Journal* 9 (January 1978); Sheldon L. Messinger, Andrew von Hirsch, and Richard F. Sparks, co-principal investigators, *A*

Report on Strategies of Determinate Sentencing (Washington, D.C.: The National Institute of Justice, 1984); Jonathan D. Casper, David Brereton, and David Neal, "The California Determinate Sentence Law," *Criminal Law Bulletin* 19 (September–October 1983): 405–433; and Jonathan D. Casper, David Brereton, and David Neal, The *Implementation of the California Determinate Sentencing Law* (Washington, D.C.: U.S. Department of Justice, 1982).

21. Ibid, p. 17.

22. Cassiou and Taugher, p. 62.

23. Ibid.

24. Messinger and Johnson, p. 19.

25. Median time served under the ISL, however, included time added by the Adult Authority for characteristics of the individual case, such as whether the offender used a gun or had a prior record. Under SB 42, these case attributes would serve as enhancements to increase the primary prison term, thus potentially increasing time served. Casper, Brereton, and Neal, "The California Determinate Sentence Law, p.410; idem, *The Implementation of the California Determinate Sentence Law,* p. 87.

26. Messinger and Johnson, p. 28.

27. Ibid.

28. Ibid., p. 27.

29. Messinger and Johnson, p. 19; Cassiou and Taugher, p. 63; Lawrence F. Travis III, *Recent Sentencing Reforms in the United States: An Examination of Change in the Justice Process* (Ph.D. dissertation, State University of New York at Albany, 1982), p. 138.

30. *In Re Lynch,* 8 Cal. 3d 410, 105 Cal. Rptr. 217, 503 P. 2d 921 (1972); *In Re Foss,* 10 Cal. 3d 910, 112 Cal. Rptr. 649, 519 P. 2d 1073 (1974).

31. *In Re Lynch,* p. 413.

32. Ibid., p. 414.

33. Ibid., p.419.

34. The United States Supreme Court has long considered the proportionality of sentences. In *Weems v. United States,* 217 U.S. 349, 30 S. Ct. 544, 54 L. Ed. 793 (1910), the Court held that fifteen years imprisonment, which included hard labor in chains, and permanent civil disabilities for falsifying a public document violated the eighth amendment's prohibition against cruel and unusual punishment. In *Robinson v. California,* 370 U.S. 660, 82 S. Ct. 1417, 8. L. Ed. 2d 758 (1962), a 90-day sentence was held to be disproportionate, and hence cruel and unusual punishment, for the crime of being addicted to narcotics. More recently, in *Coker v. Georgia,* 433 U. S. 584, 53 L. Ed 2d 982 (1977), and *Solem v. Helm,* 103 S. Ct. 3001 (1983), the Supreme Court again considered the same three-prong test enunciated by the California Supreme Court in *In Re Lynch.*

In *Coker*, the Court held that the death sentence was disproportionate to the crime of rape because aggravating circumstances surrounding the commission of the offense were absent; rape should in no instance be punished more seriously than deliberate murder; and of all of the states, only Georgia authorized the death penalty for rape. In *Solem*, the Court brought similar reasoning to bear on a statute mandating a life sentence without the possibility of parole after three prior convictions, regardless of the nature of the offenses.

35. *In Re Foss*, p. 917.

36. Cassou and Taugher, p. 60.

37. Dick Howard, *Determinate Sentencing in California* (Lexington, Ky.: Council of State Governments, 1978), p. 2.

38. *In Re Rodriquez*, 14 C. 3d 639; 122 Cal. Rptr. 552; 537 P. 2d 384 (1975).

39. Ibid., p. 646.

40. Ibid., note 6, p. 644.

41. Ibid., p. 646.

42. Ibid., p. 650.

43. Ibid., p. 652.

44. Ibid., p. 640.

45. Ibid., p. 657.

46. Ibid., p. 658.

47. *In Re Stanley*, 54 C.A. 3d 1030; 126 Cal. Rptr. 524 (1976).

48. Ibid., p. 1033.

49. Ibid., p. 1038.

50. Ibid., p. 1039.

51. Ibid., p. 1040.

52. Cassou and Taugher, p. 66; Messinger and Johnson, p. 20; Lawrence F. Travis III, *Recent Sentencing Reforms in the United States: An Examination of Change in the Justice Process* (Ph.D. dissertation, State University of New York at Albany, 1982), p. 149.

53. Messinger and Johnson, p. 21.

54. California Penal Code, section 1170 (a)(1).

55. Messinger and Johnson, p. 40.

56. Ibid., p. 46.

57. Ibid., p. 41.

58. SB 709 added the triads of two, three, and five years; two, four, and six years; three, four, and six years; three, five, and seven years; three, six, and eight years; five, seven, and nine years; and five, seven, and eleven years. SB 42's tripartite of five, six, and seven years was deleted.

59. Inmates work for five days a week for six hours a day and receive seven days credit. Programs are traditionally oversubscribed, but inmates willing to participate receive full credit even if not assigned to a program or not assigned full-time. Inmates not eligible for work-incentive credits, for example, those at reception centers and new arrivals at the prison, continue to receive a one-third reduction.

60. For example, the manslaughter triad was changed from two, four, and six years to three, six, and eleven years. The penalties for vehicular manslaughter were raised for cases involving gross negligence or alcohol or drug use. Many of the mandatory incarceration provisions contain an escape clause: in the unusual case, the court can impose a non-prison sentence in the interests of justice. The determination of the requirements of justice is, of course, left to the discretion of the decisionmaker.

61. Ibid., p. 69; von Hirsch and Mueller, p. 280. A representative from the Judicial Council admitted in a telephone interview that the council was unwilling and unable to control discretion.

62. Sentences for violent sex offenses must be fully consecutive to one another, however.

63. Board of Prison Terms, *Sentencing Patterns Under the Determinate Sentencing Law* (California: Youth and Adult Correctional Agency, 1983), pp. 64–80.

64. Messinger, von Hirsch, and Sparks, p. 99.

65. Von Hirsch and Mueller, p. 279.

Chapter 5

1. McKinney's 1960 Session Laws of New York, *Governor's Annual Message* (St. Paul, Minn.: West Publishing Co., 1960), p. 1969.

2. McKinney's 1961 Session Laws of New York, *Governor's Annual Message*, p. 2043.

3. New York Laws, Chapter 204 of the Laws of 1962.

4. McKinney's 1962 Session Laws of New York, *Governor's Memorandum*, p. 3610.

5. McKinney's 1966 Session Laws of New York, *Governor's Annual Message*, p. 2977.

6. Ibid.

7. Ibid., p. 2986.

8. Offenders convicted of murder or kidnapping in the first degree—the class A felonies—were ineligible for certification to NACC.

9. McKinney's 1967 Session Laws of New York, *Governor's Annual Message,* p. 1518.

10. McKinney's 1968 Session Laws of New York, *Governor's Annual Message,* p. 2356.

11. McKinney's 1969 Session Laws of New York, *Governor's Annual Message,* p. 2529.

12. McKinney's 1970 Session Laws of New York, *Governor's Annual Message,* p. 3053.

13. As quoted in Edward J. Epstein, "The Great Rockefeller Power Machine," *New York Magazine* (November 24, 1975), p. 71; Vincent O'Leary et. al., "Policies Toward Crime and the Criminal Justice System." In *Rockefeller in Retrospect: The Governor's New York Legacy,* Gerald Benjamin and T. Norman Hurd, eds. (Albany: The Nelson A. Rockefeller Institute of Government, 1984), p. 253; and Joseph E. Persico, *The Imperial Rockefeller* (New York: Simon and Schuster, 1982), p. 144.

14. McKinney's 1971 Session Laws of New York, *Governor's Annual Message,* p. 2590.

15. McKinney's 1973 Session Laws of New York, *Governor's Annual Message,* p. 2318.

16. Persico, p. 143.

17. James E. Underwood and William J. Daniels, *Governor Rockefeller in New York: The Apex of Pragmatic Liberalism in the United States* (Westport, Conn.: Greenwood Press, 1982), p. 139.

18. McKinney's 1973 Session Laws of New York, *Governor's Annual Message,* p. 2319.

19. *New York Times,* 4 January 1973, sec. 1, p. 29.

20. Ibid.

21. Nelson A. Rockefeller, *Public Papers of Nelson A. Rockefeller, Fifty-Third Governor of State of New York* (Albany: New York State, 1973), p. 655.

22. Persico, p. 144.

23. In addition, criminal sale and criminal possession of a controlled substance in the fourth degree were upgraded to class B felonies, with a minimum maximum of nine years and a maximum maximum of twenty-five years.

24. A companion bill, Chapter 278 of the Laws of 1973, provided an escape-hatch for offenders convicted of class A–III drug offenses. Lifetime probation could be awarded instead of imprisonment to offenders providing material assistance in the investigation, apprehension, or prosecution of another drug offender. The bill was inspired by law-enforcement officials who "expressed the fear that it would become impossible to get small fry drug dealers or addicts to cooperate in the apprehension and conviction of the bigger traffickers." Practice Commentaries of Arnold D. Hecht-

man accompanying Section 60.05 of the Penal Law, *McKinney's Consolidated Laws of New York Annotated* (St. Paul, Minn.: West Publishing, 1973), p. `85.

25. Ibid.

26. Second felony offenders convicted of class B felonies would receive a maximum sentence of between nine and twenty-five years, class C felons would receive a maximum of between six and fifteen years, class D felons between four and seven years; and class D felons between three and four years. The minimum sentence had to be set by the court at one-half the maximum imposed.

27. Persico, p. 144.

28. O'Leary, et al. p. 236.

29. Ibid., p. 245.

30. Herman Schwartz and Jerome Skolnick, "Drafting a New Penal Law for New York: An Interview with Richard Denzer," *Buffalo Law Review* 18 (1968).

31. The Bartlett Commission had not disturbed the sentencing arrangements of the Family Court Act of 1962. Under New York's rehabilitative system, children under the age of sixteen were exempt from criminal responsibility. Offending juveniles would not be incarcerated in state prisons, but rather would be treated, and hopefully rehabilitated, in facilities operated by the Division For Youth.

32. Edmund F. McGarrell, *Changes in New York's Juvenile Corrections System.* Rockefeller Institute Working Papers, No. 22 (Albany: The Nelson A. Rockefeller Institute of Government, 1985), p. 13.

33. Ibid., p. 15.

34. Governor's Panel on Juvenile Violence, *Report to the Governor* (Albany, New York: Governor's Panel on Juvenile Violence, 1976), p. 5.

35. Fourteen and fifteen year olds who committed the most serious violent offenses would receive mandatory one year placement in secure DFY facilities; placement or community supervision could be continued for up to two additional years.

36. Designated juvenile offenders were subject to sentences of three to five years, depending on the crime of conviction; six to twelve months of the sentence had to be served in a secure facility operated by DFY, during which time the youth would receive "intensive rehabilitative services." Youths would be supervised in the community upon release. The total period of placement could be extended until the youth's twenty-first birthday.

37. McGarrell, p. 15.

38. McKinney's 1976 Session Laws of New York, *Governor's Memoranda*, p. 2452.

39. McGarrell, p. 17.

40. Edmund F. McGarrell, "The Role of the Media in Juvenile Justice Policy-making: the New York Case." Paper presented at the annual meeting of the American Society of Criminology, San Diego, California, 1985. As part of a larger study of changes in New York's youth correction system, McGarrell interviewed fifty-eight people involved with the juvenile justice system. Each of his respondents commented on the role of the media in setting the stage for fundamental change. Tracing the *New York Times's* coverage of youth crime over a decade, McGarrell found that the number of articles on youth crime rose substantially during the study period: 40 to 70 articles appeared each year from 1968 to 1971; the coverage increased to 107 to 155 articles a year from 1972 to 1978. The media coverage declined thereafter. According to McGarrell, the progression went as follows: The media's focus on youth gangs prompted legislative investigations, which were widely covered by the media, which prompted more investigations, which resulted in the issue attracting the public attention, which culminated in legislative action.

41. Thirteen year olds committing enumerated crimes were made eligible for the special sentencing provisions of the 1976 act; assault in the second degree and robbery in the second degree were added to the list of designated felonies; and extended restrictive placement was authorized for recidivistic juveniles.

42. *Newsday,* 16 June 1985. After being released from DFY, Bosket promptly attacked a seventy-two-year-old blind man and was convicted of assault. Despite the subway murders committed when he was fifteen years old, the law required that Bosket be sentenced as a first offender.

43. McGarrell, *Changes in New York's Juvenile Corrections System,* p. 18.

44. Special sentencing provisions applied to juvenile offenders. Murder in the second degree, an adult offense if committed by a thirteen year old, required a mandatory maximum term of life imprisonment. The maximum term for the other JO offenses varied by crime and class: The maximum for the class B offenses of arson and kidnapping in the first degree was twelve to fifteen years; the maximum for other class B felonies was ten years; for class C felonies, seven years. The court was required to set a minimum term in all cases. The minimum for murder in the second degree was between five and nine years; the minimum for the class B offenses of arson and kidnapping in the first degree was four to six years; and the minimum for other class B and C felonies had to be set at one-third the maximum imposed. A JO conviction could serve as a predicate for sentencing as a recidivist.

Subsequent revisions in the JO law mitigated somewhat the harshness of the 1978 provisions. Chapter 411 of the Laws of 1979 specified the factors to be considered by the adult court in determining whether to waive a juvenile to Family Court, allowed thirteen-year-old murderers to plead to a designated felony in Family Court, and, most important, authorized Youthful Offender (YO) treatment for JOs, thereby making them eligible for a non-incarcerative sentence. Additional procedural rights were also stipulated.

45. For example, class B VFOs had a minimum maximum of six years and a maximum maximum of twenty-five years; the corresponding range for class C VFOs was four and one-half years to fifteen years. Minimums had to be set by the court at

one-third of the maximum imposed. An escape from the mandatory provisions was provided for offenders convicted of class D VFOs: The court could impose other than an indeterminate prison term if mitigating circumstances bore directly on the manner in which the crime was committed, if that defendant's participation in the crime was relatively minor, or where there were possible deficiencies of proof that the defendant committed an armed felony.

46. For example, a second violent felony offender convicted of a class B VFO would receive a minimum maximum term of twelve years and a maximum maximum of twenty-five years; the minimum had to be set by the court at one-half the maximum imposed. The minimum minimum sentence for a persistent violent felony offender convicted of a class B VFO was ten years, with a maximum minimum of twenty-five years.

47. State of New York in Assembly, Extraordinary Session, *Unrevised Reporter* (July 19, 1978), p. 111.

48. Ibid., p. 129.

49. Ibid., p. 137–38.

50. New York State Special Commission on Attica, *Attica: The Official Report of the New York State Commission on Attica* (New York: Bantam Books, 1972), p. xviii.

51. Staff Report, Codes Committee of the New York State Assembly, *Paul Said "But I Was Free Born": A Report on Parole Reform* (Albany: Codes Committee of the New York State Assembly, 1976), pp. 48–49 and 63–64. Even before the Assembly Codes Staff report, the legislature had made an initial attempt to control parole release by requiring, in Chapter 131 of the Laws of 1975, that inmates denied release be supplied with written reasons for the refusal within two weeks of the denial.

52. According to Chapter 904 of the Laws of 1977, the guidelines would be based on

(i) the seriousness of the offense with due consideration to the type of sentence, length of sentence and recommendations of the sentencing court, the district attorney, the attorney for the inmate, the pre-sentence probation report as well as consideration of any mitigating and aggravating factors, and activities following arrest and prior to confinement; and (ii) prior criminal record, including the nature and pattern of offenses, adjustment to any previous probation or parole supervision and institutional confinement.

In addition to the guidelines, the board could consider the offender's

(i) institutional record including program goals and accomplishments, academic achievements, vocational education, training or work assignments, therapy and interpersonal relationships with staff and inmates; (ii) performance, if any, as a participant in a temporary release program; and (iii) release plans including community resources, employment, education and training and support services available to the inmate.

53. McKinney's 1975 Session Laws of New York, Governor Memorandum, p. 2538.

Chapter 6

1. Five of the fifteen members, including the powerful chairman, were prosecutors, three others were former prosecutors. Defense interests were also well represented on the committee, which included the then-Speaker of the Assembly, Stanley Fink; the Democratic Deputy Minority Leader of the Senate, Emanuel R. Gold; a former counsel to the NAACP Legal Defense Fund, Peggy C. Davis; and Arthur L. Liman, former chief counsel to the McKay Commission.

2. Executive Advisory Committee on Sentencing, *Crime and Punishment in New York: An Inquiry into Sentencing and the Criminal Justice System* (New York: Executive Advisory Committee on Sentencing, 1979), p. 161, note 37.

3. Ibid., p. 137, italics in original.

4. Ibid., p. 120–21, italics in original.

5. Ibid., p. 118.

6. Ibid., p. 120.

7. Ibid.

8. Ibid., p. 110.

9. Ibid., p. 115, quoting from Charles Silberman, *Criminal Violence, Criminal Justice* (New York: Random House, 1978), p. 195, who was quoting criminologist Jack Gibbs.

10. The Morgenthau Committee missed the point about certainty. If deterrence operates at all, it is the certainty of arrest, the certainty of conviction, and the certainty of punishment that would seem to have the greatest effect. The certainty of whether a prison sentence is determinate or indeterminate would appear to be of significantly less deterrent value to the would-be offender.

11. The Executive Advisory Committee on Sentencing, *Crime and Punishment in New York*, p. 110.

12. Ibid., p. 123.

13. Ibid., p. 63.

14. Ibid., p. 130, note.

15. See, for example, Andrew von Hirsch, "Desert and Previous Convictions in Sentencing," *Minnesota Law Review* 65 (April 1981); idem, "Constructing Guidelines for Sentencing: The Critical Choices for the Minnesota Sentencing Guidelines Commission," *Hamline Law Review* 5 (June 1982); idem, "Recent Trends in American Criminal Sentencing Theory," *Maryland Law Review* 42 (Number 1, 1983); idem, "The Ethics of Selective Incapacitation: Observations on the Contemporary Debate," *Crime and Delinquency* 30 (April 1984).

16. The Executive Advisory Committee on Sentencing, *Crime and Punishment in New York*, p. 131.

17. Ibid., p. 138.

18. Ibid.

19. Ibid., p. 141.

20. Ibid.

21. Ibid., p. 142.

22. The testimony of the eighty-seven witnesses who appeared before the Sentencing Guidelines Committee will be discussed in Chapter Eight.

23. Defense groups were better represented in both sets of hearings.

24. No record of the testimony at the Buffalo hearings was available, and some of the appearances in Albany were not preserved for the record because of an error in the stenographic transcription.

25. Assembly and Senate Joint Codes Committee Hearings, 1979, p. 128.

26. Ibid., pp. 166–67.

27. Ibid., p. 30.

28. McKinney's 1980 Session Laws of New York, *Governor's Memorandum* (St. Paul, Minn.: West Publishing), p. 1835.

29. McKinney's 1981 Session Laws of New York, *Governor's Memorandum*, p. 2548.

30. Ibid.

31. Executive Advisory Commission on the Administration of Justice, *Recommendations to Governor Hugh L. Carey Regarding Prison Overcrowding* (New York: Executive Advisory Commission on the Administration of Justice, 1982), p. 1.

32. Ibid., p. 3.

33. Ibid., p. 7.

34. Ibid.

35. Ibid., p. 16.

36. The Morgenthau Committee had fashioned no role for the legislature, recommending instead that the sentencing commission's recommendations take effect 180 days following their promulgation.

37. Executive Advisory Commission on the Administration of Justice, p. 18.

38. N.Y. Laws, Chapter 1000 of the Laws of 1981, section 2.

39. McKinney's 1981 Session Laws of New York, *Governor's Memorandum*, p. 2642.

40. Advisory Commission on Criminal Sanctions, *Report of the Advisory Commission on Criminal Sanctions, Part One* (New York: Advisory Commission on Criminal Sanctions, 1982), p. 97.

41. Ibid., p. 83.

42. Ibid., p. 101.

43. Ibid., p. 103.

44. Ibid., p. 81.

45. Ibid., p. 84.

46. Ibid., p. 85.

47. Douglas Lipton, Robert Martinson, and Judith Wilks, *The Effectiveness of Correctional Treatment* (New York: Praeger, 1975).

48. Advisory Commission on Criminal Sanctions, *Part One*, p. 87.

49. Ibid.

50. Ibid., p. 90.

51. Chapter 1000, the enabling legislation, charged the McQuillan Commission with both study and guidelines functions.

52. When questioned about his committee's report, Judge McQuillan acknowledged that the report had said that the dual-track system was not a concession, but rather the ideal merger of two systems.

53. The *New York Times* Index was used to gather the articles from that paper. A search of all of the *Time's* articles on sentencing between 1977 to 1985 was made. A selected few of these are presented here. The *New York Post* does not index its articles, but clippings were obtained on sentencing articles from 1977 to 1985 from the paper's in-house library. While it was not possible to determine whether the selection from the *Post* was exhaustive, it certainly was revealing.

54. *New York Post*, 17 May 1977.

55. Ibid., 29 March 1977, italics added.

56. *New York Post*, 16 January 1980.

57. Ibid., 20 December 1982, italics added.

58. Ibid., 28 December 1982.

59. Ibid., 4 January 1979, sec. 2, p. 1.

60. Ibid., 7 January 1979, sec. 4, p. 20.

61. Ibid., 4 March 1980, sec. 1, p. 14.

62. Ibid., 25 January 1981, sec. 4, p. 20.

63. Ibid., 29 January 1983, sec. 1, p. 22.

64. McKinney's 1983 Session Laws of New York, *Governor's Memorandum*, p. 2732.

65. Governor Cuomo's concern for criminal-justice reform was evident in one of his first acts of office: the appointment of Lawrence T. Kurlander as the state's first Director of Criminal Justice. Mr. Kurlander was charged by the governor with coordinating the state's fragmented criminal-justice system, which the Liman Commission had labeled a great "oxymoron."

66. The negotiators no doubt remembered the uproar occasioned by the Liman Commission's recommendation of such a linkage. In an interview with this author, Mr. Liman recalled the reaction to his commission's proposal for a relief mechanism for prison crowding:

> We made a very modest proposal in my commission, and we could have been lynched for that. That was the only thing that anyone paid any attention to—just a minor escape valve. That's the only thing anyone cared about. When you explained on talk programs as I did—say suppose someone who's in there for two years gets out one month earlier, that person is going to be out one month later anyway—so is it better to make the person into an animal in that last month because you don't have room? Then people could understand it. "Yes, well now I understand, the person will be out on November 1, the only issue is whether it's October 1." But that's not the way anyone thinks, the way they think is that you're going to let someone out who would otherwise be in forever.

67. Under current law, the court can dismiss, but not reduce, an indictment. A discussion of the Bellacosa-Feinberg Committee's deliberations over inspect and reduce is presented in Chapter Eight.

68. In 1987 Mr. Miller was voted Speaker of the Assembly, replacing Stanley Fink, who declined to run for reelection.

69. New York Assembly Floor Debates on H8026, June 15, 1983, p. 15.

70. Ibid., p. 229.

71. Ibid., p. 230.

72. Ibid., p. 239.

73. Ibid., p. 233–34.

74. Ibid., p. 235.

75. Ibid., p. 236.

76. Ibid., p. 243–44.

77. The report so rejected was the dual-track system of the McQuillan Commission; the Liman Commission had not been established to recommend sentencing reform, yet it had done so.

78. New York Assembly Floor Debates on H8026, June 15, 1983, p. 246–47.

79. Ibid., p. 256.

80. Ralph J. Marino, *Determinate Sentencing: Danger Ahead* (Albany: New York State Senate Committee on Crime and Correction, 1983), p. 5.

81. Ibid., p. 15.

82 . Chapter 711 of the Laws of 1983 is reproduced in pertinent parts in Appendix III.

83. McKinney's 1983 Session Laws of New York, *Governor's Memorandum*, p. 2797.

84. Ibid., p. 2666. Mayor Koch had long been on record as supporting determinate sentencing. In 1981 the *Mayor's Survey of the Criminal Justice System* called the rehabilitative model "a failure and a fraud . . . a distorted game of chance." The Mayor's report urged the adoption of determinate sentencing based on the model outlined by the Morgenthau Committee.

85. *New York Post*, 28 December 1982.

86. Ibid., 26 April 1983, italics added.

87. Ibid., 27 April 1983, italics added.

88. Ibid., 18 May 1983. Given the *Post's* obvious preference for tough sentences, it must have been very confident that the guidelines committee would not recommend reducing penalties; otherwise, it would not have disapproved of the proposal to allow the legislature to alter the committee's product.

89. Ibid., 22 June 1983, italics added.

90. *New York Times*, 29 January 1983, sec. 1, p. 22.

91. Ibid., 29 May 1983, sec. 4, p. 13.

92. Ibid., 11 July 1983, sec. 1, p. 22.

93. Ibid., 24 September 1983, sec. 1, p. 22. One of Governor Cuomo's first official duties was to quell a prison riot at Ossining Correctional Facility. Unlike Governor Rockefeller, who remained in California during the Attica riots in 1971, Governor Cuomo was personally, and successfully, involved in ending the riot without bloodshed.

Chapter 7

1. I was employed as a staff member for the Bellacosa-Feinberg Committee. I attended committee meetings, sub-committee meetings, committee retreats, public hearings, and formal and informal policy sessions. The discussions and categorizations in this chapter are based on personal observations, as well as on interviews and a wide assortment of committee documents.

2. Several subcommittees were formed to tackle particularly troublesome issues; subcommittees met as necessary.

3. There were 16,103 inmates under custody at the beginning of 1976; by 1987 the number had risen to 38,647. At the end of 1975 the average minimum sentence of the under-custody prison population was 47 months; by 1986 the average minimum sentence had spiraled upward to 72 months—an increase of 53 percent. The time that the under-custody population had served at year's end averaged 19 months in 1975; by 1986 the average time served by the under-custody population had risen to 27 months, an increase of 41 percent. New York State Department of Correctional Services, *Trends in Time Served by the Under-Custody Population: 1975 to 1986* (Albany: Department of Correctional Services, 1986).

4. Minutes of the Meeting of the New York State Committee on Sentencing Guidelines, June 21, 1984, p. 10.

5. Ibid., January 27, 1984, p. 15.

6. Ibid., p. 16.

7. Ibid.

8. Ibid., p. 21.

9. Ibid., July 27, 1984, p. 4

10. Ibid., August 24, 1984, p. 3.

11. Where the offender was actually armed, the court can impose a minimum sentence of one-half the maximum. If the offender is not convicted of an armed felony, the minimum sentence must be set at one-third the maximum sentence.

12. New York State Committee on Sentencing Guidelines, *Determinate Sentencing: A Preliminary Proposal for Public Comment* (Albany: New York State Committee on Sentencing Guidelines, 1985), p. 49.

13. Executive Advisory Committee on Sentencing, p. 137.

14. Chapter 711 of the Laws of 1983, sec. 3 (3) (b).

15. Minutes, June 21, 1984, p. 18.

16. Ibid., pp. 40–41.

17. Ibid., June 24, 1984, p. 60.

18. Ibid., September 21, 1984, p. 7. In July 1984, Marvin Zalman resigned from the committee to return to his academic post at Wayne State University in Michigan. His replacement, Peter Walsh, had been counsel to the committee.

19. Prescriptive guidelines were ultimately rejected in favor of descriptive guidelines.

20. Ibid., December 28, 1983, p. 2.

21. Ibid., January 27, 1984, p. 9.

22. Ibid., March 7, 1985, p. 4.

23. Ibid., p. 7.

24. Ibid., August 24, 1984, p. 5.

25. Ibid., p. 3.

26. Andrew von Hirsch is a vocal proponent of the view that just deserts and enhancements for prior record are compatible. George Fletcher and Richard Singer have taken the polar view, arguing that an offender's prior record should not be considered in determining sentence length. George Fletcher, "The Recidivist Premium," *Criminal Justice Ethics* 54 (Summer–Fall 1982), p. 54–59; Richard Singer, *Just Deserts: Sentencing Based on Equality and Deserts* (Cambridge, Mass.: Ballinger Publishing Company, 1979).

27. New York State Committee on Sentencing Guidelines, Minutes of the Monthly Meetings, March 30, 1984: pp. 10–14.

28. Ibid., May 24, 1984, pp. 1–2.

29. Ibid., p. 12.

30. Ibid., June 21, 1984, p. 14.

31. Ibid., p. 16.

32. Minutes of Meetings of New York State Committee on Sentencing Guidelines, June 21, 1984, p. 13.

33. Ibid., June 23, 1984, pp. 46–48, 62.

34. Ibid., August 24, 1984, p. 9.

35. New York State Committee on Sentencing Guidelines, *Determinate Sentencing: Report and Recommendation*, 1985, p. 126–7.

36. Executive Advisory Committee on Sentencing, *Crime and Punishment in New York*, p. 136.

37. Ibid., p. 138.

38. Minutes, August 24, 1984, p. 6.

39. Ibid., October 26, 1984, p. 6.

40. Ibid., March 7, 1985, p. 13.

41. Ibid., October 26, 1984, p. 2.

42. Minutes, June 22, 1984, p. 34.

43. Ibid., October 26, 1984, p. 3.

44. Ibid., September 21, 1984, p. 2.

45. Ibid., February 24, 1984, p. 12.

46. Ibid., March 30, 1984, p. 9.

47. Ibid., November 30, 1984, p. 19.

48. New York State Committee on Sentencing Guidelines, *Determinate Sentencing: Report and Recommendations*, p. 91. The committee's final report was peppered with strong dissenting opinions.

49. Ibid., p. 88.

50. Minutes of Meetings, June 22, 1984, pp. 26–33.

51. New York State Committee on Sentencing Guidelines, *Determinate Sentencing: Report and Recommendations*, p. 89.

52. Since its first meeting, the committee had repeatedly been told by the chairman that all decisions were tentative, votes being taken solely for the purpose of moving the committee process along. Issues were frequently voted on at different meetings, the vote often changing depending on which members were present at the meeting.

53. Minutes, August 24, 1984, p. 6.

54. Ibid., August, 24, 1984, p. 12.

55. Ibid., September 21, 1987, p. 2.

56. Ibid., November 30, 1984, p. 18.

57. Ibid., September 21, 1984, p. 4.

58. Ibid., December 20, 1984, pp. 2–3.

59. Chapter 711 of the Laws of 1983, sec. 3 (3)(g). Felonies may be prosecuted by an indictment issued by a grand jury or by a prosecutor's information. Indictments are overwhelmingly the accusatory instrument of choice in New York City, which prosecutes the vast majority of felony cases in the state.

60. When it is impossible to commit a particular crime without concomitantly committing, by the same conduct, another offense of a lesser degree, the latter crime is considered a lesser included offense of the former. For example, larceny (stealing property) is a lesser included offense of robbery (forcibly stealing property); one cannot commit robbery without also committing larceny. New York State Criminal Procedure Law section 1.20 (37).

61. Minutes, June 22, 1984, pp. 37–38.

62. James Jacobs is a notable exception. James B. Jacobs, "Sentencing By Prison Personnel: Good Time," *UCLA Law Review* 30 (December 1982).

63. Prior to the 1967 law changes wrought by the Bartlett Commission, good time came off the minimum sentence.

64. Committee on Sentencing Guidelines, *Determinate Sentencing: Report and Recommendations*, p. 115.

65. Ibid., pp. iv–v.

66. Committee members Lopez, Paterson, Walker, and Williams acknowledged at the outset that everyone associated with the committee had acted in good faith to develop a viable, internally consistent proposal for the implementation of the determinate sentencing system that the Legislature in its wisdom has decided should be created, but added that, were the mandate of Chapter 711 of Laws of 1983 that created the committee otherwise, *they might have questioned whether such a determinate sentencing system should be created or would constitute a marked improvement over the current indeterminate system, flawed in part though it may be.* Ibid., pp. 83–84, italics added.

Chapter 8

1. First, the sentence ranges in the grid were decreased in two cells out of the sixty grid cells and increased in seven; the two cells that were reduced now offered the possibility of a local jail sentence rather than a state prison sentence. Second, certain crimes, most noticeably white-collar crimes and first degree sex crimes, were placed in a higher sentencing band. Third, changes were made in the good-time policy. As noted in the previous chapter, the committee ultimately voted to abandon vesting and restore restoration. Also, it allowed prison officials to retain control over disciplinary hearings, rather than having this power exercised by the parole authorities, as recommended in the committee's preliminary report.

2. See Appendix I for a discussion of the methodology used to categorize witnesses' testimony at public hearings.

3. Hearings were conducted in Albany, Buffalo, and New York City.

4. New York State Committee on Sentencing Guidelines, *Determinate Sentencing: A Preliminary Proposal for Public Comment,* p. 8.

5. The State of New York assumes the financial burden of housing offenders in state prisons. Time spent in local jails awaiting court proceedings is generally a local expense.

6. Public hearings of the Committee on Sentencing Guidelines, Albany, New York, February 7, 1985, pp. 188–89.

7. The committee made changes in its good-time proposal as a result of these comments. See note 1, *of this chapter.*

8. Public hearings of Committee on Sentencing Guidelines, New York City, February 14, 1985, pp. 48, 50, 61.

9. The reference is to the 1983 court-ordered release of jailed prisoners by Federal District Court Judge Morris Lasker. Responding to continued crowding at New York City's Riker Island jail, the judge ordered the city to reduce its jail's population. The city complied by releasing over six hundred inmates. The inmates' early release—or jail break, as it was dubbed by the media—caused a substantial and prolonged uproar.

10. Public hearings of Committee on Sentencing Guidelines, New York City, February 14, 1985, pp. 49, 72–82.

11. New York Post, 3 April, 1985, p.13.

12. Press release of Lawrence T. Kurlander, 2 April 1985.

13. There were several technical differences between the committee's bill and the Governor's bill, but only three major substantive differences. First, the governor's bill slightly changed the procedural requirements for departure at both the trial and the appellate court level. Second, the governor's bill failed to authorize the sentencing committee to review the conduct of good-time hearings or the list of Tier III violations promulgated by the prison authorities. Third, the governor's bill changed the committee's definition of criminal possession of stolen property and insurance fraud in the first degree, removing the "scheme to defraud" language that the committee had adopted.

14. Press release of Governor Mario M. Cuomo, May 8, 1985.

15. Assembly Bill 7901, May 31, 1985.

16. Ibid., p. 44.

17. Ibid., p. 9.

18. Ibid., p. 25.

19. Ibid., p. 31.

20. Ibid., p. 72.

21. Ibid., p. 74.

22. Newsday, 14 June 1985.

23. District Attorneys Association, Memorandum in Opposition to A. 7027 (Determinate Sentencing), June 11, 1985.

24. New York State Law Enforcement Council, New York State Law Enforcement Council Criticizes Determinate Sentencing Bill, June 17, 1985.

25. Chapter 711 of the Laws of 1983 charged the committee with providing "a statement of the estimated effect of the guidelines on judicial, prosecution and defense resources, prison population, jail population, probation and parole services," section (3) (e). The committee's report speculated on the impact of its proposal on local jails, but did not present the results of detailed empirical research.

26. In the Matter of Edward I. Koch, as Mayor of The City of New York against The New York State Committee on Sentencing Guidelines, Supreme Court, County of New York, July 1, 1985.

27. New York Post, 1 October 1984.

28. Chapter 711, however, charged the committee with proposing legislation concerning these and other features of the guidelines system.

29. *New York Post,* 5 October, 1985.

30. Ibid., 16 January 1985.

31. Ibid., italics in original.

32. Ibid., 23 March 1985.

33. The *Post,* which generally sided with law enforcement, was perhaps unaware that District Attorney Morgenthau and members of the Law Enforcement Council now claimed that the sentence ranges were ridiculously narrow.

34. *New York Post,* 4 April 1985.

35. Ibid., 12 April 1985.

36. The reference is to a speech by the governor on October 10, 1984 at the Governor's Conference on Law Enforcement. While praising the sentencing guidelines committee for its diligent effort to complete its assignment on time, the Governor noted that

> a word of caution is in order. When I introduced legislation in 1983 calling for the creation of the guidelines committee, I hoped it would lead toward establishing a system that promotes the public safety, and is rational and sane. I did not intend that the gains so many of you here today [law-enforcement officials] fought to achieve over many years would be undone. Clearly we do not need a system that is draconian. It is equally clear, however, that we don't need a system that slaps on the wrist our most violent repeat offenders.

Remarks by Governor Mario M. Cuomo, *Governor's Conference on Law Enforcement,* Latham, New York, October 10, 1984.

37. *New York Times,* 27 October 1984, sec. 1, p. 27.

38. Ibid., 10 November 1984, p. A–22, col. 1.

39. In selecting a methodology for determining the average length of time served in prison, the committee voted not to add in non-incarcerative sentences, reasoning that averaging in zeros for alternative sentences would vastly underestimate time served in prison. It was generally recognized that the impact estimates were far from precise. The impact of the new sentencing system on prison populations would depend on whether judges would typically sentence at the high or the low end of the sentencing range. Since there was no way of knowing what the sentencing practices would be under the grid, the committee could only suggest a range of possibilities.

40. *New York Times,* 22 January 1985, sec. 1, p. 24.

41. Ibid., 21 February 1985, sec. 1, p. 22.

42. The *Post,* on the other hand, attributed the genesis of determinate sentencing to law-and-order concerns. On March 23, 1985 the *Post* claimed that the governor promoted determinate sentencing to counter the leniency of the criminal-justice system.

43. *New York Times,* 8 April 1985, sec. 1, p. 16.

44. Ibid., May 28, 1985, sec.1, p 18.

45. Ibid., 16 June 1985, sec. 1, p. 35.

46. Ibid., June 20, 1985, sec.1, p 26.

47. Senator Ralph J. Marino, *Determinate Sentencing: Danger Ahead* (Albany: New York State Senate Committee on Crime and Correction, June 1983), p. 5.

48. In 1987 Stanley Fink resigned, and Melvin Miller, formerly chairman of the criminal-justice Codes Committee, was elected to replace him as Assembly Speaker.

49. Assemblyman Richard Gottfried told this author that he could not recall any other time during his sixteen-year tenure in the Assembly when the Speaker had tried but failed to muster support for a major piece of legislation. Regardless of the accuracy of Assemblyman Gottfried's recollection, it was apparent that the level of opposition to the Speaker's efforts was impressive and unusual.

50. Timothy J. Flanagan and Edmund F. McGarrell, *Attitudes of New York Legislators Toward Crime and Criminal Justice: A Report of the State Legislator Survey—1985* (Albany: The Hindelang Criminal Justice Research Center, State University of New York at Albany, 1986). One hundred and thirty of the 211 state's legislators replied to the survey. One hundred and five questionnaires were usable, yielding a 50 percent usable response rate. Twenty-six of the usable responses came from the Senate, 79 from the Assembly.

51. Ibid., p. 36. Based on 93 usable answers. The survey was conducted during the same legislative session in which the sentencing bill languished in the Senate and Assembly Codes Committees. Thus, while over half of the legislators answering the survey expressed support for determinate sentencing, these favorable attitudes did not translate into support for the governor's bill.

52. Ibid., p. 16.

53. Ibid., p. 10.

54. Ibid., p. 36.

55. Ibid., p. 7.

56. The C grid had been developed by committee staff with the assistance of Mr. Crosson. On December 20, 1984, the committee voted to reduce the sentences in the C grid in response to concerns raised by Mr. Smith that the sentences in the C grid overrepresented time currently being served in prison, thus resulting in intolerable increases in the prison population.

Chapter 9

1. The Temporary Commission on Revision of the Penal Law and Criminal Code, *Commission Staff Notes,* p. 277.

2. Marvin Frankel, *Criminal Sentences: Law Without Order*, p. 10.

3. The Executive Advisory Committee on Sentencing, *Crime and Punishment in New York*, p. 120, italics in original.

4. Public Hearings on determinate sentencing before the Joint Assembly and Senate Codes Committee, November 28, 1979, pp. 166–67.

5. New York State Special Commission on Attica, *Attica: The Official Report of the New York State Commission on Attica*, p. xi.

6. Citizens' Inquiry on Parole and Criminal Justice, *Prison Without Walls: Report on New York Parole*, pp. xix and 178.

7. Under the indeterminate system, prosecutors are often able to secure a conviction to the top count in the indictment by engaging in sentence bargaining. The relatively narrow sentence ranges of a determinate system, however, militate against sentence bargaining, forcing the prosecutor to engage in charge bargaining, which decreases the likelihood that the offender will plead guilty to the top charge in the indictment.

8. Todd Clear, John Hewitt, and Robert Regoli, "Discretion and the Determinate Sentence: Its Distribution, Control, and Effect on Time Served," *Crime and Delinquency* 24 (1978).

9. Minnesota Sentencing Guidelines Commission, *Preliminary Report on the Development and Impact of the Minnesota Sentencing Guidelines*. (St. Paul: Minnesota Sentencing Guidelines Commission, 1982); Minnesota Sentencing Guidelines Commission, *The Impact of the Minnesota Sentencing Guidelines: Three-year Evaluations*. (St. Paul: Minnesota Sentencing Guidelines Commission, 1984).

10. von Hirsch, Knapp, and Tonry, *The Sentencing Commission and its Guidelines*, p. 39.

11. Ibid., p. 48.

12. Ibid., p. 36.

13. Washington Sentencing Commission, *Report to the Legislature: January 1, 1986*. (Olympia: Washington Sentencing Commission, 1986).

14. von Hirsch, Knapp, and Tonry, *The Sentencing Commission and its Guidelines*, p. 29–33.

15. Casper, Brereton, and Neal, "The California Determinate Sentencing Law," p. 410.

16. *In Re Lynch*, 8 Cal. 3d 410, 503 P. 2d 921 (1972); *In Re Foss*, 10 Cal. 3d 910, 519 P. 2d 1073 (1974); *In Re Rodriquez*, 14 C. 3d 639, 537 P. 2d 384 (1975); and *In Re Stanley*, 54 C.A. 3d 1030, 126 Cal. Rptr. 524 (1976).

17. New York Criminal Procedure Law, section 450.90 (2).

18. Ibid., sections 70.02 (1) (b) (c) and 70.15 (1).

19. Ibid., sections 470.15 (3), (6); *People v. Thompson*, 60 N.Y. 2d 513, 520 (1983); *People v. Whiting*, 89 A.D. 2d 694 (3rd Dept. 1982); *People v. McDermott*, 89 A.D. 2d 748 (3rd Dept. 1982).

20 *People v. Whiting; People v. McDermott; People v. Roman*, 84 A.D. 2d 851 (2d Dept. 1981); *People v. Patterson*, 83 A.D. 2d 691 (3rd Dept. 1981).

21. The association between prison populations and type of sentencing system is difficult to determine. New York and California, just like other indeterminate and determinate sentencing states, have experienced unprecedented rises in their prison populations in recent years. Rather than being linked to a particular sentencing model, it is more likely that increases in prison populations reflect a general hardening of attitudes toward crime and punishment.

Appendix 1

1 . As a precaution, the actual testimony of witnesses assigned to ideological positions in this manner was examined for independent confirmation that they had been assigned to the appropriate category. No miscategorization was uncovered.

Appendix 2

1. This is the section that had originally contained the controversial "least severe" clause.

INDEX